D1233972

BERLIN! BERLIN!

BERLIN! BERLIN!

ITS CULTURE, ITS TIMES

Michael Farr

KYLE CATHIE LIMITED

For Emma-Victoria Anna Maria Karoline,
and, in heaven,
Hilde Karoline Maria Louise

First published in Great Britain 1992 by
Kyle Cathie Limited
3 Vincent Square, London SW1P 2LX

ISBN 1 85626 064 X

A CIP catalogue record for this book is available from the British Library

Michael Farr is hereby identified as author of this work in accordance with Section 77 of the Copyright,
Designs and Patents Act 1988.

Designed by Lorraine Estelle
Photoset by Rowland Phototypesetting Ltd, Bury St Edmunds, Suffolk
Printed and bound in Great Britain by
Butler and Tanner Ltd, Frome, Somerset

CONTENTS

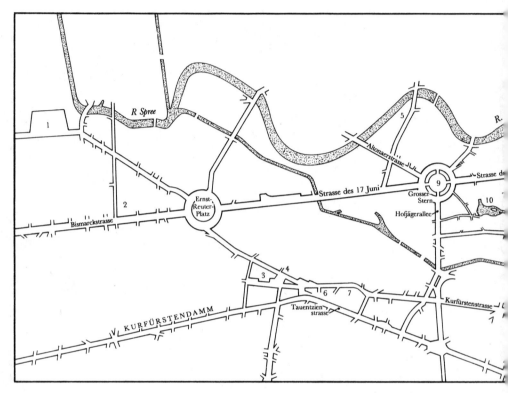

1 Charlottenburg Palace
2 Deutsche Oper
3 Theater des Westens
4 Zoo Station
5 Hansaviertel
6 Kaiser-Wilhelm-Gedächtniskirche
7 Europa Centre
8 Reichstag
9 Victory Column
10 Tiergarten
11 Neue Philharmonie
12 Matthäuskirche
13 New National Gallery

14 National Library
15 Shell-Haus
16 Potsdamer Platz
17 Brandenburg Gate
18 Deutsches Theater and Kammerspie
19 Theater am Schiffbauerdamm
20 Friedrichstadtpalast Theater
21 Komische Oper
22 French Cathedral
23 German Cathedral
24 Schauspielhaus
25 Friedrichswerdersche Kirche
26 Palace of the Republic

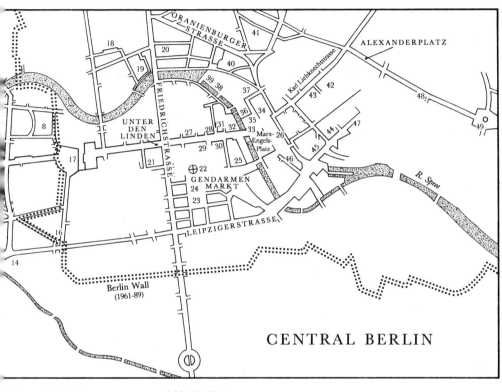

CENTRAL BERLIN

27 German National Library
28 Humboldt University
29 Altes Palais
30 Deutsches Staatsoper
31 Neue Wache
32 Zeughaus
33 Schlossbrücke
34 Berlin Cathedral
35 Lustgarten
36 Altes Museum
37 National Gallery
38 Pergamon Museum
39 Bode Museum

40 Monbijou Park
41 Sophienkirche
42 Television Tower
43 Marienkirche
44 Rotes Rathaus
45 Nikolaikirche
46 Ribbeckhaus
47 Ruins of Franciscan Monastery
48 Karl-Marx Allee
49 Strausberger Platz

ACKNOWLEDGEMENTS

To be asked to write a book about Berlin at this time is a great privilege, for which I must thank my publisher, Kyle Cathie, and my former agent, Dieter Klein, whose sudden death prevented him from seeing the completion of a project which was spurred above all by his eagerness and enthusiasm.

Berlin, restored to its rightful status as capital of a united Germany, has embarked on a hectic schedule in a bid to make up for precious time lost during the years of division. The writing of these chapters was accompanied, often coincidentally and always appropriately, by a series of memorable anniversaries, episodes and events.

Most significant for Berlin's future was the clear-cut decision by the Bundestag in Bonn, after a sometimes convoluted debate, that the restored German capital should also become the seat of government.

Schadow's Quadriga, vandalized during the first New Year celebrations after the opening of the Wall, was returned to its place on top of the Brandenburg Gate after careful restoration and the reinstatement of the Prussian eagle and Iron Cross added to Victoria's staff by Schinkel. Meyerbeer's Singspiel, *Das Brandenburger Thor*, composed to celebrate the return of the Quadriga following its theft by Napoleon, received its 177-year-overdue première. The original score was submitted too late for performance in 1814. It was found to be an indifferent work, notable only for an excess of the new-born patriotism that then swept Berlin.

Frederick the Great's wish to be buried in a vault he had had specially cut out of the top terrace of his summer palace of Sanssouci at Potsdam was finally respected and, in the presence of the head of the Hohenzollern family, Prince Louis Ferdinand, and the German chancellor, Helmut Kohl, Prussia's most remarkable monarch was solemnly interred by torchlight in a nocturnal ceremony, exactly 205 years after his death. At the last look inside the tin coffin, forty years previously, Frederick's body was found to be surprisingly well preserved.

Then, as a reminder of Berlin's heyday, its most memorable cinema star, Marlene Dietrich, celebrated her ninetieth birthday in customary seclusion in Paris. In her honour some of her best known films, including the legendary *Blue Angel* were repeated on television. Five months later, in May 1992, she died.

By the birch-lined banks of the wind-rippled Wannsee the comfortable suburban villa where Hitler's aides, fortified with generously filled glasses of fine cognac, planned in chillingly meticulous detail the mechanics of the final liquidation of the Jewish race was appropriately opened to the public as a memorial and study centre for the Holocaust.

In London, meanwhile, the Victoria and Albert Museum had shown the first major exhibition devoted to Karl Friedrich Schinkel outside Berlin, the city he had transformed with his good taste.

There were also exhibitions bringing together in his former capital a collection of the precious possessions taken into his Dutch exile by the last German Kaiser. For the descriptions of the future Kaiser as a small boy, his parents and the court of his grandfather, William I, as well as an acutely observed portrait of Berlin a decade before it assumed imperial responsibility, all penned in an immaculate copperplate hand by William Courthope, I am indebted to a successor of his at the College of Arms, Thomas Woodcock, Somerset Herald, who made available the journal of the 1861 'Garter Mission' that is in his possession.

Of similar value was a unique contemporary view of imperial Berlin by a well-connected but now forgotten young British diplomat, Lord Frederic Hamilton, which was unearthed by Stefanie Jordan, whom I must thank on this and many other counts. Not for the first time, drawing on her rich library and fired by a keen investigative talent, she provided invaluable assistance.

Michaela Neuber generously furnished an absorbing chapter on the Nazi plans to transform Berlin into the 'World Capital Germania' from her unpublished thesis on Hitler's cities which she has written at Bonn University.

Rüdiger Sawallisch helpfully found fascinating material on, among other subjects, Berlin café and intellectual life in the 1920s.

I must also thank Diana Goodman, Eastern Europe correspondent of the BBC based in East Berlin, for her frequent hospitality and her husband, Roger Wilde, for his inspiring photography. This is not the first book of mine to have been embellished by his photographs.

Similarly, I am grateful to Helen Jeffrey for her sharp eye, impeccable judgement and considerable tact as my copy editor in this, our second collaboration.

The greatest help and encouragement came from my wife, who, as Anna Tomforde, reports from Berlin and Germany for *The Guardian* and has the rare distinction of having been the only British foreign correspondent to have strolled through the Brandenburg Gate the night the Wall was opened. Finally, I cannot forget my daughter, Emma-Victoria, who watched over every page as it was written, and to whom this book is dedicated.

Michael Farr
Bonn and Berlin, 1992

PHOTOGRAPH ACKNOWLEDGEMENTS

All photographs appear by courtesy of the Landesbildstelle Berlin, except for those by Roger Wilde of: The Sophienkirche, Berlin's only surviving original baroque church; The Bode Museum in 1991; the house built at royal expense for Johann Gottfried Schadow; and of the house on the corner of Friedrichstrasse where Karl Marx once lived. The photograph of Unter den Linden in 1911 was provided by the Märkisches Museum. The Deutsches Historisches Museum provided the photographs of a catalogue cover for the Düsseldorf 'Degenerate Music' exhibition of 1938, and of the jazz band 'Weintraub's Syncopators' in 1931, while the photograph of the French cathedral in flames was supplied by the Französische Friedrichstadtkirche. The BBC Hulton Picture Library provided the still of Marlene Dietrich as Lola Lola in *The Blue Angel*. The photographs of the Friedrichswerdersche Kirche in 1991; Schlüter's imposing statue of Frederick William the Great Elector; and of Rauch's statue of Frederick the Great were taken by the author.

CHRONOLOGY

1157   Albrecht the Bear becomes margrave of the Mark Brandenburg

1237   First documented mention of Cölln, Berlin's sister city across the river Spree

1244   First documented reference to Berlin

1307   Berlin and Cölln merge

1415   Frederick VI of Hohenzollern pronounced margrave of the Mark Brandenburg

1417   Becomes Elector Frederick I of Brandenburg

1443   Elector Frederick II ('Irontooth') builds his residence in Berlin

1448   Puts down 'Berliner Unwille' revolt

1571–84   Leonhard Thurneysser, alchemist, scientist and physician, practises in Berlin

1618   Outbreak of Thirty Years War

1631   Gustavus II Adolphus of Sweden occupies Berlin

1640   Accession of Frederick William I (the Great Elector) of Brandenburg

1685   Revocation of Edict of Nantes, Huguenots welcomed in Berlin

1688   Accession of Elector Frederick III of Brandenburg

1701   Becomes King Frederick I of Prussia

1713   Accession of Frederick William I (the 'Soldier King') of Prussia

1740   Accession of Frederick II (the Great) of Prussia

1756   Outbreak of Seven Years War

1757   Austrian troops enter Berlin

1760   Berlin occupied by Russians

1786   Accession of Frederick William II of Prussia

1791   Brandenburg Gate opened

1797   Accession of Frederick William III of Prussia

1806   Napoleon marches in triumph into Berlin, loots the Quadriga

1810   Berlin (Humboldt) University founded

1814   Quadriga restored to Brandenburg Gate

1821   First performance and sensational success in Berlin of Weber's *Der Freischütz*

1838   Opening of Berlin–Potsdam railway

1840   Accession of Frederick William IV of Prussia

1841   Death of Karl Friedrich Schinkel

1847   Werner Siemens sets up Europe's first telegraph equipment plant

1848   Revolution in Germany and across Europe

1858   William, brother of Frederick William IV, becomes regent

1861 Accession of William I of Prussia

1862 Bismarck appointed chief minister in Prussia

1865 Horse-drawn trams introduced in Berlin

1870–71 Franco-Prussian War

1871 German Empire proclaimed with Berlin as capital

1878 Berlin Congress

1881 First electric tram

1888 'Year of Three Emperors'
Death of William I
Accession of Frederick III, king of Prussia and emperor of
Germany; his death after ninety-nine days
Accession of William II

1890 Dismissal of Bismarck

1914–18 First World War

1918 Abdication of Kaiser, end of Hohenzollern rule

1919 Weimar Republic proclaimed
Treaty of Versailles

1920 Kapp putsch
Berlin takes in its suburbs to become Greater Berlin

1930 Marlene Dietrich wins overnight fame in *The Blue Angel*

1933 Hitler comes to power, beginning of Third Reich

1936 Berlin Olympics, 'Hitler's Games'

1938 *Kristallnacht*

1939–45 Second World War

1945 Fall of Berlin, Hitler's suicide and German capitulation

1948–9 Berlin blockade

1949 Federal Republic of Germany (West) and German Democratic Republic (East) founded

1953 Workers' uprising in East Berlin

1961 Berlin Wall built

1963 President Kennedy visits Berlin and declares, 'Ich bin ein Berliner!'

1989 Peaceful revolution and collapse of communism

1990 Reunification of Germany, Berlin becomes capital

1991 Bundestag (Lower House of Parliament) votes for return of government to Berlin by the end of the century

INTRODUCTION

BERLIN is known, among much else, for its *Luft* (air) and for its *Witz* (wit). Both are special to Europe's youngest, sometimes delinquent capital. The air is peculiarly bracing and invigorating, a quality discovered by visitors throughout the centuries that is attributed to the extensive forests and numerous lakes of its hinterland, as well as to a decidedly continental climate. Berlin winters are crisply cold, its summers dominated by an azure sky. The famous 'Berliner Luft' did not just breeze in with Paul Lincke's memorable hit song dating from the days when Berlin took pride in being 'the fastest city in the world'. Soon after taking up his post as Hofkapellmeister (court conductor) in 1898, Richard Strauss wrote to his parents in Munich praising the capital's 'wunderschöne Luft' (marvellous air).

As for wit, Berlin has always had an abundance to sustain it through often difficult times. Even in 1830 in a city that was still placidly Biedermeier, the philosopher Georg Hegel concluded: 'Berlin wit is worth more than beautiful surroundings.' The typical Berliner was known for his cheek, irreverence and *Schnauze* (lip), his delight in giving everything a name. So the hideously pompous Siegessäule (Victory Column) put up to celebrate Bismarck's victories and the achievement of nationhood became the 'Siegesspargel' (victory asparagus) or 'Siegesschornstein' (victory chimney), and the golden, winged figure of Victoria that was perched precariously on top, the 'Siegestante' (victory aunt) or 'Gold-Else' (golden Else).

Academics still dispute the origin of Berlin humour: whether it was developed to sustain morale during the fearsome plague of 1637–9, or came later in the century with the Huguenot refugees. Or was Frederick the Great the forefather of *Kodderschnauze* (insolence)?

The Berlin lip was inseparably bound to the distinctive dialect, Berlinisch, with its pronounced 'ick' for 'ich' (meaning 'I'), its j's for

1

g's and richly variegated vocabulary, including French-derived words imported with the Huguenots and those of Yiddish origin. Goethe was not alone in having difficulties with such an impure language.

As Berlin progressively gained importance during the nineteenth century, its humour and dialect became the preserve of the city's rapidly swelling working class, Prussia's rulers preferring the perfection and seriousness of Hochdeutsch (High German). The Berliner *Witz* was immortalized in the cartoons of Johann Gottfried Schadow, Theodor Hosemann and then into the 1920s by the hugely popular Heinrich Zille, Berlin's vulgar answer to Daumier in France. It was mastered in the 1830s by Adolf Glassbrenner's irrepressible creation 'Eckensteher Nante', the people's spokesman and a model of cheek, the arch-exponent of *Berliner Schnauze*. Karl Marx came near to offering the best definition of Berlin wit, terming it 'a curious mixture of a small dose of irony with a little measure of scepticism and a large one of vulgarity'.

Berlin has also long possessed two distinctly un-German qualities: tolerance and cosmopolitan openness, explained by the highly varied backgrounds of many of its inhabitants from the seventeenth century onwards: Huguenots, Jews (later to be all but annihilated by the Nazis), over 200,000 Russians in the wake of the 1917 revolution and a sizeable Turkish community from the 1960s. To Wim Wenders, the film director who revealed his affection for the city in *Himmel über Berlin* (*Wings of Desire*, 1987), the city's appeal lies in 'its' liberal, tolerant tradition, its contradictions, the sardonic humour of its people, and the sense of a living past that it has learned to integrate'.

As a sick man only months from death, Schiller paid his first visit to Berlin in 1804. 'Berlin pleases me more than I expected. There is great individual freedom there and spontaneity amongst the middle classes. Music and theatre offer all sorts of pleasures, although their performance by no means equals the money spent.'

Berlin's late acquired status as capital was often disputed, yet it always had its champions. Friedrich Hebbel, the dramatist after whom one of the city's theatres is named, noted in the mid-nineteenth century: 'There I was once more in the metropolis of German intelligence, as Berlin so gladly hears itself called. It's true. Germany has only one city whose reputation conquers at first glance, and that one city is Berlin . . . though honestly one shouldn't look too closely, only blink, if the impression is not to be lost again.'

From the nineteenth century Berlin came to be known for its modernity. Karl Friedrich Schinkel had been the first architect of note to give the Prussian capital, still a young city, a modern face. He may stylistically have embraced both neo-classicism and the neo-Gothic, but, as an intensely original architect and designer, the emphasis was always on the 'neo'. His stated aim was to ennoble 'all human conditions through art, architecture and design'. Urban planning, which Frederick the Great and Knobelsdorff had experimented with by designing a 'Forum Fridericianum', became with Schinkel an art form which determined the city's character and appeal.

For the first but not last time in its turbulent history, Berlin during those civilizing Biedermeier years was both cosmopolitan and fashionable. 'Berlin is not a city at all, but a place where people come together,' Heinrich Heine had noted. Whether in its salons or concert halls, for literary lions or pyrotechnicians of the violin or piano, Berlin became a compulsory stop on their European tour. No longer was it peripheral; even Goethe in his advancing years had second thoughts about the city he had shunned after just one visit. In February 1832, only a month before he died at the great age of eighty-two, a witness to an extraordinary swath of German history, he wrote to the sculptor Rauch: 'I "live" in Berlin more than I can say, and try to visualize the manifold greatness of its achievement across the entire spectrum of culture and engineering, science and government.'

The Prussian capital began at last to lose the provincial image which had so irritated Frederick the Great and which, for all his efforts with pen, flute and sword, he had never quite succeeded in dispelling.

Already, then, Berlin was schizophrenic, torn between progress and reaction, between its dual allegiance to Apollo and Mars, its alternating and hardly compatible roles as either the Athens or the Sparta on the Spree. While still crown prince, Frederick had written to Voltaire promising 'Berlin will become Athens!' His overture continued: 'Leave your ungrateful fatherland and come to a country where you will be honoured. May your genius find its reward in the new Athens!'

But it was Sparta too. 'The capital of cannons,' the French writer Victor Tissot called it, adding: 'While France cultivated the world

3

with ideas, Prussia civilized Germany with guns. Therein lies the whole difference.'

Twenty years later, in the 1890s, the contrast and contradiction was unwittingly underlined by Kaiser Wilhelm II, who declared that 'there is nothing in Berlin to captivate the foreign visitor except a number of palaces, museums and the army', all of which, as it happened, formed part of his domain.

The society novelist Fedor von Zobeltitz observed that 'in no other metropolis does the soldier play so great a role . . . "military-mad" a French newspaper recently called our good Berliners – and a certain intoxication does indeed overcome them when the troops march past'.

Visiting pre-imperial Berlin, Mary Ann Evans (better known as George Eliot) had remarked on the number of 'puppets in uniform' and expressed concern at her legs being 'in constant danger from officers' swords'.

It was an uneasy city, a late developer with a troubled adolescence. Compared with European and German counterparts it was still immature by the time responsibility was thrust upon it. 'What is so surprising is that the chief city of the new empire possesses less of the atmosphere of a capital than Dresden, Frankfurt, Stuttgart or Munich. I wouldn't begin to speak of Vienna,' wrote Tissot.

'Ah, Berlin, how far you are from being a real capital of the German Reich. It is the machinations of politics that have turned you into one overnight, not your own efforts,' sighed Theodor Fontane in 1884.

Its comparative youth made Berlin a foolhardy, fast city, impatient and vibrantly modern. It was restless, short of morals and shorter of sleep, a peculiarity observed by Jerome K. Jerome: 'The Berliner has solved the great problem of modern life, how to do without sleep.'

The French painter Fernand Léger, known for his tubular, primary-coloured machine men and women, gave his impression: 'Berlin is modern, modern through its light, that is to say its battle against night. I have now been in Berlin eight days and have noticed nothing of the night. Light at six o'clock, at midnight, at four, perpetual light. Paris has the effect of a city of intermediate grey. Berlin is just one block of light.'

Oskar Kokoschka, arriving in Berlin in 1910 from still imperial Vienna, found it to be 'the watershed between the present and future'. And he remarked with reason that 'Berliners don't tolerate boredom'.

4

In 1927 Walter Ruttmann painted an unforgettable portrait in film of the bustling, sleepless city in *Berlin, die Sinfonie der Gross-Stadt*, where the neon lights make the night brighter than the day, ending in an orgasm of brilliant fireworks.

A year earlier Berlin led the way with the opening of Germany's first marriage guidance bureau, and in 1930, when Marlene Dietrich won enduring fame in *The Blue Angel (Der blaue Engel)*, the capital's first traffic light was installed in the Alexanderplatz, just three years after the black American Garrett A. Morgan had patented the world's first automatic electric traffic signal.

Marlene Dietrich, whose name, according to Jean Cocteau, 'begins with a caress and ends with a whiplash', became Berlin's most celebrated export, departing for Hollywood and turning her back on her native city. 'When I die, I'd like to be buried in Paris. But I'd also like to leave my heart in England. And in Germany – nothing,' she said in the 1960s. Though amid the euphoria of the Wall's coming down in the autumn of 1989 she admitted, as in the popular song, to 'still having a suitcase in Berlin'. In the end, aware of the approach of death, she relented completely and chose to be buried near her mother in the city in which she was born. Her last minute change of mind, according to a leading civic official, 'gave to Berlin more than the city could ever do for her.'

What Berlin lacked in terms of age, experience or pedigree, it made up for in character and excitement. In Berlin, as in no other German city, the adrenalin flowed.

'There is one reason to prefer Berlin to other cities: it changes constantly. What is bad today, can be improved tomorrow,' wrote Bertolt Brecht, a Bavarian whose body and heart, after a Nazi-imposed exile, remained in Berlin. 'My friends and I wish that the most revolutionary characteristics of this great and lively city – its intelligence, its courage and its poor memory – should remain in good health.'

PART ONE

INNOCENCE
AND
ADVENTURE

ONE

HUMBLE ORIGINS

Obscure origins can hardly enhance a pedigree, and those of Berlin seem to be lost amidst the swamps on which it was built. It is not altogether inappropriate, Rome, Paris or London could argue, that this latecomer among European capitals, this parvenu, should by all accounts have had so undistinguished and unmemorable a birth. Unlike Rome, there was no Romulus or Remus myth; it possessed not seven but only four unimpressive hills and, unlike Lutetia Parisiorum, Roman Paris, or Londinium, none of the civilizing influence that came with being an outpost of a great empire. There are even those who would maintain that, despite notoriety achieved in modern times, Berlin never has been civilized.

Of course one could try to make up an appropriate myth, something which the nineteenth-century writer and dramatist Heinrich Laube, who was not himself a Berliner, tried for amusement. 'Curiously, there is nothing certain to be said about the founding and origin of Berlin. One knows more about Rome and Palmyra. One can therefore agreeably invent a myth, that the first Berliner was suckled by a she-bear, fed by eagles and brought up by wild men. This would explain Berlin's coat of arms. The first Berliner then built a hut on the spot where the Stadtvogtei stands today and caught fish in the river Spree. Some Wends then arrived to visit and so a fishing village came into being. This then grew into Berlin.'

Berlin's beginnings were indeed on the Spree, a mean river for any future city, which it shared with the twin settlement of Cölln, facing it on the opposite bank and named after the more ancient and venerable Cologne (Colonia) on the Rhine. But it was much more than a fishing village, being perfectly placed at the crossroads of trade routes traversing east and west, north and south. Such promising geography allowed it to develop quickly as a significant centre of commerce. Berlin merchants exported grain from nearby Barnim and Teltow, and wood from the dense surrounding forests. An enormous range of goods was offered in exchange, notably cloth woven in Flanders. It was enough to justify membership of the Hanseatic League in the fourteenth century. Indeed, had it not been for the trade routes, Berlin would have had little to recommend its situation.

The name Berlin has been subject to endless scrutiny in a bid to unravel the mystery shrouding the city's origin. Indo-European as well as Slav and German roots have been suggested. The most likely would seem to be a derivation from 'birl' or 'berl', meaning 'swamp' and corresponding to 'brljaga' in Serbo-Croat. The nature of the terrain meant that the building of the first settlements concentrated on the four low sand hills that straddled either side of the river. This drier ground was easier to build on and came to be occupied by the three churches and then the town hall that together dominated early Berlin and, south of the Spree, Cölln. Although comparatively little is known of Berlin's earliest history, it appears as a model of town planning, with commerce and markets clustered around the churches. So next to the Nikolaikirche, Berlin's oldest church, was the Alte Markt (also known as the Molkenmarkt), by the Marienkirche and near the town hall, the Neue Markt, and alongside the Petrikirche, the Cöllner Markt (or Fischmarkt). The Nikolaikirche still stands, carefully but coldly restored at long last after the ravages of the Second World War, its soaring interior transformed into a spacious museum, its spirituality lost. The Marienkirche miraculously survived wartime bombs and lies incongruously amidst the gruesome grey surrounding socialist development of the Alexanderplatz as a beacon of more lasting values. But the Petrikirche, devastated in 1945 by bombing, artillery shelling, street fighting and finally flames, has vanished without trace. Its smoke-blackened remains were torn down in the 1960s, its long testimony of Berlin history bulldozed away with the broken rubble.

Berlin's early obscurity can largely be blamed on a great fire which swept through the city on the night of 10 August 1380, destroying its records and much else. As a result there is no documentary proof of its existence before a deed dated 28 October 1237 when the sister city of Cölln is referred to in connection with a priest called Symeon, whose name subsequently reappears on the first known Berlin document, dated 26 January 1244, where he is described as prior of the city. With these documents, as with a copy of an overdue birth certificate, Berlin attained a legitimacy long enjoyed by other cities.

Occasionally some archaeological evidence surfaces pointing to the earlier presence in the area of Slav or Germanic tribesmen, drawn to the windswept and wild Mark Brandenburg region by its plenteous stock of game, an attraction that was to prove more durable than the monarchy itself. The Wends came from the east and German settlers from the west. Between 1136 and 1157 the suitably named Albrecht the Bear gained the upper hand over the Wends, conquering and proceeding to 'Germanize' Brandenburg, of which he became margrave. The real colonization of the twin cities of Berlin and Cölln seems to have taken place, then, in the late twelfth and thirteenth centuries, leading to the formation of one council and the merging of the sister cities in 1307. The joint rule of the Mark Brandenburg by two brothers, the margraves Johann I and Otto III, from 1220 to 1267 was in particular a period of growth. Expansion was rapid, but Cölln, in effect an island, was hemmed in by the Spree and marshland, leaving Berlin scope to spill over its original boundaries and develop further. The area around the Marienkirche and Neue Markt gained in importance and in 1290 a new town hall was built on the spot it still occupies.

Trade-inspired prosperity brought the people of Berlin–Cölln rights and privileges, notably exemption from duties on goods traded in their markets and municipal self-government, which they were to guard jealously from erosion by their rulers. This measure of early independence seems to have stamped itself indelibly on the Berlin character, explaining the stubbornness and possibly the proverbial *Schnauze*, or lip, for which Berliners became so well known.

Like most medieval cities, Berlin was vulnerable to power vacuums and struggles. The death in August 1319 of the margrave Waldemar, who was childless, left open the question of who would rule the Mark Brandenburg. Swiftly a number of German dukes staked claims for and fought over what they saw as a lucrative source of revenue. While this allowed Berlin to strengthen its own autonomy, it led to the waste and decline of its hinterland. Robber barons formed bands that struck and broke alliances with rival dukes according to pecuniary advantage. The ensuing chaos soon began to jeopardize economic development and stability. Large areas of land constantly changed hands in often violent circumstances. Self-defence was considered prudent and in

11

1393 a number of cities in the Mark Brandenburg, including Berlin, together formed a *Landwehr* (home guard) to counter the mounting threat of the barons. Such a *Landwehr* was to be revived with considerable success over four hundred years later against another marauding enemy, Napoleon.

Most feared among these lawless barons of the late fourteenth century was one Dietrich von Quitzow, who, it was felt, was best dealt with by offering a pact. A threatening letter of his to the peasants of Lichtenberg in 1400 still exists, its evil and cynical intention masked by the impeccable hand in which it was drawn up and von Quitzow's easily legible signature, redolent of ill-won authority. Order had to be re-established, and the eventual decision to counter the barons with a strong leader was to have far-reaching consequences for Berlin and later Germany.

In July 1411 Emperor Sigismund chose his son-in-law, Frederick (Friedrich) VI of Hohenzollern, to assume authority over the Mark Brandenburg, so introducing a dynasty that was to rule for over five hundred years, until over-ambition and world war brought it to its knees in November 1918. The emperor's choice won the approval of Berlin, which offered Frederick troops and melted down the bells of the Marienkirche to forge weapons for him. The historic bells of Berlin's second oldest church were to be reduced to molten metal again for the last ruling Hohenzollern, Kaiser Wilhelm II, in 1917, a year before his abdication, to provide guns for the western front.

By 1414 the immediate threat of the bandit barons was removed and in the following year at the Council of Constance – better remembered for its treacherous solution to another problem, when it sought to exorcize the Hussites in Bohemia by having the religious reformer Jan Hus burnt at the stake despite his arrival in the city under imperial safe conduct – Frederick was pronounced margrave of Mark Brandenburg. Two years later, as Frederick I, he was made hereditary elector.

By the beginning of the fifteenth century Berlin was visibly blossoming as an independent city. There were altogether seven hundred houses, with another three hundred across the Spree in Cölln. There were three churches and two monasteries, three town halls, three hospitals, two merchants' houses, the margrave's mill and his property in the Klosterstrasse, four bishops' residences and, to complete the picture, a brothel. On an area of less than a third of a square mile were crowded some six thousand people.

Two very different orders of mendicant friars – the ascetic Franciscans practising poverty and the dogmatically rigorous Dominicans – had established monasteries on either side of the Spree in the thirteenth century. The Franciscans based themselves in Berlin, where their political solidarity with ordinary citizens gained them considerable influence over the city's spiritual life, while the Dominicans, the 'black brothers', founded their monastery in Cölln. The Gothic red brick Franciscan church survived until April 1945 when it succumbed to Allied bombs and bombardment; in 1963 it was formally preserved as a ruin. The Dominican monastery church was incorporated into the castle in the sixteenth century, becoming the burial place of the Hohenzollerns. By 1747, in dire need of repair, it did not fit in with baroque rebuilding plans and was pulled down. In the early 1960s, approximately on the site once occupied by the Dominican monastery, the communists built the placid pink and white State Council building. It was here, in his spacious office, thickly curtained from the outside world, that Erich Honecker was rudely awakened from his dream of socialism and toppled from power in October 1989, paving the way for German reunification a year later.

The arrival of the Hohenzollerns in Berlin may have offered security against the robber barons, but it also inevitably posed a threat to the city's almost republican independence. The emasculation of Berlin came with the second Hohenzollern, Elector Frederick II, whose severity earned him the grim title 'Irontooth'. Engravings show him to be clean-shaven and of determined mien. When in 1442 he was called to intervene in a dispute between the ruling patrician classes and the guilds – with whom he sided – he instituted a rigorous check of land ownership rights and a curtailment of carefully guarded privileges, which in 1448 led to the revolt known as the 'Berliner Unwille' (Berlin Indignation), another example of the stubborn character of the city's inhabitants. Frederick and his courtiers and followers were all locked out of the city, the elector's archives and mill were destroyed and the site of his castle, the foundation stone of which he had laid himself five years earlier, deliberately flooded by breaking a dam.

13

Berliners were rightly suspicious, seeing the building of the castle as the elector's most effective means of asserting his authority over them. Making fast the city wall and shutting the gates, Berlin awaited his attack and the promised intervention on its behalf of the Hanseatic League and allied cities. But help never came – only the towns of Neuruppin and Mittenwalde declared themselves for Berlin – and the patricians' attempted coup collapsed. It was to be the last attempt at overturning feudal rule for exactly four hundred years, until the equally unsuccessful 1848 revolution.

So in May 1448 Frederick 'Irontooth' was able to enter the city accompanied by six hundred horsemen and confirm Hohenzollern authority. The patricians were tried and fined and their property confiscated. Some were expelled, others left. The result was that by the mid-fifteenth century Berlin had lost the rights it had accumulated over the past two hundred years. The economic impetus that came with the city's earlier independence was gone and it would need centuries to recover.

A succession of electors followed who were distinguished by their classical second names: Johann Cicero (1486–99), who made Berlin his permanent seat and imposed the *Bierziesel*, a tax of twelve pfennigs a barrel on beer of which he took eight and the city four; Joachim I Nestor (1499–1535), who remained true to the old faith as support for the reforms of Martin Luther spread, and Joachim II Hektor (1535–71), who privately embraced Protestantism in 1539 by taking communion in two kinds, but only publically declared his change of belief in 1563.

Joachim Nestor was studious by nature and invited the learned Abbot Trittenheim from Spannheim to his city, the population of which had by then risen to just over eleven thousand. The abbot provided a vivid, almost Brueghelesque portrayal of sixteenth-century Berliners. 'The people are good, but rough and unpolished; they prefer stuffing themselves and drinking to science. Their soaking in drink is not considered by them to be a vice; though there are also many who abstain from this; and the immigrants from Franconia and Swabia, I have often noticed, are even more inclined to boozing than locals.' Such a picture of Berlin long remained recognizable.

It was Elector Johann Georg (1571–98) who cultivated one of the most original figures ever to be associated with Berlin. He had met

Leonhard Thurneysser, the extraordinarily gifted son of a Basle gold-smith, in Frankfurt-on-the-Oder, where business had brought the forty-year-old scholar and alchemist in 1571 after twenty years of incessant travel and adventure which had taken him the length and breadth of Europe: from Italy to Scotland and from Spain to Russia, and additionally to Asia Minor, Syria and Egypt. Johann Georg was much struck by the many talents of Thurneysser, a late Renaissance man far ahead of his time in backward Brandenburg.

His efforts to recover gold and precious stones from the sands and waters of the Mark Brandenburg may have come to nothing, but his horoscopes were thought unchallengeable and as the elector's phys-ician he was fortunate in his diagnoses. Thurneysser came to be con-sidered a second Paracelsus and the wide ranges of medicaments he concocted in his laboratory were valued export articles that traded throughout Europe.

Johann George furnished Thurneysser with ample accommodation in Berlin's Franciscan monastery, as well as a fully equipped labora-tory and printing works. The printing press employed up to two hundred people, including some well-known artists, and raised the art of printing and producing woodcuts to a level that for years remained unmatched. Typefaces and letters were created not only for German and Latin, but for Greek, Hebrew, Chaldean, Coptic (of which Thur-neysser had made a special study), Old Syrian, Turkish, Persian, Indian, Cyrillic, Armenian, Arabic and Abyssinian.

A Faustian figure, he had long been preoccupied with natural sci-ence and established Berlin's first natural history collection. He com-piled a volume on botany, cultivated a herb garden and kept a zoo. He was a pioneer in the analysis of mineral water and allowed himself to be distracted by female anatomy and local geography, noting, for instance, the difference between the two Berlin rivers. 'The water of the Spree is somewhat green in colour and clear. In its mud it carries gold and shines. The Havel, however, contains a heavy, unhealthy abundance of fish and foul water from which the numerous scolds who drink from it acquire the evil, sharp and lying tongues which make them speak ill of others.' He dealt in precious stones and metals and set up a glass factory, carpet-weaving mills, salt and plaster works and foundries.

As if this were not diversification enough, he embarked on art

15

restoration, leaving his mark clearly visible on the fifteenth-century relief picture of St Bernardino of Siena, which was then in the Franciscan monastery church but is to be seen today in the Marien-kirche. Thurneysser's name and the date 1584 are ostentatiously displayed on the pages of the book held open by the Franciscan saint. 'Thurneysser made me new . . . as I was old and despised,' declares the rhyming inscription in Gothic script above the date of restoration.

Fame and success allowed Thurneysser, who was in debt when he came to Berlin, to live like a prince, lavishly entertaining eminent visitors from abroad. He lent money at outlandish interest rates and by 1580 had managed to amass a fortune in cash totalling 100,000 thalers. But Fortune, on whose wheel he had risen so spectacularly, was also to engineer his downfall. Twice married, a widower and homesick, he decided to return on a visit to Basle; here he married for a third time and saw luck desert him. Divorce from his third wife, who had remained in Basle, was to ruin him completely. In 1584, penniless and pursued by his enemies who accused him of witchcraft, he secretly left Berlin and resumed a nomadic life, pausing in Prague, Rome and finally at a monastery in Cologne on the Rhine, where in 1595, on the very day he had predicted in his horoscope, he died.

Little is left of medieval Berlin; too little. The once pervasive stamp of the Middle Ages has all but disappeared with repeated redevelopment and the wholesale destruction of the Second World War. Not one of the narrow, cobbled, evil-smelling alleyways that once formed an intricate spider's web across old Berlin and Cölln is still to be found. Those with very long memories may just remember the Krögel alley that at the beginning of the twentieth century still led from the Molkenmarkt to the Spree. For a city founded in neither ancient nor modern but medieval times, this lack of visible evidence of its childhood is disturbing. Only a handful of medieval churches and buildings survives, not unscathed, in an uncompromisingly modern landscape. From the seventeenth century onwards, from the baroque to the Bauhaus and beyond, Berlin's rulers, architecturally speaking, have preferred the present to the past. It was and remains a developer's paradise, as it continues to strive to be a thoroughly modern metropolis.

At the heart of oldest Berlin its most ancient church, the Nikolaikirche (St Nicholas's), still towers but has lost its medieval soul. This began to slip away in the late nineteenth century when, after fierce debate, the architect Hermann Blankenstein had his way and replaced the church's single asymmetrical tower, one of the most distinctive features of Berlin's skyline, with two sharply pointed, rocket-like neo-Gothic spires. The task was completed by 1879, changing the face of Berlin. Nor was the interior spared Blankenstein's unwelcome attention, with his refurbishment fussily undoing much of the more tasteful work carried out in 1817 by Karl Friedrich Schinkel, the most inspired architect Prussia ever produced, and Friedrich Wilhelm Langerhans. Simplicity was not a late nineteenth-century quality.

Even before its devastation in the Second World War, the Niko-laikirche's future as a church was threatened. On 31 October 1938 – Reformation Day in the Protestant calendar – the Nikolaikirche held its last service after the Nazis had decided that Berlin's original place of worship should be converted into a secular 'Cathedral of Music'.

It is now thought that a wooden chapel first occupied the site at the end of the twelfth century. But some time before 1220 this had already become a late Romanesque basilica of stone, which in turn had gone through a Gothic transformation by the second half of the thirteenth century. After the great fire of 1380 a late Gothic church with a nave and two aisles was begun in the red brick which was being widely used in northern Germany. The church was finally completed at the end of the fifteenth century, and its peculiarly asymmetrical tower renewed three times during the sixteenth century. It was in the Niko-laikirche that the Dominican Johannes Tetzel preached reform in 1517 and where Protestantism in Berlin was consolidated under Bishop Georg Buchholzer just over twenty-two years later.

The church's wartime ordeal began with an air raid on 16 June 1944 which gutted the towers. The following April the nave caught fire during street fighting all around the church. Falling masonry from

17

the roof broke through the vaulting, and the ornate gable of the mid-fifteenth-century Liebfrauenkapelle (Chapel of Our Lady), south of the tower, was destroyed. Then in 1949, weakened further by the weather, the vaulting collapsed, tearing down with it the church's northern pillars. The building was left in ruins until 1980 when the communist authorities belatedly began a restoration programme. Blankenstein's twin towers were replaced in modified form in 1982 and five years later, in time for Berlin's 750th anniversary celebrations, the Nikolaikirche opened its doors again, but as a museum, not a church. Ranged in its cool, bright, now uncluttered interior, among the restored tombs and gravestones, are glass cases containing coins, seals and artefacts illustrating Berlin's history in the Middle Ages, but the inherent medieval mood which once permeated the Nikolaikirche more than any of the city's other churches has vanished.

The enforced secularization of Berlin's oldest place of worship is unfortunate. Yet, like the parallel rebuilding of the surrounding Nikolaiviertel, where the style could be described as 'modern medieval' as Günter Stahn and his architectural collective tried to re-create its historic character using modern materials and introducing twentieth-century facilities, the alternative could have been worse. The whole area might have suffered the fate of the bomb-damaged castle or Alexanderplatz, and been razed and brutalized by soulless blocks of concrete.

It is here, by the Alexanderplatz, that Berlin's second oldest church, the Marienkirche, stands firmly, determinedly, an island amidst the desolation of socialist city planning. Despite such a hostile and alien environment, the Marienkirche remains the last real refuge of the medieval spirit in Berlin. Its history has been happier, less chequered than other Berlin churches. Most tellingly, Berlin's leading Protestant church has been able to carry on as a place of worship.

It began as Berlin's second church, dedicated to the Virgin Mary, St Anne and St Maurice, and dates from 1270 when it was established parallel to the Neue Markt (New Market) in the northern half of the city. The early Gothic edifice was completed by the start of the fourteenth century, the sacristy on the south side being added in 1340. The Marienkirche also fell victim to the fierce conflagration of 1380, but was rebuilt along previous lines and finished in typical north German red brick by 1405. A tower was added later in the century,

18

in time for a bell to be installed in 1490. With a long, high and broad roof comfortably straddling a nave and two aisles, the church has a remarkable presence, enhanced by a solid, almost austere stone west front, its portal dating from the early seventeenth century, a note-worthy example of late north German Gothic. But the finishing touch which gives the Marienkirche its memorable profile is the brilliant completion of the tower by Karl Gotthard Langhans, best known as the architect of the Brandenburg Gate. While fittingly neo-Gothic, Langhans's two-tiered design stylishly incorporates classical touches, capping the tower with a lantern-like crown of partially gilded copper around a wooden frame. Installed in 1789–90, it succeeds in giving the church distinction as manifestly as Blankenstein's idea of substitut-ing twin towers at the Nikolaikirche robbed it of character.

Like those of other Berlin churches, the wooden structured Marienkirche tower had earlier proved highly vulnerable to lightning and fire and was repeatedly destroyed: in 1514, 1661, 1683, 1706, 1719 and 1720. Its severest test in recent times came on 3 February 1945, between 11.01 and 11.51 a.m., when two bombs dropped by the US Air Force in the heaviest wartime air raid on Berlin shook the Marienkirche tower to its foundations and peppered it with shrapnel. The Marienkirche, unlike so many other churches in the city, sur-vived, and restoration work began that autumn.

Inside the battered church, the most damage was suffered by Andreas Schlüter's magnificently extravagant pulpit, a baroque masterpiece dating from 1703, long accepted as one of the predomi-nantly medieval church's principal treasures. The blast had dislodged it and split sections apart. But Schlüter's joyous creation, with putti trumpeting god's glory from the heavens above and, at its base, two marble angels comporting themselves with a grace worthy of the school of Leonardo, was quickly restored and in use again by 1949.

The true medieval character of the Marienkirche is completed by an extraordinary late fifteenth-century wall painting that adorns the hall of the tower. A 'Dance of Death' – 1484 was a plague year – where, in a more than 24-yard-long and 2-yard-high frieze of twenty-eight scenes, the great leveller, not quite skeletal and sparsely cloaked, leads on representatives of every class. 'Ach guter Tod! Ich kann Dir nicht entweichen. Du holst den Armen und den Reichen' (Oh sweet death! I cannot escape you. You take away the poor and

19

the rich). Below the almost life-size figures is a text of originally 362 verses in Lower German dialect, the oldest surviving evidence of Berlin poetry. The wartime destruction of wall paintings in other churches in the city, notably a Last Judgement in the Nikolaikirche, has left the Marienkirche 'Dance of Death' as the only example of its kind remaining in Germany. The sequence is opened by a preaching Franciscan, illustrating the order's popularity in Berlin, before Death begins his dance, first with the clergy, sparing neither monk nor abbot, neither bishop nor finally pope, then, on the other side of a crucifixion scene, he continues his relentless procession with the laity: emperor and empress, king, duke, knight, mayor, money-lender, merchant, craftsman, peasant, landlady and fool. It is an orderly, undramatic affair enacted before a gently hilly, pale-green landscape. After being painted over with whitewash in 1730, the remarkable fresco was only rediscovered in 1860 by Friedrich August Stüler, a pupil of Schinkel.

A small stone cross outside the west portal bears witness to a particularly notorious incident during the Middle Ages and an early example in Berlin of popular indignation. On 16 August 1325 the unfortunate Prior Nikolaus Griax of Bernau was beaten to death by angry Berliners and burnt in the neighbouring Marienkirchhof after delivering a sermon in the church to which they had taken violent exception. The prior had spoken rather too bluntly against King (later to become emperor) Ludwig IV of Bavaria, who was locked in a dispute with the pope after sending his son Ludwig to govern as margrave over the then rulerless Mark Brandenburg. Pope John XXII excommunicated the young Ludwig in March 1324 and, outraged by the murder of the cleric, he responded by extending the ban to Berlin for a period of twenty years. It was then that the Franciscans won over Berliners by continuing nevertheless to minister to them.

Following an agreement of reconciliation with the brothers of the murdered prior, which included payment of an indemnity and other conditions, it was stipulated that a twelve-foot-high wooden cross should be erected on the spot of the infamous deed. In 1726 this was transferred to the position occupied by the present stone cross, which probably originated in the Marienkirchhof.

Tucked discreetly away around a corner towards the Spree, on the Spandauer Strasse, is another of Berlin's rare medieval relics, the

Heilig-Geist-Kapelle (Holy Ghost Chapel). Somehow this compact, generously windowed, red brick Gothic building defied both developers, who built uninhibitedly around it, and wartime bombs, which only slightly damaged the chapel fabric. It lies strangely sandwiched between the vast smoked-glass pile of the Palast Hotel, raised by the communists in the early 1980s to lure foreigners and their hard currency, and the grimly Wilhelmine School of Commerce of 1905–6 into which it was forcibly and incongruously incorporated as a lecture room. Yet at the time this far from satisfactory concession was only wrung after last-minute intervention by Berlin's oldest trades council. Almost suffocated by its absorption into Cremer and Wolffenstein's School of Commerce (now part of Humboldt University), the chapel – latterly used as a students' dining-room – is at least allowed a small patch of pleasant lawn as breathing space on its other side, before the presence of the Palast Hotel becomes overwhelming.

The Heilig-Geist-Kapelle, dating from the end of the thirteenth century but with a fine fan-vaulted ceiling of 1476, was originally the last building of a hospital complex first mentioned in a letter of the guild of bakers in 1272. It was a typical, clergy-run medieval hospital, performing a wide range of functions: as a place for the sick, a home for old people and a hospice for the dying. It also served as a victualler for Berlin, with a *Wursthof* (sausage yard), in effect a slaughterhouse, and a brewery, which was still in existence in 1600. A document of 1354 records the presence of a *Rüsthof* (arsenal) in the grounds, while in 1720 the adjoining powder tower at the Spandauer Gate exploded with terrific force, claiming seventy-two lives and causing the small west tower of the chapel to be so badly damaged that it had to be pulled down. With the Reformation the hospital complex was transformed into a poorhouse and finally in 1825 – apart from the chapel – it was torn down to make way for a new building.

Berlin's last medieval remnant is the sad but noble red brick ruin of the Franziskanerkloster (Franciscan monastery), officially founded in 1271 following the establishment of the Franciscans in Berlin in 1249. For a long time the uncomplicated, originally towerless building was, together with the Nikolaikirche, considered the most artistically significant and best preserved Gothic church in Berlin. Allied bombs in February 1945 and the furious fighting that followed in April destroyed much of the monastery and church, the ruins of which were preserved in 1963. A ghostly shell is left without compensation of any kind. There is no gentle rural landscape to soften the rudely broken lines, as with many ruined country churches and abbeys. And there is certainly consolation neither in the busy highway that now skirts it noisily, nor in the depressing blocks of the nearby Alexanderplatz. But, turning away from this harsh modern reality, momentary respite can still be found on a bench facing the wrecked church; a broken Corinthian capital, out of character with the Gothic ruins but not with their plight, lies on the pavement in front, weeds sprouting out of its cracks.

It had been in the monastery precincts that Thurneysser was able to carry through his experiments and innumerable activities that mesmerized late sixteenth-century Berlin, and that a famous grammar school, the Berlin School at the Grey Cloister, was founded by the elector's chancellor, Lamprecht Distelmeier, in 1574 to ensure a proper education for the city's sons. It was the first state school in Brandenburg, operating independently of the church and relying on benefactions from Berlin's more affluent citizens for its survival. Its most illustrious alumni later included Johann Gottfried Schadow, Karl Friedrich Schinkel and Otto von Bismarck.

If little remains of medieval Berlin, then traces of the Renaissance have all but vanished. Barely recognizable after heavy 'restoration' by Hermann Blankenstein and Johann Heinrich Strack, the Gerichtslaube (Court Loggia), which used to stand next to the old Berlin town hall, was removed in 1872 to the grounds of the Babelsberg Castle, near Potsdam, where it is still to be found amidst the long, uncut grass. The originally two-storeyed, thirteenth-century building had its open arcade bricked up at the beginning of the sixteenth century. In 1555 the ceiling of the upper floor was given a fan vault and the front a distinctive Renaissance gable. All this was stripped away by the irrepressible Blankenstein in his attempt to revive the Gerichtslaube's Gothic character. The result is decidedly neo-Gothic.

A solitary late Renaissance survivor is the house built out of two existing buildings for the privy councillor Hans Georg von Ribbeck on the Breite Strasse next to the royal stables in 1624. Apart from its row of flamboyant gables, however, the Ribbeck House smacks more of its 1803–4 refurbishment, when it was raised by a storey, than of the seventeenth century.

Joachim II Hektor's love of display led him to have the original Hohenzollern castle pulled down in 1538 to make way for a grander, more ornate residence. For ideas he turned to architecturally more adventurous Saxony. In April 1537 Konrad Krebs, architect of the imposing Schloss Hartenfels at Torgau on the Elbe, near Leipzig, had presented the elector with a wooden model of his proposal for Berlin and recommended that his pupil Caspar Theiss carry the work out. Only the tower known as the 'Grüne Hut' (green hat) and the chapel survived from the original Hohenzollern castle of 1451, on the foundations of which Theiss raised the first Renaissance building in the Mark Brandenburg. But the life of the Renaissance castle was itself to be limited, for by 1699 it was considered ripe for redevelopment as Berlin became baroque.

The Schlossapotheke (castle chemist) wing, a solid Renaissance extension by Peter Kummer of 1585, was to last longer, into modern times. Part of it was torn down in 1886–9 for the construction of the Kaiser Wilhelm Bridge across the Spree. The rest was razed with the bomb-damaged castle in 1950. The Schlossapotheke originally served as an alchemist's laboratory and mint run by the court chemist, Michael Aschenbrenner, a pupil of Thurneysser.

By the end of the sixteenth century Berlin's population had risen to fourteen thousand, but the city was going through a period of stagnation which today one would freely term recession. The arrival of the Hohenzollerns and their residence in the city had done nothing to promote growth; on the contrary, it was to prove an unwelcome drain on resources. From the expenses granted the castle guard to the special rights, privileges and tax exemption allowed courtiers, it was a financial liability. At the same time Berlin had lost the commercial advantage it had enjoyed during its more independent, Hanseatic days. Except locally, it had become a city of no real importance. It was, in fact, positively provincial.

While growing very gradually, the population was regularly trimmed by epidemics and disease: by almost four thousand deaths in 1576, more than three thousand in 1598 and some two thousand in 1611. With the onset of the Thirty Years War, sparked off in May 1618 by the defenestration of the Catholic councillors in Prague, Berlin was to experience a low point in its history.

The Mark Brandenburg was largely spared the worst until 1626 when it was occupied by imperial troops. In June 1620 some three thousand English mercenaries had passed by Berlin without incident. The city would have been ill equipped to defend itself, possessing only a paltry regiment of one thousand men raised by the elector. Georg Wilhelm's tactics were therefore to try to keep his land out of the conflict through a series of changing pacts and alliances. The result was that the Mark Brandenburg became a battlefield, with its rulers preferring to reside more safely in distant Königsberg.

When Albrecht von Wallenstein, the imperial generalissimo and statesman, set up his headquarters in Cottbus in 1626, he made heavy demands on Berlin to supply his armies with food. His Berlin visits in 1627, 1628 and 1630 were no less ruinous, as even in peace his troops would strip a city like locusts. In 1628 alone the occupation cost Berlin and the region around 140,000 thalers. The city was not in a position to argue; in 1623 it could muster merely 1,163 men that could be put under arms, and equip them with 498 muskets, 269 pikes and 355 halberds. The only way Berlin could insure against its destruction was by paying protection money. But economically the city had been crippled by the almost total collapse of trade in the mid-1620s, and its hinterland was devastated by the presence there of imperial troops until 1631. Completing the grim picture, disease continued to ravage the population: plague in 1626 and 1630–31 claimed three thousand lives; there was a serious outbreak of smallpox in 1628 and dysentery took its toll in 1624 and 1626.

The situation failed to improve when in May 1631 Gustavus II Adolphus of Sweden – a brother-in-law of Elector Georg Wilhelm – drove the imperial troops off and occupied Berlin, quartering himself in the castle. An agreement was reached whereby the Swedes were able to keep the Spandau citadel and receive a monthly payment of thirty thousand thalers. The arrangement was doubly unsatisfactory, for it sacrificed imperial favour and left behind a Swedish army which behaved as if it were an occupying power, continuing to extort from Berlin large payments at regular intervals.

Berlin's decline was reflected in its streets, littered with the rubble of ruined buildings. The windmills on the outskirts of the city were destroyed and cattle roamed the city centre, the ruins serving as cowsheds. It was a scene of desolation that presaged the even greater destruction wrought three hundred years later when cows would return to graze, this time in front of the opera house. Of the 1,209 houses recorded in the city before the Thirty Years War, only 999 remained by 1645. Three years later 750 houses were listed as occupied. The population, meanwhile, had sunk by more than half to less than six thousand. With the peace of 1648, Berlin faced, as in 1945, a colossal task of reconstruction.

Berlin's recovery came under Frederick William, the Great Elector and founder of the modern Prussian state, whose almost fifty-year-long rule had begun with a distinct lack of promise. Later in life, having achieved a good deal more than could have been expected, he was depicted in engravings, and most vividly in Andreas Schlüter's powerful equestrian statue of 1703, as an ox of a man: colossally corpulent, magnificently double-chinned, with a beak of a nose, a pinched mouth and long, narrow moustache. Schlüter's portrayal now dominates the great courtyard of the Charlottenburg Palace and, in a fine copy, confronts visitors in the vestibule of the Bode Museum, though it used to stand imperiously behind the castle on the Kurfürstenbrücke. The Great Elector's bulk is happily supported by a horse with rippling, classical musculature mounted upon a suitably solid and ornate pedestal glorifying Frederick William's achievement.

But coming to power as a raw twenty-year-old in the dark year of 1640, he appeared helpless before the chaos into which Berlin had sunk. He readily departed for Holland in 1646 to marry his Dutch bride, Louise-Henriette of Nassau-Orange, and then until 1650 preferred to govern the devastated land of Brandenburg from the comfort of his war-spared estates in Westphalia. This absence abroad was, however, to determine the face of the new, baroque Berlin that was to emerge after his return, for he not only brought with him Dutch ideas on town planning, but imported their architects.

Until the arrival in the early nineteenth century of Karl Friedrich Schinkel, undoubtedly Berlin's most gifted architect, the city's architecture remained with few exceptions singularly unoriginal and derivative. In the sixteenth century the castle was rebuilt by Saxon architects, in the seventeenth Frederick William turned to Holland

and in the eighteenth century Frederick the Great's architectural taste was decidedly French.

Back in Berlin, Frederick William stimulated the stagnant economy into life with fiscal measures, subsidies on construction costs and the provision of cheap building land. Levies on housing and property were lifted and replaced by thoroughly modern sales taxes. Recovery came quickly: by 1654 Berlin–Cölln had 6,194 citizens eligible to pay tax, reflecting a population of around 10,000 – still short of the pre-war total, but growing.

Berlin's vulnerability during the Thirty Years War convinced Frederick William that he should turn it into a fortress, complete with a permanent garrison. Some 2,000 soldiers were billeted on 600 families without compensation. Apart from bolstering the population figures, making every fifth inhabitant a soldier, this imparted to the city a martial character that it was never to lose. The fortifications were begun in 1658 according to the latest Dutch designs. Johann Gregor Memhardt directed a team of architects who were either Dutch or schooled in Holland; it included Michael Matthias Smids, who in addition embellished the castle with a fine arcade and was responsible for the only surviving early baroque building in Berlin, the harmoniously conceived Marstall, housing the royal stables, in the Breite Strasse.

At the same time Berlin was expanding outside its original limits, to take in Werder (immediately west of Cölln), which in 1662 became the Friedrichswerder Stadt, and further west beyond the city defences the Dorotheenstadt in 1674 and the Friedrichstadt in 1688. The woods which still extended almost to the Spree were cleared and a *Linden-allee* (lime avenue) laid, the forerunner of Berlin's most famous boulevard, Unter den Linden.

It was Frederick William's liberal immigration policy which above all laid the foundations for the flowering of Berlin in the eighteenth and early nineteenth centuries. A famous copperplate engraving of 1799 (*Le grand Électeur reçoit les réfugiés dans les États*) by Daniel Chodowiecki, Berlin's most popular eighteenth-century engraver, sometimes referred to as 'the German Hogarth', shows the bounteous Frederick William receiving the exiles: men, women and suckling babes at his feet. Merchants, soldiers and men of science display their gratitude and a hovering cherubim is poised to crown the elector with a wreath of laurels. Above, among the clouds on the left, are cameo portraits of his three successors – Frederick I, Frederick William I and Frederick the Great – revealed by a gesticulating figure of Father Time, winged and airborne. This generous approach to immigration, carried on by his successors, brought valuable labour to the population-thinned city and a wealth of talent from which it was later to profit. The granting of political and economic privileges to those who came was not so much a humane act or expression of religious freedom as a necessary means of putting life into the backward economy.

In 1671 fifty Jewish families expelled from Vienna were encouraged to settle in Berlin and the following year the first Huguenot refugees – about one hundred – came from France. Then with the revocation of the Edict of Nantes in 1685 and an end to religious toleration in France the flow quickened and altogether roughly six thousand Huguenots were welcomed, accounting at one stage for a quarter of Berlin's population. For a short time around 1700, when the population had risen to twenty-nine thousand, French was the mother tongue of one fifth of the city's inhabitants. Nearly all skilled professionals, the Huguenots formed a largely self-administrating community of considerable economic and cultural significance. A number were to attain high rank in the army and at court. By 1710 there were also immigrants from Orange as well as a sizeable number of Walloons, French-speaking Swiss and Rhinelanders, who established Berlin's important tobacco industry. In 1732 they were joined by an influx of two thousand Bohemian Protestants.

Berlin was changing; it was becoming an increasingly civilized, more open and livelier city. Trade and industry blossomed and the arts thrived. The basis was laid for the royal library and art collection. A pleasure garden (the Lustgarten) opposite the castle was set out after the Dutch manner. The Great Elector even took pride in the patch of potatoes – then considered an exotic vegetable – he had planted in the palace garden.

His colonial ambitions – inspired by the Dutch example – heralded those of the last German Kaiser some two hundred years later. He built a fleet of warships and in 1683 founded Gross-Friedrichsburg on the Gold Coast.

Frederick William was also superstitious and impressed by fortune-tellers. He was convinced that his castle was haunted by a white lady and when his favourite Kurt von Burghoff was picked up by the collar and hurled down the stairs one night, he had no doubt who was responsible. Then in 1709, twenty-one years after the Great Elector's death, building workers at the castle stumbled across a woman's skeleton. Without further delay the 'white lady' was laid to rest in the cathedral cemetery.

Berlin's quickening growth was to continue under Frederick William's son and successor, the elector Frederick III, who crowned himself King Frederick I of Prussia in Königsberg in January 1701. 'He was small and hunched; his expression was proud, his features ordinary. His soul was like a mirror reflecting every object. So that those who had gained any influence over him could excite or calm his spirit as they liked. The fulsome praise heaped on Louis XIV impressed him and he thought that by choosing the king as a model he would then also inevitably be lauded himself. Soon the Berlin court became the ape of Versailles; everything was imitated, the ceremonial, official pronouncements, the measured steps, the counted words, the grand musketeers, etc. The open-handedness that Frederick I loved was nothing but extravagance.' Such was the not exactly flattering portrait of the first king of Prussia penned in his 'Histoire de la maison de Brandenbourg' by his sharp-tongued grandson Frederick the Great, the monarch who by inventing the blitzkrieg really stamped the kingdom on the map of Europe.

But the achievement of the art-loving Frederick I, and its importance for Berlin, should not be underestimated. He expanded his territory through purchase and, acquiring the title of duke of Neuchâtel in Switzerland, for example, prompted a valuable influx of Swiss academics and soldiers. He brought the five separate city districts together into one central administration for a single Berlin. And, anxious to demonstrate equal favour to both art and science, he founded the Academy of Arts in 1694 and, at the urging of the electress Sophie Charlotte, six years later the Academy of Sciences under the philosopher and mathematician Gottfried Wilhelm Leibniz. The small, rotund and bustling Sophie Charlotte, who had become Frederick's second wife in 1684 aged only sixteen, cut a distinctive figure at court with her clear blue eyes and jet-black hair. Her grandson Frederick the Great was untypically generous in his praise: 'She combined all the attractions of her sex with the grace of her intellect and an enlightened mind. She introduced to Prussia a convivial spirit, genuine civility and a love of art and science.' Sophie Charlotte died in 1705 at the age of thirty-seven, having left her mark on Berlin like no woman before. A remarkably thick neck, double chin and buckled nose strangely do not deflect from the attractiveness of her personality and vivaciousness that emerge so strongly from Schlüter's relief portrait on her tomb. His portrayal of the king on his sarcophagus reveals a weaker, less confident personality, with a thrusting lower lip.

The work of Andreas Schlüter, 'the northern Michelangelo', as both a sculptor and architect, undoubtedly represents the artistic highlight of Frederick I's reign. The king was fortunate in his choice of architects. Johann Arnold Nering, succeeded by Martin Grünberg and then Schlüter, began work on the massively foursquare but magisterial Zeughaus (arsenal building). It was completed in 1706 by the Parisian Jean de Bodt, a pupil of Mansard with previous experience in Holland and England. The martial mood of the arsenal is celebrated by the line of statuary that adorns its parapet, the triangular stacks of trophies, banners, helmets, shields and drums, the trumpeting victories on either side of its central pediment. In 1786 the publisher Friedrich Nicolai described it as 'one of the most beautiful buildings in Europe' and, having survived the excesses of Napoleon's occupying troops in 1806–13 (which made necessary its subsequent restoration by Schinkel), being stormed during the 1848 revolution and repeated bombardment at the end of the Second World War, the Zeughaus continues today to add weight and baroque authority to the top of Unter den Linden.

The Hamburg-born Schlüter was appointed court sculptor in 1694 at the age of thirty. Recognition of his reputation was reflected in the unusually generous wage of twelve hundred thalers granted him by Frederick. He proved his worth by decorating the Zeughaus courtyard with a brilliant sculptured sequence: twenty-two intensely expressive masks of dying warriors. The agony of death is portrayed with astonishing classical realism and poignancy. In addition, his workshop produced over one hundred keystones in the form of plumed helmets or classical heads, including a petrifying Medusa, for the arsenal's arches.

His first architectural commission – to build a country palace for the electress Sophie Charlotte in the village of Lietzow – came in

29

1695. Schlüter's design now forms part of the central section of the Charlottenburg Palace, its rural setting – apart from the spacious park – swamped and lost in the past hundred years by Berlin's urban advance. In 1699, the year Schlüter completed his task at Charlottenburg, he was appointed director of building at the Berlin castle, where he was to construct a new residence incorporating the Renaissance work of Caspar Theiss. The imposingly monumental result, added to by Johann Friedrich Eosander, was to be one of the masterpieces of German baroque. Today only Eosander's portal – from which the socialist Karl Liebknecht preached revolution in November 1918 – survives, after being salvaged for political reasons and reincorporated in the State Council building of 1962–4. It was politics too that dictated that the bomb-damaged but repairable castle should be razed in 1950: an act of brazen ideological and architectural vandalism on the part of the communists. In its place they erected the vast and vulgar Palace of the Republic during the 1970s: a huge box-like modernistic monstrosity of concrete and dark reflective glass, an unwanted relic of communism which ironically is now itself under threat of demolition because of its asbestos content.

There was no questioning Schlüter's acclaim as a sculptor – his newly unveiled equestrian portrait of the Great Elector was immediately hailed as a masterpiece – but his architectural work was coming under critical scrutiny. Large cracks had developed in the foundation of the Münzturm (Mint Tower) he was building as part of the castle complex. Work had to be broken off, and a report commissioned from Grünberg and Eosander did not refrain from making embarrassing accusations. Schlüter was relieved of his post as director of building and replaced by Eosander. He was bitter about his treatment, complaining in a letter: 'For more than thirty years I have spent day and night carrying out great work; furthermore, I have already shown in Berlin, as one can clearly see, whether I had become a master, and now I have to let myself be treated so mockingly by such people, in fact just like a foolish youth.' However, the irate architect retained his post as court sculptor until February 1713 when draconian spending cuts were sought by the new king, Frederick William I. Schlüter was able to take up an invitation from Peter the Great to move to St Petersburg, where, among other projects, he worked with the tsar on a *perpetuum mobile* until he died a year later. His architect rival

Eosander also lost his position with the change of monarch and left Berlin, entering first Swedish, then Saxon service.

Frederick William I was a notoriously mean monarch, more interested in book-keeping and rigid discipline than any royal extravagance or licence. He allowed his father a suitably splendid funeral, immediately auctioned off his best wines – his own preference was for tepid brown beer with a good head of froth – and then proceeded to implement his austere regime. Karl Marx was to describe the unlovable monarch as a 'peevish mixture of sergeant, bureaucrat and schoolmaster'. No one suffered at closer quarters than the king's own son, the future Frederick the Great, whose early love of French, philosophy, literature and especially music was deemed unmanly and unsuitable for a crown prince. His own picture of his father's rule, while strongly critical, remains convincingly objective: 'Under Frederick William the State changed its character almost completely. The royal household was dismissed, high salaries slashed. Many who had maintained a coach now had to travel by foot. People say that the king even made cripples walk again. Under Frederick I, Berlin had become the Athens of the north; under Frederick William it was its Sparta. The city resembled an arsenal. In Berlin there were powder mills, in Spandau sabre manufacturers, in Potsdam arms factories and in Neustadt iron and leather workshops.

'The king granted tax concessions and rewards to all who settled in the cities of his land. In Berlin he built up the Friedrichstadt and erected houses on the old defensive walls. Every district of the city received police officers. At the same time carriages for hire were introduced. The city was cleared of idlers who spent their lives in importunate begging; they found shelter in public poorhouses. It was greatly to be regretted amid all these worthwhile innovations that the Academy of Sciences, the arts and trade were allowed to slide into so steep a decline. The Academy of Arts closed down. Stone-masons masqueraded as sculptors and brick-layers as architects.'

Frederick William I was a highly original, even eccentric figure whose parsimony was not quite all embracing. He had a weakness for which he was prepared to pay. He collected soldiers. As his father had patronized art, so Frederick William I took the greatest pride in his regiment of giant grenadiers, his 'Lange Kerls' (tall lads), for which no expense was spared. He became known as the 'Soldier King'

31

not for his military adventurism but for his love of the parade ground, its splendid uniforms and his highly disciplined, impeccably drilled troops who were far too precious to risk in battle. That great connoisseur among princes, Augustus the Strong of Saxony, was only too pleased to swap a regiment of dragoons with Frederick William for a set of priceless oriental vases that immediately became a centre-piece of the royal collection in Dresden.

Instructions were sent out to ambassadors to scour their countries for men of great height – six feet two inches was the minimum requirement – and foreign rulers knew how to gratify the king of Prussia's whim. The Prussian ambassador in London did well to obtain an Irishman who was over seven feet tall for his master, while the king of Denmark sent a Norwegian smith's son who topped six feet nine to Berlin. Frederick William exchanged with the tsar an exquisite gold ship he had inherited from his father for 150 Russian giants. Whether by gift, generous financial inducement or force, Frederick William expanded his regiment of giants, the Rothe Leibbataillon Grenadiers, to some three thousand seven hundred men by the time of his death in 1740, from the six hundred he had accumulated at the end of his time as crown prince in 1713. Untried in battle, the giant grenadiers' last duty was to provide a guard of honour for the funeral of the 'Soldier King'. Frederick the Great, who preferred deployment on the battlefield to the parade ground, had no use for them.

Though himself small (at five feet two inches a foot below the minimum height of his grenadiers), obese and generally obnoxious, Frederick William I was a monarch who meant well. He reformed the civil service and founded Berlin's most famous hospital, the Charité. But as so often, good intentions were no guarantee of popularity. A moral, upright monarch, he ordered that public performances should 'refrain from things that were Godless, annoying or detrimental to Christianity'. Instead, they should be 'innocent scenes for honest amusement'.

He decreed that inns and public houses should close at nine in the evening and toured the streets himself to see that his orders were obeyed. Berliners responded by closing their doors and fastening their shutters when they heard him come. On one occasion a Jew was caught running away at the approach of the corpulent king. 'Why?' the monarch demanded.

'Because I'm afraid,' replied the Jew.

'But you should love not fear me, you rogue!' Frederick William riposted, at the same time horse-whipping the unfortunate.

'When his Majesty took a walk,' Lord Macaulay recorded, 'every human being fled before him, as if a tiger had broken loose from a menagerie. If he met a lady in the street, he gave her a kick, and told her to go home and mind her brats. If he saw a clergyman staring at the soldiers, he admonished the reverend gentleman to betake himself to study and prayer, and enforced this pious advice by a sound caning administered on the spot.'

He would prefer adjourning to the popular King of Portugal inn for a meal than the palace. There the landlady, Frau Nicolai, would prepare him his favourite dish of ham and boiled kale, which to this day remains a north German speciality. Her husband was rewarded with a miniature portrait of the monarch.

A lover of male company, he instituted the nightly 'Tabakskollegium' (Tobacco Assembly), where over cold cuts, ale and tobacco formalities were dropped and free discussion encouraged. In such convivial surroundings he would readily consume a hundred oysters at a sitting and puff his way through up to twenty-five pipes.

Unlike his son, Frederick William could not stand the French, and he once forbade two clergymen from sending their sons to England because it was a 'land of sin'.

A number of churches were built in Berlin during his reign, including the long, low Sophienkirche in 1713; its exquisitely elegant tower, added in 1732–4, gives it an almost English quality, reminiscent of Sir Christopher Wren and his City churches. In fact Johann Friedrich Grael's tower was greatly influenced by Schlüter's design for the ill-fated Münzturm. Extraordinarily, the Sophienkirche, the city's loveliest church, survived the Second World War, emerging unscathed when buildings all around were either destroyed or seriously damaged. Grael's beautifully composed work now stands as Berlin's only original baroque tower, still delighting the eye and gracing a now ungracious skyline.

When Peter the Great belatedly took up an invitation to visit Berlin, six thousand thalers were set aside to defray the costs. So niggardly a book-keeper was Frederick William that he was able to derive the deepest satisfaction when 'only 3,127 Reichsthalers, 4 Groschen and

18 Pfennig were spent – not a Pfennig more, but in public you should say that it cost me between 30,000 and 40,000 thalers!' He lived for 'Armée und Ménage' – the army and thrift. The elegantly laid out Lustgarten was turned into a dusty parade ground and the flower beds of the Charlottenburg Palace were given over to cabbages.

In the end Frederick William preferred Potsdam, where the Great Elector had earlier established a residence, to ungrateful Berlin. There, surrounded by parade grounds and billets, he could be with his beloved battalions and build streets in the homely Dutch style he liked best.

Albeit less brilliantly than under either the Great Elector or Frederick I, Berlin continued to develop and grow, its population climbing steadily during the Soldier King's reign, rising from sixty-one thousand in 1713 to ninety-one thousand by 1740. But still provincial in European terms, the by now thoroughly baroque Prussian capital needed to attract attention abroad if it was to gain any recognition, if it was to attempt to compete with Dresden and Vienna, Paris or London. It was time for Prussia's late introduction to the complicated game of European power politics. Some sabre-rattling beyond the drill square was called for and the young Frederick II, yet to be called the Great, was eager to win his spurs.

TWO

'OLD FRITZ'

To have invented the blitzkrieg is a dubious distinction, but one that the young Frederick can claim. Invasion without declaration of war, and of an ally, was a new, far from honourable concept in warfare. Bound by pact and bond to defend the newly ascended empress of Austria, the 24-year-old Maria Theresa, Frederick sought instead to take advantage of her weakness and, on the basis of an old, tenuous claim on Silesia once harboured by the house of Brandenburg, secretly massed his army and invaded the prosperous province. 'Ambition, interest, the desire of making people talk about me, carried the day; and I decided for war,' he recalled with disarming frankness in his 'Memoirs'.

Gross perfidy and worse was the verdict pronounced by Lord Macaulay in his stirring account of the life of Frederick. 'The king of Prussia, the anti-Machiavel, had already fully determined to commit the great crime of violating his plighted faith, of robbing the ally whom he was bound to defend, and of plunging all Europe into a long, bloody, and desolating war; and all this for no end whatever, except that he might extend his dominions, and see his name in the gazettes.'

The consequences of Frederick's action were wider still, though he might understandably have been taken aback at the extent ascribed in Macaulay's splendid, sulphur-reeking invective: 'The selfish rapacity of the King of Prussia gave the signal to his neighbours . . . The whole world sprang to arms. On the head of Frederick is all the blood which was shed in a war which raged during many years and in every quarter of the globe, the blood of the column of Fontenoy, the blood of the mountaineers who were slaughtered at Culloden. The evils produced by his wickedness were felt in lands where the name of Prussia was unknown; and, in order that he might rob a neighbour whom he had promised to defend, black men fought on the coast of

35

Coromandel, and red men scalped each other by the Great Lakes of North America.'

Frederick's wars marked the birth of Prussian militarism, for his father's collecting of soldiers had been merely a game. Dangerous precedents were being hatched and set by Frederick: blitzkrieg, expansionism, grand ambitions and grander illusions. The newest of kingdoms, Prussia, was casting the mould of modern German history. Notoriety would in due course conjure up the myth of the German bogeyman, which was so unfortunately extended in the next two centuries and would prove inordinately difficult to dismantle. Prussia, previously considered an upstart nation of little consequence, came to be feared and respected. That blue patch on the eighteenth-century atlas became bigger and bigger, and as Prussian influence was extended by military might, so Berlin was forced to take itself, and be taken, more seriously.

Berliners greeted the young Frederick's accession with great relief after the exigencies of his father's reign. He did not disappoint them: he abolished torture and allowed freedom of speech and belief. A jubilant and curious crowd gathered before the castle in the hope of catching a glimpse of the 28-year-old monarch, about whom much was talked but little known. No king of Prussia was ever accorded such a welcome. Everyone pinned their own hopes on the sensitive, intellectual young man who had been bullied and beaten by his father, who had run away, been incarcerated and only narrowly escaped execution for desertion, before effecting some sort of filial reconciliation. But whatever popular expectations may have been, no one can have anticipated a monarch who was at once a follower of Apollo and Mars, a philosopher, general and statesman who earned the appellation 'Great' in his own lifetime. During his 46-year-long rule Prussia was established as a European power and Berlin as a suitable capital.

Although in the end, like his father, Frederick was to prefer Potsdam, the court remained in Berlin, and a certain presence and responsibility were required. Along with early military success, his first task was to embellish the city, to introduce a note of fashion and to give it some cultural standing beyond Brandenburg–Prussia. He had strong views on how this should be done and he had a more than capable architect in Hans Georg Wenzeslaus von Knobelsdorff, a nobleman of diverse talents who had risen to the rank of captain in

36

Frederick William's army before retiring to study under the court painter Antoine Pesne and at the Academy of Arts. By 1729 he had met and struck a friendship with the crown prince, becoming an adviser on artistic matters. Frederick had found an architect who was both amenable to his ideas and of outstanding talent.

In 1734 Knobelsdorff was with the prince on a campaign in the Rhineland and the following year he erected his first building, a temple of Apollo, at Neuruppin, north of Berlin, where he had moved with Frederick. In the tradition of the time an Italian journey followed (1736–7), after which Knobelsdorff accompanied the young Frederick to his country seat at Rheinsberg. There, from 1737 to 1740, he completed the castle and was appointed director of building. At Neuruppin and Rheinsberg the prince and his architect spent hours elaborating and developing their joint architectural ideas, particularly the project for a 'Forum Fridericianum' for Berlin.

It was hardly surprising that, on becoming king, Frederick should appoint Knobelsdorff 'Superintendent of all the Royal Castles, Houses and Gardens' and 'Director-in-chief of Buildings in All the Provinces'. His immediate duty was to design the decorations for Frederick William's funeral and to build an extension of the Monbijou Palace for his widow. A hectic programme followed through the next decade, during which Knobelsdorff was to give Berlin and Potsdam some of their finest and most distinctive buildings. These included the capital's majestic opera house, the solidly elegant Prince Heinrich Palace (which today houses Berlin's Humboldt University), a new, serenely composed wing to the Charlottenburg Palace and, in Potsdam, the architectural jewel of Frederick's reign, the delightfully original and intimate summer palace of Sanssouci.

Architecture was for Frederick an area of 'artistic self-confirmation'. Theatres, gardens and castles 'are my dolls with which I play. I am in these things like a child,' he wrote in 1742. He loved to dabble in designs and present his architects with ideas for them to execute. Inspired by Rome's Pantheon, he produced sketches for Berlin's first Catholic church to be built since the Reformation, the Hedwigskirche (St Hedwig's), with its great, broad dome. Frederick is said to have gained the idea for the church's form from turning a coffee-cup upside down. Knobelsdorff proceeded to draw up a design that was subsequently executed by the Dutchman Johann Boumann. A similar intervention was behind what was to become Berlin's loveliest square, the Gendarmenmarkt. This time, mindful of the Piazza del Popolo in Rome, Frederick suggested that the twin French and German churches on either side of the square should be crowned by matching cupolas that were then designed by Carl von Gontard.

Frederick's interest in architecture may have been awakened by a visit in 1728 to gloriously baroque Dresden, the 'Florence of the Elbe', even if his admiration did not prevent him from sacking the city in 1759. But it seems to have been his early 'thick' friendship – to use Frederick's own word – with Knobelsdorff and his introduction to Count Francesco Algarotti through Voltaire that really stimulated his architectural appetite. Algarotti, described by Voltaire as 'an exceptionally likeable Venetian and son of a stinking rich merchant', was a resolute champion of Palladio, whose influence he succeeded in extending to Prussia. In letters to Frederick during a 25-year-long friendship, he wrote on one occasion, 'I was in Vicenza where I saw what I hope to see soon again in Potsdam' and on another, 'Potsdam will become a school of the art of architecture just as it is an academy of the art of war.' Algarotti, who became a valued member of the king's Sanssouci 'Tafelrunde' discussion dinners, kept him supplied with books, prints, works of art and architectural advice. Frederick's admiration for the art-loving Italian, who had also served the rival court of Dresden well by obtaining priceless pictures for its royal collection, was expressed in the memorial he had erected in 1764 at Algarotti's grave in Pisa. It bore the memorable epitaph, 'Algarottus non omnis', which may be translated as 'Here lies Algarotti, if not all of him.'

Frederick had an infamously difficult character. He was moody and stubborn, he could be petty and mean, but, yearning for the affection he was denied as a child, he sought, valued and rewarded friendship. The closer the bond, however, the harder it proved to maintain. The falling out with Voltaire, with whom he had corresponded since 1736 and who was his guest and chamberlain in Potsdam and Berlin from 1750 to 1753, proved mutually unedifying. The souring of the long-standing association with Knobelsdorff was deeply disappointing. In 1746 Knobelsdorff withdrew from the direction of the building at Sanssouci on health grounds. Frederick took this as a personal affront and Knobelsdorff's authority was gradually whittled away, though he still retained ministerial rank in 1748. Another possible cause of friction was Frederick's abhorrence of basements, despite the advice of his architects, and his resistance to Knobelsdorff's suggestion that one should be built at Sanssouci. References to his chief architect in his letters lost their warmth: 'I don't get anywhere with him these days. He doesn't carry things out as I wish, and he's as lazy as an artillery horse.' Yet for all the irritation and upset on the surface, Frederick retained a deep affection for an old friend and after the architect's death in September 1753, in an act unprecedented between monarch and architect, himself wrote a tribute to Knobelsdorff which was read at the Academy of Sciences in January 1754. 'He embellished architecture through his painterly taste, which lent grace to ordinary ornaments. He loved the noble simplicity of the Greeks, and his finesse would allow no decoration that was out of place.'

The opera house on Unter den Linden stands as Knobelsdorff's Berlin masterpiece, its classical form and noble proportions adding considerable grace to the city's great avenue. It was already conceived in Rheinsberg by Frederick and his architect as a key element in their plan for a Forum Fridericianum at the head of Unter den Linden, only part of which ever came to be realized. The Royal Opera House, its grand portico supported by six Corinthian columns, was a revolutionary building in its day – the first theatre to be free standing and separate from the castle. Work began on this true temple of art in 1741 and, though only completed two years later, it was given an early inauguration in December 1742 when Frederick, returning in triumph as the conqueror of Silesia, held a glittering investiture in his new opera house followed by a masked ball that lasted the night long.

While leading his troops in the field, Frederick had written to Berlin hungry for more news of his projects, even though he was receiving almost daily reports. 'Tell Knobelsdorff that he should write to me about my buildings, my furniture, my gardens and the opera house, so as to distract me.' When his chief architect did write, it was not enough. 'I have got a letter from Knobelsdorff with which I am very satisfied. But everything is too dry, there are no details. I would like the description of each bit of column at Charlottenburg to fill four sides of quarto: that would entertain me highly.'

Knobelsdorff had simultaneously worked on the extensions to the Monbijou and Charlottenburg palaces, the royal apartment and court theatre in the castle, the lay-out of the Tiergarten park and the plan for the Hedwigskirche before adjourning to Potsdam by 1745 to carry out his great commission at Sanssouci. Apart from the opera house and the fine new wing he added to the Charlottenburg Palace, little of the Berlin work of Frederick's most distinguished architect has survived. Not a trace remains of Monbijou, which once gracefully hugged the curve of the Spree's north bank. Its site is now occupied by a drab park dominated by children's playgrounds, where in the wake of East Germany's peaceful revolution and the overthrow of communism young women celebrated their new-won liberty by going topless and sunbathing the moment summer came.

After Knobelsdorff, Frederick's relations with lesser architects were no less fraught. With advancing age he became increasingly despotic and impatient, his demands more unreasonable and his economies more radical. Frederick found the estimate excessive for the theatre at the Neues Palais in Potsdam, so he suggested that four thousand thalers could be saved by using papier mâché for the decoration instead of plaster. The elder Boumann was arrested after a building of his at the royal porcelain works collapsed. Instructed in July 1765 to complete it by the end of the year, he continued work during the frosty winter months, injudiciously ordering the mortar to be mixed with warm water. The building was in place when the king, delighted that it had been completed on time, inspected it. But a year later it collapsed, one person was killed and Boumann was for a while put behind bars.

Neither did Frederick spare Carl von Gontard, the designer of the matching towers and cupolas for the French and German churches in the Gendarmenmarkt, whom he described as an 'ass'. Gontard was forced to surrender responsibility for the project to Georg Christian Unger after the cupola of the German church came down in July 1781.

Frederick's obsession with architecture, and his pronounced views and ideas on the subject, ensured the transformation of Berlin during his reign into an altogether more elegant, some might say effeminate city. Knobelsdorff had the gift of originality, but his successors were inclined to imitate the French or Dutch. Frederick himself, while partial to both these styles (in 1755 he travelled incognito to Holland to undertake his own study), also looked to the Roman example with which he was familiar from the prints provided by Count Algarotti. It was elevations which the king loved; ground plans and practical details he left to his architects.

The masculinity of Schlüter's baroque buildings was missing from the largely derivative style of 'Friderician rococo' that succeeded Knobelsdorff's more substantial achievement. Always decorative and often attractive, it was a taste of formal, florid, sometimes brittle elegance that matched in stone the golden notes that Frederick elaborated in the adagios of his flute concertos. There was style but no muscle. But then, except on the field of battle, it was not a muscular age.

Typically, Berliners were amused rather than impressed by the royal library raised between 1774 and 1785 by Unger as another element in the long planned Forum Fridericianum. It looked, they rightly thought, like a giant chest of drawers, so Berlin's first library building became known as the royal 'commode'. In 1747 the dilapidated old Dominican church was pulled down to make room for a new cathedral at the Lustgarten. A number of architects were involved in a project which strangely was never successfully resolved. Christian Friedrich Feldmann, Knobelsdorff himself and the elder Boumann had a say, but the result was disappointingly weak until redeemed in the next century by Schinkel. Even then the cathedral was considered flawed and had eventually to give way to its bombastic and vulgar Wilhelmine successor.

The Hedwigskirche (the Catholic cathedral which was also begun in 1747, but being church funded, took the best part of thirty years to build) was, on the other hand, an impressive building by any reckoning, with six massive Ionic columns supporting a pediment of some magnificence and the huge dome capping the circular church like a great comestible mushroom. Gutted by fire during an air raid in March 1943, it now has a duck-egg green and white painted interior – with double columns like giant gold-tipped cigarettes – as modern as the new Roman liturgy, though the exterior has retained its classical character.

Commendable too is the Prince Heinrich Palace, which was built between 1748 and 1753 for Frederick's brother by the elder Boumann to a plan of Knobelsdorff in lieu of the royal palace that was originally intended to complete Frederick's Forum. A freeze on spending during

41

the Seven Years War left Carl Ludwig Hildebrandt to add the finishing touches in 1764–6. The central part is set back from Unter den Linden behind a court enclosed by two forceful wings. The gentle rustication, the tall arched first-floor windows, a balustrade of agreeable lightness and the six fluted Corinthian columns carrying a rectangular pediment crowned by as many statues prevent the creation of too solid an impression. The palace's easy classicism suggests rather a mood of civilized scholarship, something that suited it well from 1809, when it became the home of the university founded by Wilhelm von Humboldt.

Friedrich Schleiermacher, the first head of the university's theology faculty and an outspoken champion of the patriotism awakened by Napoleon's occupation of Berlin, noted of his lectures: 'Mainly students, women and officers come to me. The students have to hear me preach, the women wish to eye the students, and the officers come on account of the women.'

Since 1883 the courtyard entrance has been overseen by large marble statues of the Humboldt brothers, Wilhelm and Alexander, by Reinhold Begas and Martin Otto. The distinguished German academics, one a brilliant philosopher and humanist, the other an outstanding geographer and explorer, are portrayed seated, books in hand, and looking distinctly weary from their academic labour.

The university, which developed a reputation for conservatism as the century progressed, was the last one in Germany to admit women, only opening its doors to them in 1908. During the forty years of communist rule that led to the 1989 revolution it was a bastion of Marxism, which was not entirely inappropriate as the author of *Das Kapital* had studied there from 1836 to 1841.

In front of the Prince Heinrich Palace and across from the square formed by the opera house, the Hedwigskirche and the royal library, Frederick the Great is mounted on his faithful charger, Condé – he was in the habit of naming his mounts after hostile statesmen, enabling him at various times to sit astride Kaunitz, Brühl, Choiseul, Pitt the Elder and Lord Bute. His shoulders bent with fatigue, his head and tricorn tilted, he surveys what became of his Forum Fridericianum. Christian Daniel Rauch's inspired equestrian statue of the 'Alte Fritz' ('Old Fritz', or 'Old Fred' if anglicized further) stands as a small island in the midst of Unter den Linden, at its aesthetic apex, the traffic parting on either side like the flow of a forceful river. His generals, ministers, counsellors, members of his family and notable contemporaries are portrayed around the base of the monument, which was unveiled in 1851 and has been an integral part of Berlin's grand boulevard almost ever since. It was absent for a while under communism. After being put away for safekeeping as the wartime Allied air raids on Berlin intensified, Frederick eventually surfaced again in 1950 in the park of Sanssouci. By the early 1980s Prussia's conquering hero was rehabilitated and returned to his familiar spot, having been granted political acceptability by the communists. It was then that East Germany's élite regiments, like battleships earlier in the century, were given the names of Prussia's greatest generals.

Frederick's desire to improve Berlin's appearance was not restricted to its most prestigious edifices. He had several hundred palace-like buildings put up to provide housing for officials and ordinary citizens. But as in Potsdam, where around the castle he had houses and workplaces built for artisans employed by the court, his munificence was not always practical. Visually attractive, the buildings were sometimes ill suited to living or working.

Indefatigable in his efforts as 'first servant of the state', the king encouraged industry, notably the manufacture of silk and porcelain (founding the Königliche Porzellan Manufaktur), and supervised the construction of the necessary factories and canals for the transport of raw materials and finished goods. The industrial revolution was not such a distant prospect. In 1781 the first spinning-jenny machine was introduced to Berlin.

Frederick's transformation of Berlin was such that by the time Boswell reached it on his European tour in 1764, he could describe the city as the finest he had ever seen. But while it was considered pleasant to look at, doubts were expressed about its inhabitants. In 1772, for example, the English minister based there considered Berlin a city bereft of 'either an honest man or a chaste woman'. Three years later the poet Christian von Stolberg found the tone of society 'affected and imitative of the French, the minister arrogant and the women silly and unnatural, rouged and decorated with feathers like sleigh-horses'. And the eighteenth-century travel writer Georg Forster concurred: 'I found the exterior much more attractive, but what was inside much blacker than I had imagined.'

Beyond his duty, Frederick did not care for life in Berlin either, preferring Potsdam and the intimacy of Sanssouci, where, instead of the court he despised, he could surround himself with chosen intellectuals and discuss literature, philosophy, art and music, with which he would regale his guests every evening.

Music was for Frederick a necessary and, if possible, daily distraction. He would even take a portable clavichord and flute on his military campaigns, finding time between battles to compose and play for his own pleasure. Individual members of the court orchestra were put into uniform and sent to accompany him at field headquarters.

He seems to have inherited his musical gifts from his grandparents, for Frederick I had been a talented flautist and Sophie Charlotte an outstanding harpsichord player. It was to his great-uncle, the margrave Christian Ludwig, youngest son of the Great Elector, that Johann Sebastian Bach dedicated his Brandenburg Concertos in March 1721. Living in a wing of the Berlin castle, the margrave maintained a modest orchestra which provided at least a glimmer of culture during the barren years of Frederick William's reign.

As a seven-year-old Frederick was already receiving his first musical instruction and keyboard lessons from the cathedral organist Gottlieb Heyne. At one stage the violin was introduced into his programme, but it was the flute which became the crown prince's favourite instrument and which his irascible and philistine father once cracked over his head in a rage at his son's artistic pursuits.

On the trip to Dresden in 1728 the sixteen-year-old Frederick was introduced to the virtuoso flautist Johann Joachim Quantz, but his mother's subsequent attempt to secure the musician's services with a generous salary foundered on the unwillingness of Augustus II of Saxony to part with his first flute. He did, however, allow him leave twice a year, during which he could give lessons to the prince of Prussia. A bond was forged which proved more durable than almost any other formed by the notoriously difficult Frederick. Soon after becoming king he was able to take Quantz into his service on an annual salary of two thousand thalers for life. His duties included directing the evening chamber concerts and supervising the royal practice. He was also responsible for procuring flutes for his master and for their production. Other than his own work, Frederick would play only compositions by Quantz, who alone was permitted to applaud the king's performance. Over the years he was to compose three hundred flute concertos and two hundred pieces of chamber music for Frederick, who honoured his teacher by himself completing Quantz's last unfinished work following his death in July 1773.

Contemporary accounts relate that Frederick's particular strength lay in his playing of adagios with their drawn-out decorative passages. The singer Elisabeth Schmehling, who clashed with the king, none the less spoke of his strong sound and his great skill with the instrument, and Charles Burney found Frederick in some respects excelled all he had heard 'among amateurs, or even professional flautists'. The king went on playing until 1779 when, at the age of sixty-seven, his teeth were too rotten to continue. At the same time he ceased going to the opera.

Frederick himself wrote 121 sonatas for the flute as well as the 4 concertos, 2 sinfonias, a serenade and 3 marches which have survived. All were written in a flowing hand for his own performance and pleasure and were not meant for publication, though without his knowledge or approval the spirited Sinfonia in D minor did find its way into print. It is a bouncing, festive work scored for two flutes, two oboes, two horns and string orchestra written between 1742 and 1747, when it was performed as an overture to the serenade *Il rè pastore* performed for his mother's birthday. The lyrical flute parts would have been taken by Frederick and Quantz, the basso continuo played by one of the most gifted of Bach's sons, Carl Philipp Emanuel, who had come to Rheinsberg in 1738 and was engaged two years later as court harpsichordist. In his autobiography he noted that he accompanied the king's first 'flute solo . . . in Charlottenburg, quite alone at the keyboard'. But C. P. E. Bach was never really content during his long, thankless years directing the court orchestra from the harpsichord, his own compositions remaining unappreciated by the king. Finally, in 1767 he managed to free himself from his obligations and move to Hamburg, where he took over from his godfather, Telemann, as director of music.

The king's musical taste was markedly conservative and secular; he was unmoved by innovation. His famous meeting with Johann Sebastian Bach in Potsdam in 1747 proved a disappointing anti-climax. It began promisingly enough with 'the old Bach', as Frederick called him, taking a theme played by the king and improvising brilliantly on the wide selection of keyboards, including the new Silbermann 'forte e pianos' available in the Potsdam Stadtschloss. On his return to Leipzig the Thomaskirche cantor recalled the royal theme in his deeply original *Musical Offering*, which was published with a dedication to Frederick. Bach's industry and invention received neither recognition nor, despite the custom, reward from the king, whose interest in the composer had been only fleeting. In the end the great Bach's compositions were really too complex and intellectual, too hard to reconcile with the king's gallant view of music.

Frederick's cultural autocracy let notable developments in the world of music slip by: the Mannheim school had established a new classical style in the 1740s that was to be an important influence on the young Mozart; in opera in the 1760s Christoph Willibald von Gluck's modern music dramas were proving revolutionary. Both were ignored.

The same was true of German literature, which scarcely interested a king who could only speak the language with difficulty. He himself described his broken German as 'like a coachman's!' French was his preferred language; his personal library was filled with French books, among them translations of the classics, and it was in French that he wrote his verse and prose. He was so blinkered that he overlooked the budding of a new German literary spirit that included the young Goethe. His verdict on *Götz von Berlichingen*, Goethe's early Shakespeare-influenced play, which enjoyed considerable popular success when it was performed in Berlin in 1774, was devastating and made typically in French: 'Here is a Götz de Berlichingen on stage, a detestable imitation of those bad English plays, and the parterre applauds and calls enthusiastically for these disgusting platitudes to be repeated.'

The king's taste in opera was decidedly Italian and conventional. The two principal court composers, Carl-Heinrich Graun, who had directed Frederick's orchestra since 1735, and Johann Adolph Hasse, whose *Cleofide* in Dresden in 1728 was the first opera heard by the then crown prince, both created works exclusively in the Italian manner. Their operas – Graun was to write no fewer than thirty-one for Berlin – completely dominated the repertoire. Frederick would occasionally compose arias himself for insertion into the operas and he wrote several libretti, such as that for Graun's *Montezuma* in 1755. His interference was inescapable. He would give his composers advice, would himself determine the repertoire, supervise rehearsals and decide on the sets and costumes. He allowed an annual budget of forty thousand thalers for the opera.

No sooner was his unmusical father buried than Frederick dispatched Graun on a nine-month-long trip to Italy to raise an ensemble of singers for the Berlin opera house that Knobelsdorff was building. Graun succeeded in reaping a rich crop of talent, attracting to Berlin such stars as Benedetta Moltenie, Felice Salimbeni, Antonio Romani and the castrati Giovanni Carestini, Antonio Uberti, known as 'Porporino', and Paolo Bedeschi, or 'Paulino'. In 1747 the celebrated Giovanna Astrua, at the tender age of seventeen, was secured for a salary of six thousand thalers. There was no question of German singers being engaged, the new king declaring memorably that he would sooner hear a horse neigh on stage than a German sing.

Much later in his reign, however, he was to be astounded by the discovery by Count Zierotin, his 'directeur des spectacles', of the young German singer Elisabeth Schmehling, who became known as 'Mara'. A pupil of Paradisi in London and Hiller in Leipzig, she staggered the doubtful king with her vocal ability and in 1771, aged twenty-two, was engaged at an annual salary of three thousand thalers for life. Her partnership with the castrato Concialini revived for a while the flagging fortunes of the Berlin opera, which reopened in 1764 after closure during the Seven Years War, but had, it was generally agreed, lost its glamour. There was little doubt that Mara, the first German soprano of class, outshone the Italian prima donnas both in her singing and her capriciousness. In 1773 the king's anger was so aroused by signs that she intended to marry that a power struggle developed between the two which soon became a minor court scandal. It was only ended by her escape to Vienna in 1780.

Her flight confirmed Frederick's belief that all singers and dancers were 'whores'. A frightful misogynist, Frederick had no time for women except for his mother, whom he respected greatly, and his sister, Wilhelmine, margravine of Bayreuth, to whom he was to remain very close. He completely ignored Elisabeth Christine of Brunswick, the wife thrust upon him by his father, who, restricted to the royal palace at Niederschönhausen – appropriately, Frederick remarked, as she was 'neither low [nieder] nor beautiful [schön]' – and banished from Potsdam, was queen only in name. Her appearances at the Berlin castle were limited to official functions. Frederick loved his grey-hounds more.

It was with them – with Alcmene, Thisbe, Diane, Phillis, Arsinoe, Biges, Pan, Achilles, Superbe, Chloe, Biche, Amourette and Mylord – that he planned to share his tomb, a wish that was not fulfilled until August 1991 after a delay of 205 years. As early as 1744 he had had the vault laid out that he intended for himself and his greyhounds above the vine-trailed terraces of Sanssouci, on to which he looked from his study window. But his will was ignored and, until its removal for safekeeping during the Second World War, his body remained in a tin coffin in Potsdam's Garrison Church next to his father, the 'Soldier King', for whom he held so little affection.

Frederick's weakness for his sleek greyhounds knew no bounds. He sometimes called them his 'Marchionesses de Pompadour' – after Louis XV's influence-wielding mistress and Prussia's sworn enemy – but always remembered to add that they cost him less. He would sleep with his current favourite, or take her riding tucked snugly under his coat. He would read to Arsinoe and write a letter on Biche's behalf to Folichon, the preferred hound of his sister Wilhelmine. It was his adored Biche who saved Frederick's life at the battle near Soor by remaining silent when he hid from the passing enemy under the arch of a bridge. Her image was perpetuated in a painting by Pesne that hung in Sanssouci's music room, where she died.

Johann Gottfried Schadow was later, in 1821, to produce a famous bronze group of Frederick, cane in hand, walking with Alcmene (named after the mother of Hercules) and Hasenfuss (Harefoot), which now aptly stands in the Sanssouci study where in the early hours of 17 August 1786 Prussia's eccentric but formidable king breathed his last.

One of the very few women accepted by Frederick was the dancer Barberina, a beauty whose graceful portrait, tambourine in hand, by the dependable court artist Antoine Pesne, decorated Frederick's room in the Berlin castle. A Venetian, unlike most of the dancers, who came from Paris, she was engaged in 1744 on a salary of seven thousand thalers. Voltaire noted how Frederick had 'the most beautiful voices and the best dancers in his service' and recalled: 'Barberina used to dance in his theatre: she later married the son of his chancellor. The king let this dancer be abducted in Venice by soldiers who brought

1. Berlin in 1635. The oldest known view, accompanying an equestrian portrait of Elector Georg Wilhelm, probably engraved by Albrecht Christian Kalle. George Wilhelm, who ruled from 1619 to 1640 and pursued a policy of fluctuating neutrality during the Thirty Years War, was the father of the Great Elector.

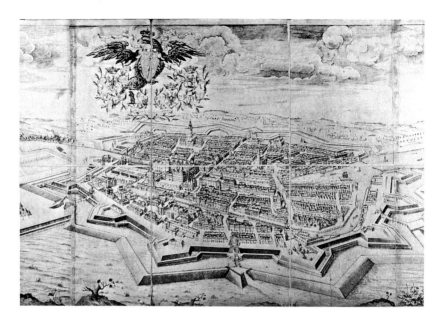

2. View of Berlin in 1688, the last year of the Great Elector's rule, during which the city's population had been significantly bolstered and its future character determined by the influx of Huguenot refugees from France. From an engraving by Johann Bernhard Schultz.

3. Berlin viewed through English eyes almost a century later, in 1780, by the engraver Thornton. As a result of the long and eventful reign of Frederick the Great, which was about to draw to a close, Prussia and its capital had achieved recognition across Europe and won inclusion on the gentleman traveller's itinerary.

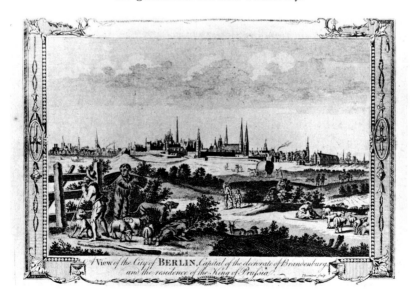

A View of the City of BERLIN, Capital of the electorate of Brandenburg, and the residence of the King of Prussia.

4. Berlin from the Rollberge, an idyllic pre-industrial pastoral setting portrayed in an aquatint of 1800 by Florian Grosspietsch.

5. Schinkel's monument in cast iron to the Wars of Liberation on the Tempelhofer Berg, subsequently renamed Kreuzberg – at two hundred feet, Berlin's highest natural hill. Erected in 1821, the neo-Gothic edifice is reminiscent both of the then still uncompleted Cologne Cathedral and English Eleanor Crosses. Overlooking the Prussian army's exercise grounds, the Kreuzberg for many years provided a favourite vantage point from which to view the city. This engraving of 1825 is based on a drawing by Calau.

6. Berlin at the dawn of the industrial revolution when smoking
chimney-stacks rose between long familiar church spires.
Engraving by A. H. Payne.

7. (*Left*) The Marienkirche in 1832, with its delightfully eclectic late
eighteenth-century lantern, incorporating both Gothic and classical
elements, by Langhans, architect of the Brandenburg Gate.
8. (*Right*) The Marienkirche over a hundred years later in 1939,
rising magisterially above Berlin's distinctly industrial skyline and
hemmed in by close-clustered buildings that were soon to be reduced
to ruins by relentless wartime bombing.

9. (*Above*) The Sophienkirche, Berlin's only surviving original baroque church and its loveliest. Grael's wonderfully elegant tower, erected in 1732 – twenty years after the main body of the church – has an almost English quality, reminiscent of Wren or Hawksmoor.

10. (*Above right*) The Nikolaikirche, Berlin's oldest church, depicted in 1832, showing its original, engagingly asymmetrical tower, which fell victim to late nineteenth-century taste, and the lace-like Liebfrauenkapelle, which was destroyed by wartime bombardment.

11. (*Right*) Rebuilding the ruined church in 1982.

Prospect oder Weg, gegen dem Thier=Garden vor Berlin

1. Obrist von Weilers Haus. 3. Königl Ställe
2. Saldamms Brücke

Linden Allee
1691.

Johann Stridbeck ad vst.

2. (*Above left*) The newly laid Unter den Linden in 1691, described as 'Linden Allee' in Johann Stridbeck the Younger's drawing.

3. (*Below left*) Unter den Linden in 1804 – already Berlin's most cosmopolitan boulevard.

4. (*Right*) A drawing of 1739 by Knobelsdorff, Frederick the Great's most notable architect, showing the 'Forum Fridericianum' at the head of Unter den Linden. Frederick has himself inked in corrections.

5. (*Below*) Napoleon Bonaparte's triumphant entry into Berlin through the Brandenburg Gate in 1806. Among the squadrons of cavalry accompanying him was an enthusiastic young officer, Henri Beyle, who was later to adopt the name Stendhal after the town in the Mark Brandenburg and to achieve enduring fame as a novelist.

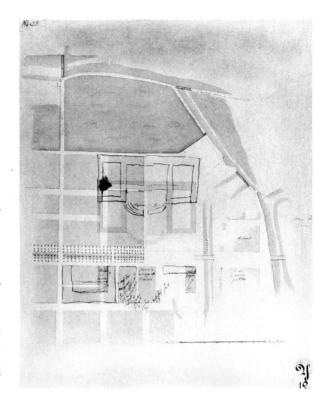

16. The 'Horse Thief of Berlin'. Napoleon carries off Schadow's Victoria and her Quadriga as a trophy to Paris. 'Arrogance took her – courage brought her back', according to the inscription on the satirical print.

17. The Brandenburg Gate without the Quadriga in an engraving of 1813 by F. A. Calau. The following year Blücher brought Victoria and her carriage back, to the delight and acclaim of Berliners.

18. The Friedrichswerdersche Kirche in 1835. The red brick neo-Gothic church, dating from 1824, is Schinkel's most English creation.

19. (*Left*) The Friedrichswerdersche Kirche in 1931.

20. (*Above*) The church sixty years later in 1991, carefully restored after wartime bomb damage.

21. Karl Friedrich Schinkel. Oil portrait by C. F. Schmidt.
22. (*Below*) The Bauakademie (1832–5), Schinkel's late masterpiece, described here as the 'Berlin School of Architecture'. It was in the apartment set aside for Prussia's chief architect that Schinkel died in October 1841, never having regained consciousness from a stroke suffered as a result of overwork in September 1840.

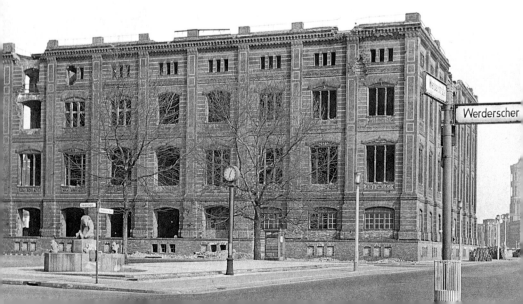

4. (*Right*) Door frame with terracotta reliefs from the Bauakademie, salvaged and later incorporated into a building behind the Friedrichswerdersche Kirche as an entrance to the Schinkelklause restaurant. In 1990, on the eve of German reunification, chewing-gum was stickily smeared across the nose of the sphinx-like figure on the bottom right, and two years later it had still to be removed.

5. (*Below*) Drawing by Schinkel (1823) of his Altes Museum and the former cathedral, which he improved. Though much maligned, and later demolished, the cathedral fitted in with the finely balanced proportions of the Lustgarten more happily than its bombastic early twentieth-century successor, in which Christopher Isherwood detected 'a flash of that hysteria which flickers always behind a very grave, grey Prussian façade'.

3. (*Left*) The Bauakademie, battered and gutted by bombs and artillery fire but eminently restorable, immediately before the communist authorities pulled it down in 1961 to make way for their lamentable Foreign Ministry building. In the background is the strikingly Italianate tower of the 'Rotes Rathaus', so called because of its red brick, built between 1861 and 1869 to a design by Hermann Friedrich Waesemann, clearly and inevitably influenced by Schinkel's important late work.

6. (*Opposite page*) Schinkel's drawing of the staircase hall of the Altes Museum, completed in 1830. Built to house the royal collections, it was conceived as a museum in the modern sense and immediately became a focus of Biedermeier elegance and erudition.

7. The Altes Museum, with its breathtaking colonnade of eighteen Ionic columns, in 1920.

---

8. (*Right*) One of the two statues adorning the sweep of stairs at the museum entrance, A. Wolff's *Young Man on Horseback Spearing a Lion*, pictured in 1935. In the background rises Julius Raschdorff's restless cathedral, completed in 1905. 'Extinguished by its absurd dome, it is, at first sight, so startlingly funny that one searches for a name suitably preposterous – the Church of the Immaculate Consumption' (Isherwood).

9. (*Below*) The shattered columns and ruins of the Crown Prince's Palace in 1945. To the left lies the bruised Zeughaus and in the background the wrecked cathedral and castle.

30. The Gendarmenmarkt in 1815 in an aquatint by Calau. On the left is the German cathedral (not to be confused with the Berlin Cathedral already illustrated) and partially depicted on the right the French cathedral, an ensemble planned by Frederick the Great and, with its matching domes and breadth, once considered one of the loveliest squares in Europe. The centre-piece here is Langhans's worthy National Theatre (1800–1802); it was destroyed by a fire in 1817 and replaced by Schinkel's masterful Schauspielhaus, which, for reasons of royal economy, had to incorporate the theatre's old columns in its raised portico.

31. The square in 1822, painted in oil by Wilhelm Hasenpflug, showing Schinkel's recently completed Schauspielhaus.

2. The French cathedral in flames after an air raid in 1944. On the left are the ruins of the German cathedral. The Schauspielhaus also suffered extensive damage.

3. In 1952, and for the next thirty years, the square remained in ruins.

4. The restored Schauspielhaus in 1990, with work well advanced on the German cathedral. Behind lies the newly built Dom (now Hilton) Hotel and the huge apartment blocks erected by the communists on the Leipziger Strasse in the 1970s. The French cathedral was the first of the Gendarmenmarkt's fine trinity of buildings to be reopened, impeccably restored, in 1983. Reinhold Begas's untypically sensitive marble statue of Schiller was later returned after an absence fifty years to its place in front of the Schauspielhaus.

35. Schinkel's Neue Wache and the Zeughaus on Unter den Linden in an oil painting of 1828 by Wilhelm Brücke. The Schlossbrücke leading to the castle lies at the end of Unter den Linden. In front to the right, amidst the bustle of Biedermeier Berlin, Rauch's statue of Blücher, sabre in hand and foot resting on a broken French cannon, may be seen; in front of the guardhouse the sculptor's marble likenesses of generals von Bülow and Scharnhorst occupy their original positions. Behind lie the horse-chestnut trees beloved by the poet and playwright Gerhart Hauptmann.

36. A similar scene in 1902, complete with fashionable couples, smart officers and delivery boys barely distracted by the changing of the guard.

her to Berlin via Vienna. Incomprehensible was only that he paid her thirty-two thousand pounds salary.'

The inaugural performance in December 1742 in the still incomplete opera house was Graun's *Cesare e Cleopatra*, the composer in his red conductor's coat directing the thirty-seven-man orchestra himself. The building was clad in scaffolding, the unfinished ceiling covered with a tarpaulin, the balustrades of the boxes unpainted, the corridors hastily covered in an undercoat wash. The king arrived to a fanfare and took his seat in the middle of the front row of stalls; the dress circle box was reserved for the queen, the stalls boxes for diplomats and foreigners of note who could report home glowingly on Berlin's first opera house. Culturally, the Prussian capital had come of age with such a fine building dedicated to music.

Those who had watched the young Frederick had expected as much. In 1725 the Austrian minister at the court of Prussia wrote an assessment of the thirteen-year-old prince that ended with a prediction that was to prove devastatingly erroneous, especially for Austria. 'He was a musician, a moralist, physician, mechanic. He will never be either a general or warrior.'

A stream of musicians had headed for Berlin on Frederick's accession, hoping for advancement in an Apollonian age. Even Georg Friedrich Händel, comfortably settled in London, his name long anglicized to Handel, considered departing for what promised to be Europe's new musical capital. None could realize that Mars was to hold his sway and that it would be Prussian cannon that accompanied the royal flute. 'The prince cast his philosopher's coat aside and reached for his sword the moment he spied a province that pleased him,' Voltaire wrote unapprovingly.

Given new artistic and political standing by a king who was at once a philosopher and warrior, Berlin had still to pay for his policy of conquest and war. In 1757 and 1760 it suffered the indignity and discomfort of occupation: first by Austrian and then by rapacious Russian troops. Battle, and particularly the Seven Years War from 1756 to 1763, brought hardship as well as glory. Men were lost and taxes, billets and rations were demanded, but Frederick's strong hand was admired by a people who always looked up to firm leadership. The 'Alte Fritz', for all his faults, certainly inspired loyalty, even affection among his subjects. He used to say that he wanted the people of Berlin to have surroundings that would uplift them and distract them from their humdrum, sordid lives. Not only princes should survey splendour.

During Frederick's reign Berlin grew into one of Europe's major cities. When he had come to the throne there were 5,400 houses, many of them built of wood and no more than hovels; by the time of his death, forty-six eventful years later, the number of houses had more than doubled and solid brick had largely replaced wood. Fine palaces reflected the prosperity of the ruling classes. The city's population, despite the deprivation of war, had meanwhile risen to 145,000 from 90,000 at the start of his reign. Soldiers and their dependants accounted for some 30,000, giving the city the distinctly martial air it was to retain as long as Prussia existed.

It had been an exhausting reign for both Frederick and Berlin, but much had been achieved. When it had finally run its course and Frederick passed away quietly in his favourite, greyhound-pawed, pale-green silk upholstered chair in Sanssouci, there was almost a sense of relief in anticipation of less demanding times.

So cultivated a king that he could at one moment argue philosophy with Voltaire and the next adjourn to compose and play the flute accompanied by one of Bach's sons, Frederick had been the most enlightened of despots. He had wanted and created a capital that would vie in elegance, grandeur and importance with the great cities of Europe. The dazzling courts of Paris, Vienna, Dresden and St Petersburg were confronted with a new rival that required more serious consideration than they might have wished. Prussia had proved by deed that it was more than just an upstart among European states and monarchies. Frederick had succeeded in turning a previously minor power into a major force.

There were undoubtedly many sides to Prussia's great king that were far from attractive, but to Berlin's benefit he was that rarest of beings, a German leader with taste. Others later tried hard to emulate him, whether the bombastic Kaiser Wilhelm II or an evil Austrian demagogue called Hitler. But, while they achieved power, they always lacked taste.

THREE

THE HORSE THIEF OF BERLIN

I T was a remarkable accident of history that the paths, or swords, of two of the greatest military tacticians of their age so narrowly failed to meet. When, twenty years after Frederick's death, Napoleon, having won Berlin and ridden in triumph at the head of twelve thousand men through its Brandenburg Gate, stood before the great Prussian king's tin coffin in Potsdam, he remarked with some reason, 'If that man were still alive, I would not be here.'

Napoleon held Frederick in the highest esteem as a military strategist and, significantly, had made a study of his battles. He singled out Leuthen, the small Silesian village west of Breslau where in December 1757 the Prussians trounced a numerically superior Austrian army, as Frederick's most notable victory. 'That battle,' commented Napoleon, 'was a masterpiece. Of itself it is sufficient to entitle Frederick to a place in the first rank among generals.'

Lord Macaulay, in his account of the battle, identified its Bonapartist appeal. 'The King, who was, in general, perhaps too much inclined to consider the common soldier as a mere machine, resorted, on this great day, to means resembling those which Bonaparte afterwards employed with such signal success for the purpose of stimulating military enthusiasm. The principal officers were convoked. Frederic addressed them with great force and pathos; and directed them to speak to their men as he had spoken to them.'

Napoleon received his commission as an artillery officer in 1785, the year before Frederick died. Eight years later, aged but twenty-four, he was promoted to general. The proximity of the French Revolution – a mere three years – to the close of the reign of the Prussian despot and exponent of 'enlightened absolutism' is extraordinary.

Berlin was not yet ready for revolution; it was still seeking to establish its identity, a process which was completed by the time Napoleon arrived in the city in 1806 and earned the people's scorn by carrying

51

off the Quadriga that crowned the Brandenburg Gate. 'Napoleon, the horse thief of Berlin' was portrayed in caricatures sneaking away across the Spree, hunched, bearing the famous horse-drawn chariot on his back. Of course, Napoleon had frequently and unashamedly looted before; the horses of St Mark's in Venice were packed up and taken to Paris to join obelisks from Egypt and prize works of art lifted from collections the length and breadth of Europe. But the Quadriga had in its thirteen years surmounting the Brandenburg Gate, Berlin's first great classical landmark, achieved a popularity among the people which made its removal rash. Theodor Fontane put it into verse: 'Warte Bonaparte, warte Kujon, andere Woche, wir kriegen dich schon' (Just you wait, Bonaparte, just you wait, scoundrel, in another week, we'll get you).

The theft of Berlin's most visible symbol provided a rallying cause that stirred the new-found patriotic spirit which was to lead to Napoleon's defeat at Leipzig and the Quadriga's triumphant return in 1814. In December 1806 the victor had taken his trophy, leaving the gate bare for seven and a half years. In the spring of 1814 the sculpture was brought back from Paris in a convoy of six vehicles drawn by thirty-two horses. 'Arrogance took her, courage brought her back,' the celebrating Berliners declared. The Königliche Porzellan Manufaktur produced a fine bone china cup and saucer depicting Victory and her chariot with the words, 'Welcome Back to Berlin 1814'. Giacomo Meyerbeer, whose action-packed operas were later to be the rage of Paris and London and who in 1842 became director of the Berlin opera, composed an oratorio, *Das Brandenburger Thor* (The Brandenburg Gate), to mark the joyous occasion. Born in Berlin in 1791 and in reality called Jakob Liebmann Beer, the future master of grand opera was as old as the gate itself.

Johann Gottfried Schadow's figure of a bare-breasted Victoria, staff in hand, riding a chariot drawn by four prancing horses, provided the necessary finishing touch to the severely classical, Doric-columned gate which Karl Gotthard Langhans modelled on the Propylaea in Athens and completed two years earlier, in 1791, at the bottom of Unter den Linden. As his model for the redoubtable goddess Schadow took a local Berlin girl, Ulrike Jury, a relative of Emmanuel Jury, the Potsdam coppersmith with whom he was working on the project. He had wanted to portray her quite naked, but the king disapproved and the sculptor settled for flowing drapery that offered only scant cover to Victoria's proud breasts. 'The good woman has had her share of fate. Though one wouldn't see it; the courageous chariot driver,' Heinrich Heine said of Victoria. Her kidnapping by Napoleon was but the first of a number of adventures.

On her return to Berlin the wreath of oak leaves – symbolic of peace – which adorned her staff was made to frame the Iron Cross designed by Karl Friedrich Schinkel, and a Prussian eagle, crowned and with wings outstretched, was perched upon it. Her more militant bearing suited the century as it unfolded. Victorious troops returning from the 1870–71 Franco–Prussian war marched through a Brandenburg Gate which, to commemorate their success at Sedan, was draped in banners with the inscription, 'What a turning-point through God's leadership'. As he was borne to the Charlottenburg Mausoleum in March 1888, Kaiser Wilhelm I, under whom Germany was unified with Berlin as its capital, passed for the last time through the gate which was suitably clad in black with the valedictory message, 'Vale Senex Imperator'. His grandson, Wilhelm II, would trot through it surrounded by his aides-de-camp on the way to his morning ride in the Tiergarten. Passage through the centre columns of the gate was reserved for the Hohenzollerns, until the overthrow of the monarchy in November 1918. A few months later, in the ensuing political confusion, Bolshevik revolutionaries mounted a heavy machine gun below Victoria's chariot in their unsuccessful bid to grab power and held the gate for a day – the first but not last time the red flag was raised above what Langhans had originally intended to be a 'gate of peace' (*Friedenstor*). Victoria, her chariot and horses were left riddled with bullets. A year later during the abortive Kapp putsch the top of the gate was again seized as a vantage point and during a lull in the confused proceedings an inscription was carved on the Quadriga: 'Four machine gunners lay here, hungry.'

The Kaiser's troops had marched confidently through the gate on their way to war in August 1914, sweet-smelling nosegays in their lapels, flowers stuffed down the barrels of their Mauser rifles, bugles blowing, drums beating, trailed by exuberant small boys, admired by their ladyfolk and watched from above by Victoria. In their patriotic enthusiasm they chalked the words 'Nach Paris!' (To Paris!) on the railway wagons which were to take them to the front and probable death. It was the latest instalment in the Franco–German duel that had been opened over a century earlier by the 'horse thief of Berlin'. In 1870 French troops were cheered through the streets of Paris amid shouts of 'À Berlin! À Berlin!' (To Berlin! To Berlin!), as Émile Zola noted at the close of *Nana*. This time, after the harsh terms of the Treaty of Versailles, the troops returned to the Brandenburg Gate 'undefeated', they were told, with battle-tried steel instead of their old leather spiked helmets and a weary tread. The gate itself had had its copper roof stripped away for war production.

The Brandenburg Gate and Quadriga had become the apex of Berlin's turbulent history and its best known symbol. Hitler's *Machtergreifung* (seizure of power) on 30 January 1933 saw endless columns of brown-shirted, torch-bearing Nazi stormtroopers stream through the gate like a searing flow of molten lava. Goebbels's propaganda machine hijacked the image of the Quadriga for the posters of the 1936 Berlin Olympics, and soon the cavernous hollow of the gate, adorned with classical reliefs alluding hopelessly to the triumph of peace, echoed to the steel-heeled jackboots of Hitler's strutting regiments. The goddess who had been intended as a harbinger of peace was unwillingly transformed into a Valkyrie.

The goose-step returned to the height of military fashion. The ceremonial march past with unbent leg had been devised by Prince Leopold of Anhalt-Dessau, variously known as the 'old Dessauer' or 'old Snoutnose', who served as a field marshal and military adviser to the 'Soldier King' and subsequently under Frederick the Great, drawing up the fifty-four movements of Prussian drill and taking inordinate pleasure from setting psalms to march music. Hitler's wheeling, kicking troops soon proved themselves more menacing than any Prussia had previously produced.

In the summer of 1940, after the fall of Paris, fair-haired, pig-tailed Teutonic maidens strewed roses before the victorious Führer's motorcade as it swept through the gate and down Unter den Linden. But the sweet taste of triumph was to turn sour. Soon Victoria was enveloped in the flames of war as Allied bombers took the conflict to the heart of Berlin. Her symbolism was such that the Nazis dared not risk morale by removing her to safety; instead, in 1942 they had detailed plaster casts made and put into storage. And so a battered goddess, her staff broken, her chariot riven, her horses mutilated, the gate

54

beneath her blistered and pockmarked but still standing, was left to survey the grim, haunting scene of destruction when the shooting finally stopped in May 1945. In the moment of victory Red Army troops had scaled the gate to hoist their hammer and sickle flag.

In the immediate aftermath of war, as old men, women and children picked, scraped and fended to feed themselves, amid the wasteland which was the hub of bomb-devastated Berlin, the city's principal black market grew around the Brandenburg Gate. There anything which had been saved or salvaged from the rubble could be obtained for a few cigarettes or Allied rations, for a packet of Lucky Strike or a bar of Hershey chocolate.

In 1950 young communists ignominiously hurled the remains of the Quadriga to the ground, where the last of Schadow's fine horses shattered in a cloud of dust. Once again, as in Napoleon's day and for as long, the Brandenburg Gate stood stripped of its crowning glory.

The workers' uprising in the East of the city, which was bloodily suppressed by Russian tanks and the loathed Volkspolizei (People's Police) in June 1953, saw an eighteen-year-old, Lothar Nitsche, scramble to the top of the gate and tear down the hated red flag. Five years later, as the eastern authorities worked on restoring the gate, in the West a new Quadriga was cast in copper from the plaster impressions that had been made during the war, and handed over to the communists in whose sector the gate stood. Before they returned Victoria to her rightful place, they took from her staff the Iron Cross and eagle, 'symbols,' said Waldemar Schmidt, East Berlin's mayor at the time, 'of Prussian–German militarism'. He added that 'since soldiers of the victorious Red Army raised the flag of socialism over the Brandenburg Gate, it is no longer a symbol for chauvinistic excess or Prussian glory.'

On 13 August 1961 the communists acted to stop the crippling exodus of workers to the West and sealed off their half of the city with the infamous Berlin Wall, leaving the Brandenburg Gate desolately trapped in the middle of a well-patrolled no man's land. For more than twenty-eight years only bored border guards and the rabbits which thrived in the empty space could approach Langhans's classical masterpiece. The loneliness of Berlin's best known symbol ended on the night of 9 November 1989 when the crumbling communist regime finally relented and allowed its citizens free passage to the West.

55

Incredulous East Germans wandered in a daze around the gate, testing their new-found liberty to see if it was not merely a dream. Meanwhile, on the western side, thousands massed – many climbing on to the Wall and dropping into the East – and began their chant, 'Die Mauer muss weg!' (The Wall must go!) Lothar Nitsche, who had ripped the red flag from the gate in June 1953, took a day off from his job as a lorry driver in Giessen, near Frankfurt, and returned to the scene of his youthful escapade. 'Berlin is one city again', he said with emotion.

Six weeks later the Wall was opened at the Brandenburg Gate, in time for Christmas, and all Berlin and the world rejoiced. A wild fireworks party followed on New Year's Eve when the good nature of East Germany's peaceful revolution was first soured by the over-exuberance of young people who climbed on top of the gate and vandalized the venerable Victoria. They stole her crown of laurels, tore off the reins and bridles of her horses and carved their names in the Quadriga. For the third time in its chequered existence it was removed. The massive, one-ton sculpture was dismantled and transported to West Berlin for restoration.

By the time the Quadriga was reinstalled in August 1991, in time for the celebrations marking the two hundredth anniversary of the Brandenburg Gate, Berlin and Germany were formally unified again. Their new-found confidence was reflected in the return of the Iron Cross and eagle to Victoria's staff. Since her rape by Napoleon, her history had been Berlin's. And now the Brandenburg Gate and its Quadriga had become the symbol of German unification.

From the Brandenburg Gate to the house Schadow had built at Frederick William III's expense in the Kleine Wallstrasse (today Schadowstrasse) is no distance at all. The originally two-storeyed, since 1851 three-storeyed building, lightly rusticated in beige stone and adorned by his pupils with decorative reliefs outside and stucco medallions in its hallway, was built between 1802 and 1805 and lies in a small street off Unter den Linden, a hundred yards or so before it culminates in the Pariser Platz (as it was named in 1814) and the historic gate. From an upstairs back window Schadow would have been able to keep an eye on Victoria steering her Quadriga. It was one of a number of reasons that the deputy director of the Royal Academy of Art felt strongly about the French. Apart from packing Victoria off to Paris (which they might have argued was flattering), while on a looting spree they vandalized a gently poetic earlier work of his, the movingly classical monument he executed for the Dorotheenstädtische Kirche to the memory of the nine-year-old son of Frederick William II, the count of the Mark, who died in 1787. The marble sculpture, completed in 1790, depicts the young prince lying as if asleep, his grip released on the sword resting against his knee, his discarded antique helmet propped against his pillow, the folds of his cloak falling haphazardly over the edge of the small tomb. A classical relief below shows a boy being led reluctantly to another world, while above, over a rich garland of oak leaves framing the inscription, are seated three grief-stricken women.

In addition to artistic injury, Schadow had to put up with French troops billeted in his house and, as its owner, stiff war taxes. Since the pen is invariably mightier than the sword, the French were taking on a dangerous adversary. But Napoleon did not mean to. As an admirer of both Frederick the Great and Schadow's Victoria, he suggested temptingly that with French funds Berlin's leading classical sculptor should continue the work he had begun in 1786 on an equestrian monument to Prussia's most memorable monarch. Schadow refused, and, as Frederick William III did not share Napoleon's enthusiasm for the project, it came to nothing.

However, a distinctly patriotic commission from the Bavarian crown prince, Ludwig, led to Schadow's exhibiting his compelling marble portrait bust of Frederick the Great at the Academy in 1808. It was one of fourteen busts of famous Germans which Ludwig ordered from Schadow for a planned German temple of honour on the Breuberg near Donaustauf in Bavaria, the 'Valhalla' which his court architect Leo von Klenze designed and built between 1830 and 1842. As well as Frederick, those depicted by Schadow for Ludwig's gallery of fame included the philosopher Kant and the poets Klopstock and Wieland.

Schadow was not just Berlin's leading sculptor, though; as a draughtsman he was the sharpest observer of Berlin life since Daniel Chodowiecki, the 'German Hogarth', had portrayed the fashions and morals of Frederick the Great's reign so vividly. Schadow, the 'onlooker on the Spree', was, according to Theodor Fontane, 'also a representative of Berlin irony'. Strongly influenced by his English comtemporaries Thomas Rowlandson and James Gillray, between 1813 and 1815 Schadow pilloried Napoleon in a savage series of satirical sheets mocking the diminutive emperor and French ways. Some were mischievously signed 'Gilrai à Paris', others 'à Paris chez Blaise', clearly to irritate and confuse the censor. The prints caricatured the 'great' exploits of the 'Great Nation' (Grande Nation), its pomposity, greed and ultimate failure. The French are lampooned for their revolution, their military miscalculations and above all for their self-indulgence, their obsession with the joys of the flesh: women, food and wine. The ample-bosomed, fair figure of fame is twice depicted with a bare bottom: in *La retraite de la Renommée*, where on the retreat from Moscow she crashes down from her stumbling mule, scattering the leaves of her crown of laurels and breaking her trumpet, and in *Joie de la Grande Nation*, riding a wild pig backwards while blowing the trumpet, her prominently exposed posterior carefully examined by three decidedly seedy-looking Frenchmen. The humiliation of Napoleon's Grande Armée, which set out for Moscow in 1812 with 600,000 men and came back with only 50,000, is grimly highlighted in *Le Déjeuner à la fourchette*, where the ravenous invaders – gourmets by nature – carve up a dead horse and roast two rats and a dog for food. In *Emparez-vous de Berlin* an imperious Napoleon stands dictating orders for the take-over of the city to a note-taking marshal while his faithful Mameluke Rustan stands guard, hand on scimitar. The marshal has barely noted the word 'Berlin' before the new government, with its administrators, decrees and regulations, including the billeting and taxation from which Schadow was to suffer, sets out in a procession for the city, accompanied by serried ranks of soldiers in the background.

Schadow's resistance to Napoleonic authority was not restricted to satire. In 1813, at the ripe age of forty-nine, he joined the Berlin Landsturm (Home Guard) which, together with the Landwehr (Volunteer Militia) and the occasional Cossack of exotic appearance, also featured in his satirical prints, representing the allied opposition to the French. Earlier in the year he had contributed to the appeal for donations to fund the war of independence from France, noting in his diary how he handed over his 'hard-won gold medal gained in Rome and a couple of French gold coins'. Then, when the Landsturm was formed, he offered his services. 'I could arm myself with a French carbine which had been forgotten during the billeting. On the nineteenth [of May] the Berlin Landsturm gathered for the first time all together on the parade ground. After a few marches an old colonel let us charge with fixed bayonets and pikes, when it became very clear who could run and who could not.'

In 1813 Berlin managed to provide more than half the Prussian volunteers who went to fight the French, as well as 1.6 million thalers in war donations.

After 1815, when Schadow became director of the Royal Academy of Art, Berlin neglected him as a sculptor. For the Baltic port of Rostock he completed a memorial to Field Marshal Blücher and for the Reformation town of Wittenberg a statue of Martin Luther, but despite his great talent they were the last major commissions. Fashion and favour had passed to his former pupil Christian Daniel Rauch, which prompted Schadow to comment ironically that 'sein Ruhm sei in Rauch aufgegangen' (his fame had gone up in smoke [Rauch]). He wrote dejectedly in December 1820: 'What help is it to me that I am a member of so many foreign academies if I am forgotten in my Fatherland while I still – thank God! – enjoy an abundance of good health which enables me yet to pursue my art.' But Schadow was to continue to draw and in 1823, after a meeting in Weimar, he produced a marble bust of Goethe which remains the finest portrayal of the poet. His set of lithographs of Berlin jokes dating from 1827–8 had a wide appeal. In 1838, two years after a cataract operation and at the age of seventy-five, Schadow drew a self-portrait in wash – wearing bed-cap and spectacles – that brims over with character. He was, as his friend Fontane noted, one of Berlin's great personalities. He lived for another twelve years.

In 1851, a year after Schadow's death, the largest and most popular work of his one-time pupil Rauch was unveiled on Unter den Linden, the equestrian statue of Frederick the Great which had superseded Schadow's own unrealized plans for such a monument. The foundation stone for Rauch's design had been laid in 1840 on the one hundredth anniversary of Frederick's accession. Also on or slightly set back from the great boulevard stood five larger-than-life, full-length statues by Rauch of Prussia's leading generals in the war against

Napoleon: Scharnhorst and Bülow in marble in front of Schinkel's perfectly proportioned Neue Wache guardhouse on one side, and Yorck, Blücher and Gneisenau cast in bronze on the other side of Unter den Linden, between the Princesses' Palace and the opera house. Clutching his drawn sabre, Blücher stands victorious, his coat draped like a toga over his uniform and his left foot resting on the barrel of a French cannon, in a superb martial pose. 'Marschall Vorwärts' (Marshal Advance), Berliners liked to call him. Schinkel collaborated on the placing of the statue, which was unveiled in 1826, and the design of its base, where with a Biedermeier love of detail bronze reliefs recount the final phase of the fight against Napoleon, including the triumphant return, bands playing, of the Quadriga. Yorck and Gneisenau were positioned on either side of Blücher in 1855 and all three have since remained in place. The figure of Bülow has not survived however, and a pensive but determined Scharnhorst, also in marble and dating from 1822, has been moved to a patch of lawn by the opera house. Without actually joining them, he is now on the same side of the avenue as his fellow generals in bronze.

Rauch's fame was justifiably based on his serene marble effigy of the beautiful and popular Queen Luise of Prussia (who died in 1810 aged only thirty-four) for her tomb in the sombre mausoleum designed by Heinrich Gentz in the style of a Doric temple in the Charlottenburg park and completed by Schinkel. Rauch worked on the memorial in Carrara and Rome in 1812–13 and it was widely admired when it was finally unveiled in 1815.

Twenty years earlier Schadow had portrayed Luise with her sister Friederike in a famous double statue that stunningly combined grace, movement and beauty, causing a sensation. Luise, then princess of Mecklenburg-Strelitz, married the Prussian crown prince, Frederick William, in 1793. A year later Schadow produced clay busts of the princesses, described by Goethe as 'two heavenly creatures', which were remarkable for their liveliness and lifelike modelling. The commission for the life-size double statue followed and it was completed in 1797, the year Frederick William III became king and Luise queen. But now that a state portrait was expected, the king found the immediacy of the likeness, as well as a certain erotic quality and its unidealized presentation, to be 'unfortunate'. Frederick William was indignant that the sculptor had taken the exact measurements of the two young princesses, and he complained that Luise's breasts were too small, finding the fuller bosom of her sister much more attractive. In future the queen would have to do something about her figure, he insisted.

Frederick William's lack of enthusiasm led to Schadow's lively masterpiece being ignored until 1810, the year of Luise's premature death, when it was brought out and displayed in one of the darkest rooms in the royal castle. After the Second World War the two princesses for a long time graced the gloomy entrance hall of East Berlin's National Gallery. Recently the original plaster model has been given a central place of honour, among other sculptures of the period, in the bright interior of Schinkel's Friedrichswerdersche Kirche.

Berlin after Frederick the Great, liberated from his all-embracing controlling influence, went through a period of hectic cultural activity under much lesser rulers. Architecture and sculpture thrived especially, moving quickly on from baroque and 'Friderician rococo' to a new, fashionable classicism that suited the city as it entered the nineteenth century. Indigenous painters of note were still lacking, but they would come, and with a growing sense of national awareness German theatre and literature, so long ignored or stifled by Frederick the Great with his pronounced French taste, began to blossom. The new climate was marked by Schiller himself, the greatest of German playwrights, visiting Berlin in 1804, shortly before his early death, and having his likeness recorded in Schadow's sketchbook. The French Comedy in the Gendarmenmarkt became the Royal National Theatre, and the German Garrick, August Wilhelm Iffland, appointed Berlin theatre director in 1796, filled the house. Music too was no longer dictated by the royal prerogative and works by Gluck and Handel belatedly superseded the perpetual performances of Graun's stiff operas. Mozart dedicated his last string quartets to Frederick William II and the young Beethoven was given a warm welcome.

Frederick William II was, like his flute-playing uncle, Frederick the Great, musically gifted, though neither so conservative nor so autocratic in his taste. He was an able cellist – well taught by the highly regarded Frenchman Jean-Pierre Duport, a master of the instrument and the king's director of chamber music – and would himself occasionally play in the court orchestra. It was enough to raise the hopes of the increasingly desperate Mozart that he might finally gain the appointment at the Prussian court which had eluded him for so long in Vienna. 'When I shall go to Berlin, I hope indeed for great honour and fame,' the composer wrote. Accordingly, he set out for Berlin in April 1789 at the invitation and in the company of Prince Karl Lichnowsky, who had business in Prussia. This was swiftly concluded and the prince ended up inconveniently asking the impecunious Mozart for a loan he was too proud to refuse. News of the composer's arrival led the National Theatre to change its programme hastily and stage his *Entführung aus dem Serail*, for which he was given a badly needed hundred Friedrichs d'Or, though he complained about the 'slackness' of the violins.

Frederick William, while expecting Mozart, did not rush to receive him. The composer was sent instead to Duport, and only at the end of the month, after Mozart had been to Leipzig, did he play for the king. While in Potsdam he paid the royal teacher the compliment of composing for the piano Nine Variations in D on a Minuet by Duport (K573), the manuscript of which bears the date 29 April 1790.

'When I return you will have to be looking forward to me rather than money,' Mozart wrote almost a month later to his pregnant wife, Constanze. No position in Berlin had been forthcoming, but Mozart did not leave empty-handed, for Frederick William had commissioned six string quartets for himself and six 'easy' piano sonatas for the same Princess Friederike who was to be so engagingly portrayed by Schadow with her elder sister Luise. Despite his urgent need of funds, Mozart only completed part of the commission: one sonata (in D, K576), which was far from easy and never apparently reached the princess, and three quartets, the first of which (in D, K575) he composed in Vienna in June 1789 and described as being 'for His Majesty the King of Prussia'. This at least found its way to Berlin and elicited a timely reward of one hundred Friedrichs d'Or stuffed into a gold snuffbox; exactly the kind of payment J. S. Bach could have expected for his *Musical Offering* had Frederick the Great not been such a skinflint. The other two quartets (in B flat, K589, and in F, K590), Mozart's last, were hurriedly and carelessly published in Vienna, without further dedication, soon after his death in December 1791. As might be predicted, the three 'Prussian' quartets, particularly the first two, give prominence to the cello part intended for the king and as a result have an almost concertante character, being rich in melody and in their sunny mood at times reminiscent of the opera *Così fan tutte* which was composed around the same time.

Neither did Beethoven, aged twenty-one when Mozart's life was tragically cut short, ignore the Prussian capital, though he was at first unsettled by the way it demonstrated its musical appreciation. 'In Berlin a few years ago I gave a concert for which I made every effort, and believed I was doing right. I hoped for a good deal of applause, but to my astonishment there was not a hint of it to be heard; that, I thought, was really too much, I didn't understand why; the riddle's explanation lay in the entire Berlin public being so very sophisticated that they showed their appreciation instead by waving with considerable emotion their wet handkerchiefs'.

But Berlin was by no means in the vanguard of musical taste, nor was it to be for another hundred years. When Beethoven completed his Ninth Symphony in March 1824, the summit of his symphonic achievement, and dedicated its manuscript score to Frederick William III of Prussia, he received in recognition only a simple gold ring set with a worthless stone. Though the London Philharmonic Society had commissioned and paid for the work as early as 1822, it was fobbed off with a copy of the full score headed 'Grand Symphony written for the Philharmonic Society in London' that was only dispatched in December. The symphony had already received its first performance, with the composer conducting, in Vienna in May.

Beethoven dedicated his Third Piano Concerto, composed in 1800 and published in the summer of 1804, to the most musically promising of all the Hohenzollerns, Prince Louis Ferdinand, whom he first met in Berlin in 1796. The prince, born in 1772, was the favourite nephew of Frederick the Great, who liked his ready wit and admired the exceptional musical ability he showed from a very early age. Despite such talent, Louis Ferdinand was destined to be a soldier, joining the army at the age of seventeen and quickly earning a reputation for valour in the campaign of 1792–4. By 1795 he commanded an infantry regiment in Magdeburg, where he continued to study philosophy, military science and music. The following year he returned to Berlin for instruction in 'pianoforte playing and composition' and there struck up a firm friendship with the visiting Beethoven, who described his playing as being 'not that of a king or prince but rather of a competent pianist.' When it came several years later to the Third Piano Concerto,

Beethoven significantly did not bother to simplify the most difficult passages for the prince as he had for his own pupil, the accomplished pianist Ferdinand Ries, who turned the pages for the composer at the work's first performance in April 1803 in Vienna. Louis Ferdinand's skill in improvisation may also be reflected in the concerto, with its deeply poetic slow movement.

He had tried to persuade the Bohemian musician Antonín Rejcha to give him lessons and accept a post as Kapellmeister in Berlin, but he declined, preferring Paris, where Berlioz, Gounod, Liszt and Franck were to number among his pupils, and so Louis Ferdinand soon afterwards welcomed Jan Ladislav Dussek as his teacher. In spite of being a commoner and just a 'poor musician', Dussek became a close friend and constant companion of the prince, which was ill understood at a court that failed to grasp Louis Ferdinand's generous and unaffected nature. Beethoven described him as 'the most human of men'. The prince's own compositions, which were greatly admired by Liszt, among others, reveal Beethoven to be the decisive influence, especially in the most notable work, the Piano Quartet in F minor, opus 6. Robert Schumann described Louis Ferdinand as 'the Romantic of the Classical period'.

In 1804 the prince travelled to Vienna for a conference of the general staffs, and one evening at the Lobkowitz Palace he insisted on having the recently completed 'Eroica' Symphony played to him three times in succession. Shortly afterwards Louis Ferdinand and Beethoven found themselves invited to the same dinner party given by an ageing countess. But the temperamental composer left in a huff on discovering that he was not seated at the same table as the prince. Louis Ferdinand responded by himself arranging another dinner at which Beethoven sat on his right and the countess on his left.

The 'Eroica' Symphony so admired by Louis Ferdinand had been intended by Beethoven as a tribute to the comet-like rise of Napoleon, and as a possible passport to finding a position in Paris. Beethoven called his Third Symphony, composed in a new heroic–dramatic style, a 'Grand Symphony entitled Bonaparte', but when it was completed in May 1804, he learned with disgust that Napoleon had declared himself emperor. In a rage he tore out its title page, scratching out the name of the enlightened leader who had turned into a tyrant. Instead, the composer retitled the work 'Heroic symphony to

64

celebrate the memory of a great man', though he continued to refer to it as 'written on Bonaparte'.

Two years later – on 10 October 1806 – Napoleon's burgeoning ambition was to seal the fate of Prussia's most promising prince. After an evening delighting his fellow officers with his improvisations at the piano, Louis Ferdinand rode out the next morning at the head of a corps of eight thousand men, the van of the Prussian army, only to be cut down by the French with a force more than twice the size at the battle of Saalfeld. Just over two weeks later – on 27 October – to the echo of cannon fire and the pealing of church bells, Napoleon, on a grey mount and escorted by his victorious foot regiments and cavalry, rode triumphantly through the Brandenburg Gate on his way to take up temporary residence in the royal castle. The 'horse thief' had arrived in Berlin.

FOUR

PRUSSIA'S INSPIRED BAUMEISTER

N o architect left his stamp more magically on modern Berlin
than Karl Friedrich Schinkel. He was undoubtedly the greatest architect to have emerged in Prussia in the nineteenth
century, and his admirers would argue that in Germany his genius
has never been equalled, or surpassed. He was to German architecture
what Beethoven was to music. Like the incomparable composer, he
embraced and embodied a classical–romantic age and sought not
merely to capture its spirit, but to give expression to its deeper, more
spiritual values.

He mastered the harmonies of ancient and modern building and
created architecture which, if any, is 'music in stone'. The Altes
Museum (Old Museum), with the magnificent breadth of its portico –
a colonnade of eighteen Ionic columns with as many brooding Prussian
eagles perched on the cornice above – and the Schauspielhaus, with
its carefully calculated and imposing proportions, are his classical
Berlin symphonies, the Neue Wache guardhouse and Schlossbrücke
(Castle Bridge) his perfectly argued and balanced sonatas. The Friedrichswerdersche Kirche, reminiscent of an English country church,
has a pastoral quality, while his last great work, the Bauakademie
(Architectural Academy), which the communist authorities barba-
rously pulled down in 1961–2 to make way for their frightful foreign
ministry building, was the glorious culmination of a lifetime's learning, stretching building techniques as much as Beethoven tested the
orchestra with his Ninth Symphony.

The solar plexus of Berlin, that climactic point where Unter den
Linden comes to a head before the site ponderously occupied until
1950 by the royal castle, is, despite architectural abominations later
in the nineteenth and twentieth centuries, visually still determined

more by Schinkel and his impeccable taste than by anyone or anything else.

Schinkel was more than an architect of genius; he was an all-round artist: a painter, draughtsman, watercolourist, designer and interior decorator of rare talent. In any one of these specialized fields he would have been remembered for his achievement, if family connections and friendships had not led him to the finding of his vocation in architecture. Bringing together all his diverse gifts, he sought to create a complete work of art, from the broad concept of a building to the smallest details, whether door handles, lamps or curtain rails. The result was remarkable. He was a Renaissance man in a neo-classical age.

Fluency and facility in art do not necessarily give a work depth or, in terms of fashion, durability, but the intellectual rigour applied by Schinkel to his creations ensured their lasting quality. His mind was bursting with ideas in need of expression, no day was long enough for him to capture them all. In the end his creative energy was to prove too much, exhausting him and leading to his death, aged sixty, from overwork.

Schinkel's all-consuming industry set him apart from his contemporaries. He did not share Schadow's ribaldry or pronounced, disrespectful Berlin humour. He had none of Beethoven's tempestuousness. Rather he was sternly Protestant and Prussian, a hardworking, patriotic, family man who saw his work as his duty. But whatever colour may have been lacking in his own upright life was more than made up by the exhilarating and joyful inventiveness of his creations. Without them, Berlin would have been a duller, drabber place.

Like the writer Theodor Fontane, Schinkel was born (on 13 March 1781) north of Berlin amidst the haunting lakes and forests of the Mark Brandenburg in the garrison town of Neuruppin, where the streets have a breadth deliberately designed for marching and wheeling regiments, and where small boys in rabbit-skin jackets still fish by the lakeside. Today, statues of the town's two most famous sons recall their achievement. Among Neuruppin's churches is the former Dominican Klosterkirche, a red brick Gothic edifice overlooking the wide Ruppin lake and skirted by the town wall, its twin pencil-point spires visible for miles around. Dating from 1300, it is hardly surprising that Schinkel, by now responsible for all buildings in Prussia, carried through its restoration and decoration between 1836 and 1840. The soaring church, which became Protestant with the Reformation, had suffered grievously during the Napoleonic wars when it was variously misused either to accommodate prisoners of war or as a warehouse for bread and flour.

Schinkel's father, Johann Cuno Christian Schinkel, was a Protestant priest who had risen to the position of archdeacon and local inspector of schools; his mother came from a family of chemists and teachers, one of whom taught Fontane. Schinkel's childhood was spectacularly disrupted by the great fire of August 1787 which razed much of Neuruppin: altogether 386 private houses, including the Schinkels', and 24 public buildings were destroyed. Two months later his father died of pneumonia contracted as a result of his unsuccessful efforts to extinguish the flames. It took up to 1806 for the town to be rebuilt in a restrained, pleasing neo-classical style by Bernhard Matthias Brasch, whose friendship with the Schinkel family offered Karl Friedrich an introduction both to architecture and to Friedrich Gilly, a youthful colleague who was also working on Neuruppin's reconstruction. Architecture had something of a tradition in this sedate lakeside town, where at the height of his friendship with Frederick the Great Knobelsdorff raised his first building in 1735, the Temple of Apollo; together with an array of baroque statues from Dresden, it continues to grace Neuruppin's Tempelgarten.

From 1792 to 1794 the young Schinkel attended the local grammar school (a typically two-storeyed neo-classical building by Brasch of 1790 that still stands as the Kulturhaus), then he moved with his mother to one of the houses in Berlin set aside for priests' widows. His schooling was continued at the Grey Cloister school of the former Franciscan monastery, where Leonhard Thurneysser had excitingly dabbled in alchemy, printing and much else at the end of the sixteenth century.

In 1797, aged sixteen, Schinkel saw the wildly extravagant and never to be executed design by Friedrich Gilly for a monument to Frederick the Great and was convinced that he should become an architect. A year later Schinkel moved in with and became a pupil of Gilly's architect father, David. The young Gilly had come from Paris, greatly stimulated by designs he had seen of French revolutionary architecture, and the enthusiasm rubbed off, though Friedrich Gilly's tragic early death was to leave the field for innovation open to Schinkel.

Following private instruction with Gilly's father, in 1799 he went on to the newly founded Building Academy where both the Gillys taught; there he quickly established himself as one of its most promising pupils. By 1800 he had received his first commission, for a garden pavilion on the Pfingstberg near Potsdam. The result was the exquisitely graceful, thoroughly classical Pomona Temple with a portico of four slender Ionic columns made of oak painted to look like stone and a viewing platform on the roof that was intended to be covered by a tented canvas canopy. The delightful building stood until 1965 when it finally succumbed to years of vandalism, not least – as borne out by the Cyrillic graffiti – from a neighbouring Soviet army barracks. Some parts have been salvaged and its restoration is planned.

Besides this first building, the dawn of the new century also brought Schinkel a double bereavement: his mother died, and Friedrich Gilly never returned from a cure at Carlsbad which it had been hoped would restore his flagging health. His premature death aged only twenty-eight ended a career which had promised much, and when in 1801 the twenty-year-old Schinkel went to visit his grave at the fashionable, forest-enclosed Bohemian spa, he vowed to carry on Gilly's work, subsequently completing several of his unfinished commissions.

Among these early projects was the house in the Friedrichstrasse (number 103) for the builder Gottfried Steinmeyer, with whose son, Johann Gottfried, he set out in 1803 on a two-year European tour which took him through architecturally rich Dresden, Prague and Vienna to Italy and as far south as Sicily, returning via Paris, Strasburg and Weimar. The elder Steinmeyer, whose construction firm – later involved in many of Schinkel's buildings – was taken over by his son several years after the Italian expedition, supported the young architect financially, making the trip possible by providing the necessary funds. It was a journey of great discovery for a mind as eager and receptive as Schinkel's. During his sojourn in Rome he produced some four hundred drawings of landscapes and architectural subjects. While it was above all the marvels of antiquity which had made an 'Italian journey' so fashionable, even obligatory, from the late eighteenth century onwards, Schinkel looked further and discovered ahead of his time the wonders of medieval architecture in Italy and France. He began painting in oil, which he continued during the lean years of French occupation when architectural work dried up. His oil paintings, created solely for himself or his friends, were for the most part strongly romantic architectural landscapes; the influence of Claude, particularly in the dramatic use of light, was clear. There is symbolism too, and a number of his paintings bear comparison with the romantically brooding works of his contemporary Caspar David Friedrich.

Back in Berlin, with no architectural commissions forthcoming, Schinkel resorted to drawing decorative parts for Schadow's sculpture, though soon even this fell victim to the recession that gripped the Prussian capital under Napoleon. Yet during these difficult days Berliners were only too keen to be distracted, and Schinkel did just that with a series of panoramas and dioramas he devised. Through these 'mechanical pictures' Schinkel was able to instruct and entertain the people with geography and art. At Christmas time in Berlin it was customary for confectioners and other shops to display pictures, incorporating transparencies and moving figures, on fashionable or topical themes; none was more sophisticated than those provided by Schinkel, though of the forty-odd 'optical perspective' pictures he designed from 1807 to 1816 only preparatory drawings or contemporary descriptions survive. The perspectives were so effective that astoundingly realistic illusions of space were created. In 1807 there were stunning views of such exotic cities as Constantinople and Jerusalem, and in 1808 Schinkel himself financed a much admired 360-degree panorama of Palermo, where he made use of his Sicilian sketches. What he had omitted to record from nature he did not hesitate to invent. Steinmeyer's firm was responsible for erecting the wooden construction that housed the panorama on the Opernplatz. Schinkel continued with a series of famous buildings and landscape scenes, the presentation of which was sometimes accompanied and highlighted by a choir, music and commentaries. A visit by the king and queen to one of his spectacles only enhanced their popularity and helped secure him a civil service appointment in 1810, as senior assessor (Oberbauassessor) in the Royal Office of Works (Oberbaudeputation). In 1812 he showed the 'Seven Wonders of the World' and the 'Burning of Moscow', which, portraying the momentous contemporary event that presaged Napoleon's downfall and Berlin's liberation, enjoyed a huge popular success.

Although after 1816 architecture once more became his principal activity, he never abandoned the idea of the panorama with its broad appeal. Just before his physical and mental collapse on the evening of 8 September 1840 he outlined a plan for a vast panorama depicting the history of architecture. That afternoon Schinkel had gone for a walk in the Tiergarten beyond the Brandenburg Gate, where he met the set designer Carl Gropius, with whom he had worked on his earlier panoramas. He told him of his idea for a new panorama measuring ninety feet across that would represent the most important monuments of as many countries as possible set in their appropriate landscapes: Asia, Egypt, Greece, Rome and medieval Germany, where the Gothic style was then thought to have originated. He brushed aside Gropius's doubts on the impracticability of such a project. It would represent the summation of his work as a painter and his experience as an architect. Alas, it was not to be, as Prussia's most brilliant artist was immediately afterwards struck down by a stroke that left him in a coma from which he never awoke.

Fascinated by new possibilities and techniques, in 1809 Schinkel was one of the first artists to experiment with lithography, completing altogether more than twenty lithographs, a number of which were shown at the 1810 autumn exhibition of the Royal Academy of Art.

A tradition of working for the stage established by eighteenth-century architects was carried on with enthusiasm and understanding by Schinkel. From an early age he was fascinated by the theatre and in 1802 his first work to be shown at a Royal Academy exhibition was a set design for Euripides's *Iphigenie in Aulis*. Though there was already more than enough theatricality about his panoramas, or 'scenographic spectacles', he was impatient to extend his design skills further, to the stage itself. In 1813 he approached the Berlin theatre director Iffland about the vacant post of set designer, spelled out his ideas in a 'Memorandum' and even offered to work without a salary, but all to no avail. It took a new, more adventurous and sympathetic theatre director, Count Karl von Brühl, for him finally to gain the appointment in 1815. The collaboration was to prove excitingly fruitful, with Schinkel producing more than a hundred sets for over thirty plays during a period of almost fifteen years.

71

None surpassed the dozen superb designs he produced in 1815 for Mozart's *Magic Flute*, revealing a profound knowledge of Mozart's music and Schikaneder's libretto. The design for 'The Hall of Stars in the Palace of the Queen of the Night' achieved instant and lasting success. Reviewing the set of *Magic Flute* designs in March 1816, *Das Dramaturgische Wochenblatt* found: 'The second set design, the great inner vault of the Palace of the Queen of the Night, is astounding when the Queen herself appears. Even if the décor has little artistic merit – a blue heavenly vault spangled with regular arches of stars – the way the designer conceives the Queen of the Night's appearance could yet prove to be sublime and inspired.' The powerful image of the queen enthroned on a crescent moon riding on fiery clouds, while above, cascading rows of bright white stars pierce the dark-blue vault of sky, has not lost its force with time and is still regularly resurrected for productions of the opera. In the 1980s, for example, it was chosen by the Czechoslovak film director Miloš Forman for his representation of *The Magic Flute* in his acclaimed film on Mozart, *Amadeus*.

If not quite so memorable, other designs for the opera are as magical: one, 'The Palm Grove', depicts a dark palm-shrouded gully opening on to a pale pink lit valley backed by cool blue mountains; another, the final design for the series, 'The Inner Court of the Temple of the Sun with the statue of Osiris', has a mesmerizing quality, displaying both a sure understanding of ancient Egyptian architectural styles and the opera's masonic significance. Schinkel had made a point of studying and digesting the latest literature, notably the travel journals, *Voyage dans la Haute et la Basse Égypte*, published in 1802, and *Description de l'Égypte* (1809–13), of Dominique Vivant Denon, who had accompanied Bonaparte on his 1798–9 Egyptian campaign. In 1812 Schinkel had already produced a sketch for a scenographic spectacle entitled 'The Egyptian Labyrinth', demonstrating the synergy between his panoramas and the later stage designs. As for the masonic element, this is evident in the heavy symbolism of the sets for Mozart's operatic fairy tale, reflecting the struggle between the powers of darkness and light, good and evil. With such forward-looking compositions Schinkel succeeded in leaving behind the flat, static designs of the baroque theatre, instead pointing ahead to Carl Maria von Weber's romantic and revolutionary *Der Freischütz*, which before long was to take Berlin by storm, and even to the later music theatre of Richard Wagner.

Among Schinkel's other evocative stage sets were those for the French revolutionary composer Méhul's most romantic opera *Ariodant*, where the architect–designer portrayed a forbidding moonlit Scottish setting, with a gloomy castle and tall dark fir trees scarcely silhouetted against a black night sky illuminated only by a mean crescent of a moon. For the king's – if not the public's – favourite composer, the Italian Gaspare Spontini, and his opera *Fernando Cortez*, Schinkel provided an even more sinister scene for the Peruvian Fire Temple two years later (1818). A statue of the God of Evil stands in the foreground, gripping a double brace of snakes and perched on a golden ball flanked by two tigers of fierce aspect. Above this fearsome figure rises a steep, stepped pyramid, dotted and decorated at intervals by fire-breathing serpents, its doorways flanked by narrow towers studded with human skulls. From such a scene of unmitigated horror, it is a relief to find from the same year Schinkel's gentle, soothing design for Act IV of Schiller's *Maid of Orleans*: an appealing open Gothic portico looking on to the city of Rheims and its great cathedral, a highly realistic, if romantic scene.

As in architecture, Schinkel's impact on stage design in Berlin proved revolutionary, with sets and costumes – combining historical accuracy with artistic imagination – henceforward becoming an integral part of any play or opera. And if this were not enough, Schinkel earned a place in theatre history by being the first to depict on stage a room with three walls and a ceiling above, something he managed in 1820 for Gretchen's chamber in one of his sets for scenes from Goethe's *Faust*.

But, most significantly Schinkel had the chance to apply his reformist ideas on theatre architecture to an actual building. In April 1818, over stiff competition, he gained the commission to rebuild the fire-gutted National Theatre on the Gendarmenmarkt. The rapport he had already established with Count Brühl through his pioneering set designs clearly counted in his favour.

As a nineteen-year-old he had sketched the long, box-like building which Karl Gotthard Langhans completed in 1802 and which Berliners had quickly dubbed the 'Koffer' (trunk). Langhans's design was plain – alleviated only by a portico of six Ionic columns – but not unattractive. However, its rather ponderous dominance of Berlin's most elegant square, flanked by the great domes of the French and German cathedrals, was to prove short-lived. In July 1817 a fire broke out during a rehearsal for Schiller's *Die Räuber* and the theatre burnt down. Only part of the outer walls and the six Ionic columns survived the blaze, and these, the king insisted for reasons of economy, were to be incorporated into any new design.

Schinkel's aim was to fuse auditorium and stage into a unified whole and create a building that combined function with art. He noted that the first priority was for the theatre 'to have good acoustics and visibility'; secondly, it should be attractive both inside and outside; and thirdly, it should have agreeable entrances and exits. He also stressed the importance of fire security – hardly surprising in view of the fate of the earlier building and too many contemporary theatres – and the need for cost-saving, in consideration of the parsimonious king, who, maintaining a Prussian tradition established so emphatically by Frederick the Great and his 'Soldier King' father, kept the tightest control on expenditure; hence the order to conserve the columns and walls of the previous theatre, with the limitations this inevitably imposed on the architect, and Schinkel's original cladding of the building in plaster, which was then customary for cost reasons but was not durable. A building as fine as the Schauspielhaus deserved better and some sixty years later sandstone was substituted.

Schinkel turned to ancient Greece to provide suitable inspiration for what was intended as Berlin's second largest theatre after the opera house. In addition to a stage 'for comedy and small dramas' there was to be a concert hall. In his explanatory notes for the king, Schinkel wrote that 'the building will be able to present a noble style on the lines of Greek edifices'. As for the six columns that were to be reused, they would be set 'more worthily' . . . 'with a fine flight of steps, and will thus have a greater effect, as befits a public building'. It took the king only two days to approve Schinkel's plans.

One of the delights of the Schauspielhaus was the protected entrance under this generous sweep of steps which allowed carriages to pass underneath and deposit their passengers under cover during inclement weather. Inside, Schinkel was able to combine his experience of stage set design with his flair for interior decoration. No detail – whether lamp or door handle – was too small for his attention. Based on designs provided by Schinkel, Rauch and Christian Friedrich Tieck executed the statues and sculpture decorating the building's exterior, including, most strikingly, the griffin-drawn sun chariot ridden by Apollo surmounting the front of the building and the sleek Pegasus peering over the back. It was just over fifteen years earlier that Schinkel had noted in his Italian diary: 'The ideal of architecture is only fully attained if a building's purpose in all its parts and as a whole is reflected in its spirit and appearance.' There can be no doubt that with the Schauspielhaus this ideal had been achieved.

On 26 May 1821 the theatre opened with Goethe's *Iphigenie auf Tauris* preceded by a specially written dedicatory prologue which Count Brühl had asked the great poet to write for the occasion. Brühl, himself a man of diverse talent familiar with the theatre in Paris and London, was a friend of Goethe who had trod the Weimar boards under his direction, quite apart from playing the horn in the orchestra and designing stage scenery. But poor health prevented Goethe from delivering the prologue or attending the opening. The oration was given in front of a backcloth designed by Schinkel, which was itself a *coup de théâtre*, depicting the Gendarmenmarkt with the newly unveiled Schauspielhaus at its centre and the French and German cathedrals on either side. The dramatic effect was enhanced by the theatre's scaffolding only being taken away the evening before. The audience was thrilled and at the end of the performance the king was cheered and there were calls for Schinkel. With typical modesty, however, he had already slipped away discreetly and it was necessary for Count Brühl to lead a band of academicians, artists, colleagues, students and members of the public to Unter den Linden, where they serenaded and acclaimed him outside his house.

Repeated renovation later in the nineteenth century obscured or replaced much of Schinkel's original interior. Then in February 1945 the building was severely damaged in Allied air raids, which also left the French and German cathedrals in ruins. In April that year heavy street fighting almost completely destroyed the Schauspielhaus. What had been Berlin's – and one of Europe's – finest squares was reduced to a desolate space marked by the broken shells of its once fine trinity of buildings. These remained ruins until a restoration programme was belatedly embarked upon by the communist authorities in the early 1980s, tackling first the Schauspielhaus and French church and finally the German cathedral, which was only finished a decade later.

To a great fanfare the Schauspielhaus was reopened in October 1984, meticulously restored from Schinkel's original plans and drawings. Inside, a large concert hall, derived from his design, replaced the previous theatre and the interior was further modified to meet modern requirements with rehearsal rooms and a small chamber music hall. Where Schinkel patterns were not available, suitably neo-classical decoration was chosen. The result was stunning; on no other restoration project had communist East Germany lavished so much attention with such success. It made it all the more distressing that other less war-damaged buildings by Schinkel, notably his great Bauakademie, had earlier been callously pulled down to make way for crass examples of socialist building.

In 1815, three years before Schinkel's plans for the Schauspielhaus were accepted, he was commissioned to build a guardhouse on Unter den Linden, almost directly opposite Knobelsdorff's regal opera house and next to Schlüter's solid Zeughaus. It was to be the first Prussian state building begun since the Wars of Liberation and Napoleon's defeat, in which Schinkel had played his own small part, signing up for the Landsturm in 1813. More memorable than such patriotic commitment was the fact that it was Schinkel who met the king's demand for a medal that could be issued to those who had distinguished themselves in the war, regardless of rank – a novel idea emulated forty years later with the introduction of Britain's more exclusive Victoria Cross. He designed the most famous medal ever conceived, the Iron Cross, which quickly became Prussia's most potent military symbol. The war aroused patriotic feelings in Schinkel which architecturally he felt were best expressed in a Gothic style. He had a grandiose idea for a massive neo-Gothic cathedral to the Wars of Liberation, which never went beyond the drawing-board because of the huge costs that it would have entailed. The more modest Kreuzberg memorial, cast in iron at the Royal Foundry between 1818 and 1821, survives as a descendant of the unexecuted cathedral project. The pinnacled spire, crowned by an Iron Cross and inscribed with Prussian battle honours, seems to derive its inspiration not only from Cologne Cathedral, which Schinkel acknowledged, but also from English Gothic Eleanor crosses whose form it matched.

But as the need for patriotism faded with peace and as a consequence of the classical taste and commissions of Frederick William III, Schinkel moved with ease from the neo-Gothic to the neo-classical and with his Neue Wache guardhouse, completed in 1818 and so Berlin's oldest surviving building by him, created a masterpiece of classicism.

After toying with several ideas of startling originality, though not of such perfection or gravity, Schinkel finally gave the cube-like block of a building, which he described as 'designed more or less in accordance with a Roman castrum', a Doric portico reminiscent of a Greek temple. The ten free-standing columns of Saxon sandstone form a colonnaded hall of great dignity that contrasts effectively with the unplastered brickwork of the sides and back of the building which underlines its character as a 'fortification'. The commission fitted in with Schinkel's conception of a 'via triumphalis' dedicated to the Wars of Liberation at the east end of Unter den Linden that would include Rauch's series of statues of Prussian generals. The brilliance of this earliest of his Berlin masterworks is that so compact an edifice stands its ground comfortably between the mighty baroque Zeughaus and the distinguished Prince Heinrich Palace, which had become the university. Almost surprisingly, it defies any suggestion of being over-shadowed. Schinkel achieves this by setting the Neue Wache slightly back from the line of the Zeughaus, giving prominence to the area in front that was to be flanked by Rauch's marble statues of Scharnhorst and Bülow. At the same time this classical jewel among Berlin architecture is allowed space to assert itself in a setting shaded only by the horse-chestnut trees clustered behind. This, to the poet Gerhart Hauptmann, was Berlin's most magical spot. Few would argue.

The building had an immediate impact. 'The new guardhouse is almost complete and has become a splendid building,' Rauch wrote to Tieck in 1818. To Schinkel's design, Schadow modelled ten cast zinc figures of Victories for the frieze, one placed over each column, adding a lighter touch. The pediment relief, depicting Victoria awarding victory, was only completed, also in cast zinc, by August Kiss in the 1840s.

With elegantly uniformed soldiers striking poses outside, or as a focal point in any military march past, it was to be included in innumerable contemporary paintings. Describing how at midday officers assembled here, the 1878 Baedeker guide to Berlin

77

recommended the military music. Even today, its interior transformed into a shrine 'for the victims of fascism and militarism' and its previously steel-helmeted, goose-stepping sentries removed on German reunification, it is as much a focus of tourist attention as Horse Guards in London.

The final point of the 'triumphal avenue' envisaged by Schinkel came with his design for the Schlossbrücke that would span the Spree in place of the inadequate Hundebrücke (Dogs Bridge), issuing before the Lustgarten on the left and the royal castle on the right. The design for the new stone structure, a superb example of bridge engineering with its broad sweep and great breadth of 104 feet, dates from 1819 and was executed between 1821 and 1824. Its building was not, however, without incident. Before completion in March 1824 it was provisionally secured in November 1823 for the passage of the crown prince's bride, but disaster struck and twenty-two people were killed when auxiliary railings collapsed.

Chief among the bridge's charms are the cast iron railings of disporting seahorses, tritons and dolphins linking the pedestals, which were later to be occupied by marble groups of Greek gods and warriors executed by sculptors of the Rauch school, also after Schinkel's designs. Their appearance in the 1850s led to the bridge becoming in popular parlance the 'Puppenbrücke' (Dolls Bridge), with scant regard to the far from doll-like martial poses of the figures.

The Lustgarten is completely dominated by the heroic Altes Museum, almost symphonic in its span, which makes such a splendid show of its favoured site. 'The front facing the Lustgarten has so excellent a situation, one could say the finest in Berlin, that it requires something of a very special kind. A simple columned hall in a grand style, and proportionate to the importance of the location, will most certainly give the building character and ensure a fine effect,' Schinkel noted in January 1823. 'The beauty of the area will attain its perfection with this building, as the fine Lustgarten will at last have a worthy conclusion on its fourth side.'

The idea for a museum to house the rapidly expanding royal art collections was one Schinkel had played with since his student days. Now he finally had a chance to realize his grand and well thought out concept. In April 1823 Frederick William III had 700,000 thalers assigned for the commission, and work – complicated by the marshland on which the museum was to be built – began in earnest in 1825. It was opened on the king's sixtieth birthday on 3 August 1830.

So majestic a building was not spared from bombing in the Second World War and it went up in flames on 30 April 1945 after a tanker exploded outside. Its exterior faithfully restored, it reopened again in 1966, though restoration work continued into the 1980s.

Apart from the mesmerizing colonnade of eighteen towering Ionic columns – their effect heightened by being raised – and the regal sweep of steps, it is the museum's Pantheon-inspired rotunda which is its chief glory. Applying a lesson learned perhaps from Friedrich Gilly and his impressions of French revolutionary architecture, or else displaying dazzling originality of his own, Schinkel encased the rotunda's dome in a quadrangle so that it cannot be seen from the outside. Its discovery on entering the museum is meant and comes as an exhilarating surprise. 'So mighty a building, as the Museum will certainly be, must have a worthy centre. This must be the sanctuary, where the most precious objects are located. One first enters this place coming from the outer hall, and the sight of a beautiful and sublime room must make the visitor receptive and create the proper mood for the enjoyment and acknowledgement of what the building contains,' Schinkel explained in February 1823. Twenty Corinthian columns support a gallery, the doors of which open on to the first floor of the two-storeyed building. Between the columns and in the niches of the gallery there is space for the display of antique sculpture, and the whole great area is lit like the Pantheon by natural light from the top of the dome. The dome itself is divided into four rows of cofferwork with painted figures, signs of the zodiac and rosettes standing out in golden yellow against a background of deep red.

In front of the steps leading up to the museum's colonnade stands a huge stone bowl which Christian Gottlieb Cantian cut from an Ice Age granite block to a classical design of Schinkel. But Cantian went further than the architect expected, giving the bowl, which was originally intended to be placed inside the rotunda, a twenty-three-foot diameter that made it too large to fit. Instead, in 1831 the eighty-ton curiosity was positioned outside to be celebrated only three years later as 'a Biedermeier wonder of the world'. With their customary lack of respect, Berliners were less impressed, calling it simply the 'soup bowl'.

In 1826, as work was under way on the Altes Museum, Schinkel travelled to London to inspect, among other English innovations, Sir Robert Smirke's British Museum, where work had begun three years earlier and which was considered the most modern building of its kind in Europe. It too boasted a formidable, uninterrupted Ionic colonnade. Schinkel was looking for new ideas for the interior of his museum and returned hoping to upgrade some of the materials, using marble and granite, for instance, instead of stucco and sandstone. Such extravagance was predictably turned down by the ever cost-conscious king.

But the trip to Britain was to have a much more fundamental significance for Schinkel as he absorbed the lessons of its industrial architecture, its factories, roads, canals, bridges and workers' housing. His notebooks overflow with observations, sketches and drawings – of Manchester cotton mills, for example – which he could later put to use. The widespread employment of brick was a particular inspiration to him and, reviving a neglected north German tradition, he was to turn increasingly to this practical and cheap material. His ten-week stay took him beyond London to the Midlands, where he sketched the Potteries with their rows of distinctively shaped kilns, the north, Wales and Scotland. He was fascinated by the industrial revolution and its architectural implications. In Edinburgh he drew and took notes on a new gasworks and gasometer, while a textile factory at Stroud in Gloucestershire did not fail to catch his attention. He made a point of studying technical problems such as iron frame construction and the use of glass, recognizing that industrialization was the great challenge of the age. Yet he saw too how it could lead to oppressive social conditions that clashed with his humanistic ideals.

His visit was not only concerned with what amounted to open industrial espionage; he also let himself be distracted by more obviously uplifting sights: St Paul's, which he drew from across the Thames, Westminster Abbey, the colleges and spires of Oxford, where he sketched All Souls from the Radcliffe Camera, or the force of nature at Fingal's Cave, the ebb and flow of whose thunderous tide he captured in pen, ink and pencil three years before a similar visit was to inspire Mendelssohn's *Hebrides Overture*. In London he was especially interested by Nash's new terraces on Regent's Park, his Clarence House, Sir John Soane's Bank of England and the theatres at Covent Garden and Drury Lane. The British journey was quite as important in its way as were his three trips to Italy in 1803, 1824 and 1830. Like other Germans in the nineteenth century, he was greatly impressed and influenced by what the British achieved, their inventiveness and not least their way of life. Prussia could and would learn from the British example, and Berlin would benefit. As early as 1827 an English company installed gas lighting in Berlin at Schinkel's suggestion.

The most visible English influence came with his neo-Gothic, twin-towered design for the Friedrichswerdersche Kirche, which was approved in March 1824. Originally Schinkel had suggested classical alternatives modelled on a Roman temple, but the crown prince rightly thought the restricted site and the irregular street pattern favoured a design 'in the medieval style'. The Englishness of the unplastered red brick church which was completed in 1830 is not in doubt; Schinkel himself described it as being 'in the character of an English chapel'. Even before his rewarding expedition across the Channel he was familiar with English Gothic churches from engravings. The result was a church of some loveliness, great lightness, with its long, pointed windows, and considerable character. After being pounded by artillery fire in April 1945, the already bomb-damaged building was left in a piteous state until its restoration was begun in 1982. As if in contrition for their unnecessary and scandalous pulling down of the neighbouring Bauakademie twenty years earlier, the communist authorities meticulously refurbished Berlin's first neo-Gothic church, transforming it affectionately into today's Schinkel Museum.

Previously, until the end of the Second World War and its gutting by bombs, a Schinkel Museum had been housed in the Bauakademie, his late and most modern masterpiece. There he brought together art and science, fusing the styles he had mastered, classical and Gothic, with the latest building techniques – some learned from English industrial architecture – to create his most original work. The square, four-storeyed dark-red brick building, decorated with violet brick for banding and terracotta reliefs around the windows and doors, was called 'the box' by its critics, but became an architectural encyclopaedia to students. As was fitting for the first representative brick building in Prussia, it enjoyed a superb site, one side facing the Spree and royal castle and another the Werdersche Markt, where his 'English chapel' occupied one corner in its pleasantly contrasting lighter-toned red brick. Construction began in April 1832 and was completed exactly four years later. Schinkel, by now head of building in Prussia and its provinces, moved into the upper-floor flat set aside for the director and, after his collapse into a coma in September 1840, died there thirteen months later without regaining consciousness.

'It goes against my sense of duty to pretend to be more than I am. The sphere of the artistic, which alone appeals to me, is of such a limitless dimension that the span of a man's life is too short. I feel troubled that, under different circumstances, I could have achieved still more had I not been torn within by work which snatched away time I could have used to fulfil my intended purpose,' Schinkel wrote revealingly in 1832. Thirty-five years later the art critic Herman Grimm noted: 'Whoever leafs through Schinkel's portfolios gains the impression of a man who could have built twenty times what he did.'

The weighty Bauakademie itself can be said to be his testament, though he is known today for those earlier buildings of his that survived late nineteenth-century development and twentieth-century destruction. The Bauakademie, the proud palaces of the Wilhelm-strasse and Pariser Platz, his highly habitable private houses, his eminently appropriate and always elegant institutional and administrative buildings are all gone. And yet, leaving aside the marvellous profusion of his non-architectural artistic activities, those few Berlin buildings of his that do still stand, clustered around the top of Unter den Linden, are enough to testify to a remarkable genius that more and better than any other fashioned the face of Prussia's capital. Not only his friends, and the thousands who attended his funeral, were of the opinion that he had 'turned Berlin into a city of beauty'.

FIVE

ROMANTICISM AND REVOLUTION

I T was the summer of 1821 and Harry Heine, as, perhaps surprisingly, Heinrich was originally called, had a complaint: a too pervasive popular song. The Düsseldorf-born poet was visiting Berlin and, though himself an arch-romantic of a radical disposition, he found its insistency irritating. During those hot summer months, and for a while after, everyone in Berlin, 'from schoolgirl to barber', had but one tune on their lips: the 'Jungfernkranz' (Bridal Wreath) 'hit' from Weber's *Freischütz*. 'You now hear eternally the same melody, the song of songs – the "Jungfernkranz",' he wrote in a 'Letter from Berlin'.

Napoleon's defeat had awakened new self-confidence in the Prussian capital, bringing democratic expectations and aspirations. Berliners had put up with enough absolute rule and despotism, enlightened or otherwise. The French Revolution – too early to be followed in Germany – pointed to new political possibilities and alternatives. Republicanism was revealed. Attitudes were changing in a Berlin which was no longer so backward; romance and revolution were in the air.

Frederick William III had a chance to adjust and stave off a future crisis by granting the constitutional rights which were demanded and had apparently been promised. But, dissuaded by the Russian tsar and Austrian emperor, who were fearful for their own absolutism, he listened to the conservative voice of the power-mongering Metternich in Vienna and shelved any progressive plans, returning to the reactionary ways of his predecessors, as if there had been no French Revolution or Napoleon. In a Berlin which had become a hotbed of questioning intellectual activity, while daily being transformed by industrial innovation, this was bound to be unrealistic. Sooner or later the stifled democratic forces would erupt and demand more radical change. They did in 1848, the year revolution swept the continent,

83

when his father's procrastination finally caught up with Frederick William IV.

Well before the barricades went up in that momentous year, the popularity of the first performance of *Der Freischütz* in 1821 derived not merely from its memorable melody. It symbolized the new national awareness: a German opera with broad appeal eclipsing the continued Italian preference which the king and court had maintained rigidly ever since the autocratic days of Frederick the Great. Significantly, the date chosen for the première was 18 June, the anniversary of Waterloo, when Blücher's Prussian regiments had played a late but not unimportant role in dashing once and for all Napoleon's hopes of a comeback. It was given not in the Royal Opera House, frequented by the court, where Weber's simultaneously completed *Preciosa* was at that very time enjoying considerable success, but in the Schauspielhaus, which, rebuilt by Schinkel, had opened to such acclaim only three weeks earlier.

The theatre was packed with young people who fervently admired Weber for his patriotic songs and by members of the 'German' camp in opera. The composer conducted and Schinkel designed the evocative scenery, notably the suitably ghostly 'Wolf's Glen' where the magic bullets are cast. The court was conspicuously absent, but the intellectual élite was out in force, including Heine and Felix Mendelssohn. E.T.A. Hoffmann wrote a famous review: 'The public appreciated the worth of the brilliant music from start to finish, from the overture to the final chorus each piece without exception was loudly applauded and at the end the composer was given a tumultuous reception.' The gripping blend of romance and the supernatural was a winning combination which Weber would later find hard to repeat. That night musical history was made in Berlin and romantic opera was born. Nationalists, not only in music, savoured a moment of triumph and every barrow-boy who whistled or hurdy-gurdy that played the popular melody of the 'Jungfernkranz' was, in true Berlin fashion, cocking a snook at the Establishment. And that, if not the quickly hackneyed tune, Heine would have appreciated.

Weber followed the triumph of *Freischütz* with *Euryanthe* composed while he stayed in the Pariser Platz, in the shadow of the Brandenburg Gate. But his attempts to stage it in Berlin were repeatedly blocked by the jealousy of the dictatorial Italian court composer

Gaspare Spontini. Finally, taking advantage of Spontini's absence on a ten-month holiday, the new opera, admired by Beethoven – who saw in it another victory for German over Italian music – and Schumann, but condemned for its poor construction (among other criticisms) by Schubert, was given its Berlin première in December 1825, more than two years after its first staging in Vienna and following performances in Dresden and Leipzig. Buoyed by the popularity of *Freischütz*, *Euryanthe* was bound to be acclaimed at first, but its cumbersome, laboured libretto by the eccentric poetess Helmina von Chezy was enough to ensure its disappearance from the repertoire before long. Nevertheless, it was to herald quite obviously the early romantic operas of Richard Wagner, particularly *Tannhäuser*.

After Bonaparte's fall, Frederick William had seen Spontini's *The Vestal Virgin* and *Fernando Cortez* in Paris and been so impressed that he offered the composer, who had just taken French nationality and had been a favourite of Napoleon and his empress, the most generous terms to come to Berlin and resume the eighteenth-century tradition of annually furnishing a new opera. As an additional inducement he was given, despite the opposition of the Royal Theatre director Count Brühl and the anti-Italian lobby, the newly created title 'Director-General of Music' with effect from September 1819. By express wish of the king *Fernando Cortez* was to be performed on the royal birthday.

Only five weeks before the momentous première of *Freischütz*, Spontini's *Olympia* had a markedly less memorable first night at the opera house, despite forty-two rehearsals, an enlarged orchestra, sets designed by Schinkel, a libretto based on Voltaire translated by E.T.A. Hoffmann, the appearance of live elephants on stage and a technical perfection and polish excelled only by the amount spent on the production. Eight years later *Agnes of Hohenstaufen* was given on an even grander scale. Although technically accomplished, the poverty of inspiration of Spontini's compositions has seen them consigned to theatre archives. He was a poor choice for a newly self-aware Berlin and everyone but the king, and the conceited composer, knew it. Dresden had made a wiser selection in picking Weber as musical director of its opera.

Frederick William III hated court pomp, preferring to live in the Kronprinzenpalais (Crown Prince's Palace), opposite the Zeughaus, than the castle. He would behave like an ordinary citizen, taking walks in the Tiergarten beyond the Brandenburg Gate, where by chance he would come across the irrepressible Schadow and be sketched by him. Particularly later in life, he would adjourn nightly to the theatre, occupying a side box dressed in a simple soldier's coat. There he was concerned over the moral reputation of his actors and surprised at the public's critical faculties. 'The public is forever dissatisfied, and everything pleases me so much!' he noted. But when in 1838 Mephisto in *Faust* delighted the public with his 'flea song', the king was so shocked that he suspended the play. He was a monarch who lacked imagination, who failed to grasp the significance of world events and their effect on his own authority, while showing little interest in the great minds that were then shaping a new Prussia and Berlin.

One of the more remarkable characters at the centre of Berlin's burgeoning musical and cultural life was Karl Friedrich Zelter. Born in 1758, he had as a young man lived through the years when culture was still dictated by a culturally opinionated and conservative king. With the death of Frederick the Great, artistic judgement began to pass to a rising middle class. The king remained the key but not the sole figure in patronage.

In September 1791 a mixed choir assembled in the Marienkirche, which to this day has a reputation for music-making, for a public performance that was to mark the birth of a Berlin institution, the Singakademie. It was the first time in church that women had sung alongside men in a choir. Among those from very varied walks of life who joined the choir – as a tenor – was the 32-year-old building contractor Zelter. Since 1790 music lovers had been gathering for their personal enjoyment under the guidance of Karl Friedrich Fasch (a composer who also held the position of court harpsichordist and had played for Frederick the Great) for singing lessons at each other's homes. In 1793 Fasch led the newly founded Singakademie into rooms in the Royal Academy of Arts building, and a year later the gradual rediscovery of Johann Sebastian Bach began what was to be the great achievement of Zelter's directorship. By 1796 the Singakademie's reputation was sufficient for Beethoven to attend a rehearsal on his sole visit to the Prussian capital.

Despite his background as a builder, and his involvement in his father's construction business, which he took over in 1787, Zelter was passionately attracted to the arts and had been attending music and drawing classes at the Academy of Arts since 1774. At the same time he forged friendships with leading writers, artists and intellectuals, and none was closer than Johann Wolfgang von Goethe, with whom he was in regular correspondence from 1799. Failing to lure Goethe to Berlin, Zelter went to see him frequently in Weimar. Schiller too was a friend, as were Hegel, Wilhelm von Humboldt, Schadow and Rauch.

Fasch, the Singakademie's founding father, died in 1800 and Zelter succeeded him as its director, a post he was to hold for thirty-two years, during which time its membership rose from 148 to 240. An orchestra school was added in 1806 and in 1827 it moved into the beautiful building based on a Schinkel design behind the Neue Wache. This exquisitely refined, two-storeyed classical creation, distinguished by the four Corinthian pilasters that support a pediment of great simplicity, survives today as the Maxim-Gorki-Theater, tucked away behind that beautiful grove of horse-chestnut trees, so admired by Gerhart Hauptmann, that lies in the shadow of the Neue Wache. Schinkel had first put forward a design for the Singakademie in 1812 and this was to be the basis for the building put up between 1825 and 1827 by Carl Theodor Ottmer. Idols of the romantic movement such as Paganini and Liszt were later to play there. The choir soon attained a European reputation with its performances of Bach, Handel, Haydn and Mozart, quite apart from Graun, a hangover from the time of Frederick the Great, and the local aristocratic talent of Prince Radziwell, whose quite creditable *Faust* had its scenery designed by Schinkel.

By then advancing in years, the bulbous-nosed Zelter wrote to Goethe with evident pride: 'If only you were now here with me for four weeks in my corner room. From three sides I can survey the whole of Berlin pass by me, without anyone seeing me. The most beautiful guardhouse in the city lies between me and the king. From my house I can observe the king at his window. He can't see me. At midday when the guard parades, there is the very best military music, yes, the most beautiful pieces by Beethoven, Mozart, Cherubini, Spontini, Rossini, all without taking a step from the house.'

For all Zelter's entreaties – the builder turned musician was the only friend with whom he was on familiar 'Du' terms – Goethe resolutely resisted the invitations to come to the Prussian capital, which he knew only from his one visit in 1778 with the young Carl August, duke of Weimar. Zelter, who had withdrawn from the building business completely in 1815 to concentrate on music and eight years later was appointed director of the newly founded Institute for Church Music, had a love for his city which he wanted to share with the sage of Weimar. 'That I would very much like to have you here, you can imagine . . . In the end, quite frankly, all you fine gentlemen far away know nothing about Berlin, where, like everywhere else, a lively actuality gives the lie to every preconceived idea and notion. It is debatable whether there is anywhere in Germany where you have as many honest admirers as here,' Zelter wrote to him in 1818.

Like Schadow, Zelter was at the centre of Berlin life as it embarked on the new century and was associated with those lively minds seeking equality and freedom for its citizens. In 1806–7 he had closed down the Singakademie in protest at the French occupation; from 1806 to 1809 he was a member of the administrative committee that ran the city and in May 1809 he was named a professor at the Royal Academy of Arts. He promoted the prodigious talent of Felix Mendelssohn, who joined the Singakademie in 1820 at the tender age of eleven and under whose baton nine years later, on 11 March the historic first modern performance of Bach's *St Matthew Passion* was given in the choir's fine new premises. 'Never have I felt a more holy inauguration stir an audience as I did on this evening,' wrote Mendelssohn's friend Eduard Devrient. The pioneering performance opened the way for the belated appreciation of the largely forgotten legacy left by Bach. On the morning after the performance Zelter excitedly sent off another letter to Goethe. 'Our Bachian music went off successfully yesterday and Felix made a calm and efficient impression as conductor. The king and the whole court saw a full house before them; I sat with my score in a corner next to the orchestra from where I could keep an eye on my people and the public at the same time . . . If only the old Bach could have heard our performance!'

But Felix Mendelssohn was, despite his precocious genius and his pedigree as the grandson of Moses Mendelssohn, the enlightened eighteenth-century philosopher who had done so much to assure the acceptability of Jewry in the reign of Frederick the Great, to be passed over by Berlin, like other composers who were better rewarded beyond the Prussian capital. When the redoubtable Zelter died at the age of seventy-four in 1832, fittingly the same year as the 82-year-old Goethe breathed his last, Mendelssohn would have dearly liked to be chosen as his successor at the Singakademie. Instead, the appointment – made by the choir itself – went to Karl Friedrich Rungenhagen, a safe, uninspired choice which ensured continuity without adventure. 'Berlin is the sourest apple one can bite,' wrote the disappointed young composer. Berlin's loss was Leipzig's gain, as it had been Dresden's with Weber. And as Berlin let them pass, London too, musically always advanced, recognized and profited from both.

It was a similar story with other leading German romantic composers. Even local talent was misjudged. The Berlin-born Meyerbeer, whose youthful *Singspiel* celebration of the return of the Quadriga to the Brandenburg Gate, *Das Brandenburger Thor*, arrived too late for performance, was first to achieve fame abroad, in Paris and London. He too came from a prominent Berlin Jewish family and was a pupil of Zelter. One brother, Wilhelm, was a noted astronomer who built his own observatory in a house on the Königsplatz and drew up a widely used map of the moon, while another, Michael, was known as a poet. The Brandenburg Gate composition, for which he had no great enthusiasm, had been urged on him by his mother in a flush of patriotism and had to wait until 1991 and the two hundredth anniversary of both his birth and the building of the Gate for a musical première of purely historical interest. Such a youthful experiment apart, he was to be remembered as the exponent *par excellence* of the fashionable grand opera that was to take by storm Paris and London, where, like Mendelssohn, he was to find Queen Victoria among his many admirers. The hallmarks of his operas were their length, melody, drama and the superfluous ballets that allowed the dancers a chance to delight their Jockey Club admirers. Such was Meyerbeer's standing – he had Italianized his first name to Giacomo from Jakob – that the unquestionably greater talents of Wagner and the young Verdi for years had to compose in his shadow. It was Wagner who offered the memorable description of Meyerbeer's orchestration as 'effects without causes'. And yet he also frankly acknowledged the impact of the grandiose opera productions of works by Spontini and Meyerbeer that he had witnessed in the Prussian capital. 'Berlin engraved its mark on my development.'

Spontini's rigid reign at the opera came to an overdue end in 1842 and the new king, Frederick William IV, moving with the times in a fashion that would have been beyond his father, appointed Meyerbeer as musical director. But hardly had the celebrated composer returned to his native city than Knobelsdorff's opera house went up in flames, providing a spectacle that Berliners talked about for years, a 'Vesuvius' illuminating Unter den Linden. Restoration was swift and the gentle glow of candlelight was replaced by the white glare of gas lamps. For the theatre's reopening in December 1844 the creator of *Robert le Diable* (1831), *Les Huguenots* (1836) and *L'Africaine* (1865) composed a markedly inferior work: *Das Feldlager in Schlesien* (The Bivouac in Silesia). Based on a suggestion of Frederick William IV, it was an unsubtle attempt to evoke the Friederician past, with 'Old Fritz' himself rather too predictably represented by a flute in the background. Its only merit was as the vehicle that launched the soprano Jenny Lind, the 'Swedish Nightingale', in Berlin. Fortunately, Berliners were also treated to *Les Huguenots*, or *Die Hugenotten* as the opera became in German, a highly suitable offering in view of the city's sizeable Huguenot community. With its marches, dances and wealth of memorable melody, colour and visual spectacle, it appealed equally to the court and the general public.

While Meyerbeer was heaped with honours at home and abroad, another Berlin-born composer was making a name for himself, if not a fortune, with his popular comic operas, including *Zar und Zimmermann* (1837), *Der Wildschütz* (1842) and the romantic opera *Undine* (1845). Albert Lortzing finally gained well-deserved recognition with performances of his work in 1850 on the summer stage of the Kroll, the people's theatre. But it was too late. Early the following year he died at the age of fifty in the poverty he had become accustomed to. His operas had a light appealing touch, anticipating the operettas that captivated Berlin later in the century. They could also be topical and extraordinarily modern, like his now forgotten opera, *Regina*, composed in the revolutionary year of 1848, which in its opening scene showed striking factory workers. Romance mingled with revolution, as in the streets of Berlin.

Recognition at home also came too late for another local talent, Otto Nicolai, the son of a musician who had taken to drink. The omnipresent Zelter intervened early on, sending Otto to the German choir at the Vatican so that he could learn 'holy music'. The young man had other ideas, however. To finance his urge to write opera he took to conducting in Italy and made his way to Vienna, where he composed his spiritedly romantic and comic opera after Shakespeare, *Die lustigen Weiber von Windsor* (*The Merry Wives of Windsor*). By the time he was brought to the Berlin opera and the *Merry Wives* received its first performance in 1849, his life had all but run its course. He died later that year of consumption, aged thirty-nine.

It was at this time that the most literary of contemporary composers – his memoirs are as scintillating as any of his compositions – arrived in Berlin and was captivated. Hector Berlioz, the leading exponent of musical romanticism in France, the champion of Gluck and Beethoven, wrote enthusiastically of Prussia's capital: 'Music is in the air, one breathes it, it penetrates one. One finds it in the theatre, in church, in concerts, in the street, in public parks, everywhere. For music in Berlin is valued by all.' But this musical electricity, which had already been noted by Heine, did not help promote any of Berlioz's revolutionary works. Nor did it much benefit Wagner, despite the hopes he set on Berlin's progressive thinking. In the end there was a tendency, except in the case of Schinkel and architecture, to encourage mediocrity, to reject real genius so as to allow the cosily second-rate to continue undisturbed.

So culturally more alert Dresden could claim Weber, and Leipzig Mendelssohn, though neither came from Saxony. Dresden had a long tradition of artistic supremacy stemming largely from the munificence of that avid connoisseur of all things beautiful – whether objects of art or women – Augustus the Strong, while Leipzig, Saxony's next city, was loath to play second fiddle. Frederick the Great did not even try to lure Johann Sebastian Bach from his post as cantor at Leipzig's Thomaskirche, or respond to the *Musical Offering* dedicated to him.

Berlin was different and its repeated inability to recognize real talent could be blamed, as during Frederick's long rule, on the inherent conservatism of the court or monarch. Its lack of experience as a capital may also have been responsible. Times were changing, though, and the increasing influence wielded by the middle classes with their profusion of intellectually stimulating salons and pianos in every drawing-room, was not necessarily more discriminating and could be all the more disappointing. It was, after all, the members of the Singakademie, not the king, who bypassed Mendelssohn.

The accession of Frederick William IV in 1840 after a long

apprenticeship as crown prince raised expectations and hopes of cultural and political change. He had a reputation for being jovial by comparison with his unimaginative father; he understood and shared the Berlin sense of humour. He was artistically aware, holding in equal regard the antique and the Italian Renaissance. He was fascinated by architecture, on which he had all manner of ideas; as crown prince he had regularly supplied Schinkel, whom he regarded as something of a mentor, with drawings and instructions for projects. It was his good taste and judgement that resulted in the Friedrichswerdersche Kirche being built according to Schinkel's neo-Gothic and not his less suitable classical design. He was a sensitive, many-sided character, whose reign degenerated into mental illness, leaving his brother William to take over as regent in 1858. There is a portrait by Franz Krüger dating from 1846 which captures well this searching but insecure monarch – he is leaning informally, legs crossed, against the table in his study in the Berlin castle, his military frock-coat unbuttoned, handkerchief and pince-nez in hand, surrounded by paintings, statuettes and fussy little *objets d'art*.

In 1841 he tried to break through the circle of mediocrity that gripped Berlin's musical life by winning Mendelssohn back, but there was not really a post to offer him. Nevertheless, during this brief spell of misleading calm before the political storm, Mendelssohn's incidental music to *A Midsummer Night's Dream* and *Antigone* could still delight audiences at the Schauspielhaus. As for opera, Frederick William recognized contemporary European taste by securing the services of Meyerbeer. In architecture, it was Berlin's loss that Schinkel slipped into his terminal coma just as Frederick William IV came to the throne. Between them much more could have been achieved than had been possible under his cost-conscious father.

It was in politics that demand for change had become strongest; there could hardly be an industrial revolution without a political one. The hopes of some sort of a constitutional monarchy raised in 1815 were rudely dashed by Frederick William III, who resolutely blocked all attempts at reform and, despite the fundamental and evident social change that was under way, remained firmly committed to outdated Prussian absolutism. The lessons of the 1830 July Revolution in Paris were ignored by the king, if not the people, as stubbornly as had been those of 1789. Surely, Berliners asked, his son, conversant with

92

leading liberals and artists, a man of much broader outlook, would not continue to be so short-sighted? But Frederick William IV vacillated, which made matters worse. Expectations were only fuelled and the disappointment was all the greater when in the end the king's unshakeable belief in his divine right made any meaningful reform impossible. He was prepared to give the people a voice, summoning a parliament to Berlin in 1847, but not a say. Such an inability to accommodate political change could only delay, not stifle, the prospect of a popular outburst. Meanwhile, the industrial revolution was continuing apace.

At the very end of the eighteenth century and at the dawn of the industrial revolution in Prussia, Frederick William III and Queen Luise paid a visit to the iron foundry at Gleiwitz in Silesia, which had become the talk of Europe. Even Britain, who was unchallenged in the vanguard of industrialization and whose iron and steel industry had provided the model for the foundry, was eager to learn its secrets. As well as more traditional products, Gleiwitz was able to produce filigree iron work of such delicacy that it became fashionable in Prussia to wear iron jewellery in place of gold or silver. The success of the Gleiwitz iron works led to the setting up of the Royal Berlin Iron Foundry in the Invalidenstrasse by the Neue Tor (New Gate) in 1804. A canal connecting with the Spree allowed the transport of coal and iron ore from Silesia, and the Panke, a tributary of the main river, provided the power. The first locomotive to be cast on the continent was produced here in 1816 and employed for mining. During the Wars of Liberation the foundry provided cannon and munitions and followed Gleiwitz's example in meeting domestic and foreign demand for fine iron jewellery, which was exported as far as North America. Schinkel's love of iron for architectural ornamentation and interior decoration (stairs, candelabra and even furniture), quite apart from its use in construction, ensured full order books at the foundry, which was also known for its 'fer de Berlin' wickerwork (using iron wire), reduced scale models of the works of popular sculptors and, between 1805 and 1848, its popular iron 'New Year cards'. Iron had become the material of the new century and the pillars of Prussian and later German industry were forged from it.

If in the rapidly developing Ruhr, which after 1815 was appended as a valuable province to Prussia, Krupp in Essen came to be the

93

byname of the increasingly mighty iron and steel industry, then in
Berlin it was Borsig who began the city's transformation into the giant
industrial metropolis between the Atlantic and the Urals.

August Borsig was born in Breslau in 1804, in the age of Goethe,
Schiller, Beethoven and Caspar David Friedrich, and grew up in the
still cosy world of Biedermeier Berlin, where he began modestly as a
journeyman carpenter. He went to the school of industry, then worked
in the Egells machine factory and took over the direction of a new
iron foundry there before setting up his own works near the Oranien-
burger Tor (Oranienburg Gate) in 1837, initially employing only fifty
workers. Soon that first factory was too small and in the 1840s the
sprawling Borsig locomotive works were built by the Spree in Moabit,
incongruously near the gardens and greenhouses laid out so carefully
by Peter Joseph Lenné, the Bonn-born landscape gardener who was
Schinkel's great collaborator. What had been a favourite, unspoiled
recreational spot was turned into a chimney-punctuated industrial site.
Borsig had produced his first locomotive in 1841; by 1854, the year
of his death, the five hundredth was fêted. In the meantime, the
imperious industrialist, who cut an imposing figure, according to contemporary descriptions, with his flashing eyes and considerable frame,
amassed a fortune that allowed him to live like a prince. And so he was
pictured by the royal painter Franz Krüger in a valedictory portrait of
1855, a faithful hound at his side and the chimneys of his factory
smoking in the background.

In coincidental proximity in the middle of Berlin are the graves of
three of the men who fashioned the city in the first half of the nineteenth century. An avenue gently lined by melancholy birch trees and
edged by moss runs down the centre of the Dorotheenstadt cemetery,
off the busy Chausseestrasse. Some way down on the left is the short,
simple, Egyptianized column that friends placed on Schinkel's grave;
fifty yards further on is a more conspicuous memorial to the sculptor
Rauch, followed by the suitably grand tomb of Borsig, on which
slender Corinthian columns support a canopy over his bust. More
imposing still is the muscular Borsig building that stands opposite the
cemetery entrance, a reminder that this was once part of Berlin's
Scheunenviertel (slums), where day and night, as in Wagner's Nib-
elheim, the furnaces burned and hammer beat anvil. Whoever climbed
to the top of the Kreuzberg in 1840 to survey Berlin from in front of

Schinkel's iron memorial to the Wars of Liberation would have been confronted with a skyline which had altered dramatically in only a few years. Between the graceful and long familiar church spires had sprouted an array of cigar-like, constantly fuming chimneys.

The railway was at the heart of the industrial revolution. Where but recently horse-drawn wooden coaches had creaked and rocked over dusty country roads, iron locomotives now pulled iron-wheeled carriages smoothly along iron tracks. In October 1838, a year after Borsig had set up his machine works, the first Berlin railway line was opened to Potsdam. The pioneering project had been planned since 1835 by August Leopold Crelle. In its fashion the steam engine was the most romantic of inventions and there was a tremendous sense of excitement and adventure during these early days. Nor were its artistic implications ignored; Lenné was commissioned to landscape the route to Potsdam and leading architects competed to build the growing number of railway stations required. By the 1850s the first phase of railway expansion was completed with direct links to Dessau (1841), Frankfurt-on-the-Oder (1842), Stettin (1843) and Breslau, Magdeburg and Hamburg (1846).

In October 1847, ten years after the beginning of Borsig's locomotive works, a shrewd 31-year-old artillery officer called Werner Siemens took Berlin's next great industrial step when with the mechanic Johann Georg Halske, in a house in the Schöneberger Strasse, he became the first in Europe to manufacture telegraph equipment. The father of electronics was bewhiskered and bushy-haired, a man of most romantic appearance who combined sheer inventive brilliance with business acumen like no other German of his time. By the turn of the century the company he founded could boast a turnover that exceeded Frederick the Great's state budget.

First, however, just six months after Siemens embarked on making telegraph equipment, there was the not so minor matter of a political revolution. The clouds of discontent had long been massing. A storm was about to break over the continent of Europe which would no longer be delayed locally by any ridge of high pressure over a Berlin which had ceased to be backward, except politically. Earlier, in 1844, a strike by starving Silesian weavers had been bloodily suppressed by Prussian troops. Now news of the toppling of Louis-Philippe in France and revolution in Vienna and other German cities ignited a very short fuse. It was a clumsy and in the end unsuccessful affair whose achievements were soon reversed. Social and national aspirations were again to be dashed. Yet the uprising had heroic appeal – recorded in the drawings of Theodor Hosemann – as the people of Berlin seized the initiative, armed themselves, ripped up paving-stones and upturned carts to build rough barricades, and instead of burning down the palace of the revolutionaries' arch-opponent Prince William (later the first German Kaiser), they scrawled 'National Eigenthum' (national property) on its portal. Disguised as a coach-man, he wisely slipped away from Berlin at night and under the alias of Müller embarked from the port of Hamburg for the safety of England.

There was short-lived victory too as the king, wavering, ordered troops out of Berlin for fear of further bloodshed, and there was his humiliation as the people demanded that he remove his helmet when he witnessed the passage of the funeral cortège of the 'March Revolutionaries' from a balcony of the royal castle.

But the aristocracy and army ensured that conservative reaction would ultimately prevail over the prospect of a new democratic order. Within months the wave of romanticism and revolution which had so enlivened Biedermeier Berlin had ebbed. Shocked, the city recoiled, and braced itself for what must have seemed a more than usually uncertain future; yet it was to be one that in less than a generation would place Berlin at the head of a new German empire.

PART TWO

THE
TRIBULATIONS
OF A
METROPOLIS

SIX

IMPERIAL GRANDEUR

D ESPITE appalling weather, William Courthope discovered much to admire during his visit to Berlin in March 1861. As secretary of the Garter Mission sent to the city to invest King William I with the Order following his succession to the throne, the assiduous herald, appointed 'Rouge Croix' in 1839, found time to mix pleasure with duty. A conscientious tourist, he made a point of exploring the city on foot, taking in its best buildings and enjoying the picture galleries. On such sorties from the Hôtel de Rome, where the delegation was quartered – 'the king thinking we should be more comfortable at an hotel' – he 'made some purchases . . . including divers Berlin wood articles' to bring home. The Mission also departed with gifts: 'Snuff-boxes for Garter [Sir George Young], myself and Dendy [Chester Herald], – gold with the W and crown in diamonds, – Garter's with six, and the others with four large diamonds besides. The Marquess [of Breadalbane] had a beautiful marble bust of the king on marble pedestal; – Lord Frederic Paulet, – a statue of Frederick the Great on bronze pedestal, and Lord Hinchingbrook, a bronze model of the group of the Elector Frederick, standing on the Schloss bridge; Mr Vivian a porcelain vase.' The Anglophilia in Berlin was almost tangible.

Having weathered the storm of revolution so uncertainly, Prussia and its rapidly expanding capital had embarked on a period of consolidation that was to bring without much delay the valued dividend of an enhanced standing in Europe. The Frederick Williams had proved erratic, sometimes weak and ultimately disappointing kings and – as the failed 1848 revolution made clear – a case could now be argued for a return to the strong direction which had been lacking since the days of Frederick the Great.

As it happened, William, prince of Prussia, whom the revolutionaries had rightly identified as their chief opponent was made of sterner, if not necessarily more attractive stuff. He was a dyed in the wool conservative of distinctly Prussian character. With the mental health of his elder brother, Frederick William IV, in decline, William took over as regent in 1858; little more than two years later, on 2 January 1861, he succeeded to the throne. For the first time since Frederick the Great Prussia had a king who would exceed – not disappoint – expectations. Though unlike his more remarkable ancestor, William's achievement was not his own. The unification of Germany and his declaration, ten years after coming to the throne of a crisis-ridden Prussia, as German Kaiser amid the splendour, the mirrors and gilt of the palace of Versailles, 'borrowed' for the purpose from a defeated France, were the work of his masterful 'Iron Chancellor', Count Otto von Bismarck, supported by an increasingly confident military machine.

It was Britain above all other nations which inspired the rising Prussia. Its industry and inventions, its martial prowess, its court, its architects and fashions, indeed everything, except its constitutional monarchy based on a much older revolution, was admired and imitated. Frederick the Great, who had a wit rare among the Hohenzollerns, had once remarked that rather than an eagle the Prussian coat of arms would more appropriately include an ape. And the British, who by nature considered the French to be the traditional threat and enemy, viewed the Prussians favourably. They had, after all, displayed an early enthusiasm for Frederick the Great. Major General Lord Frederic Paulet, accompanying the 1861 Garter Mission, was probably well pleased with his gift of a statue of 'Old Fritz'.

The links with Britain were cemented by marriage. William's eldest son, Frederick, had married Victoria, the eldest daughter of Britain's queen, in 1858. The following year they had a son, William, who fifty-five years later would lead his armies in a devastating war against his mother's land that ended in his abdication and the collapse of what turned out to be a short-lived German empire. But as a two-year-old playing around his parents' dinner-table, under the supervision of his English nurse Mrs Hobbs, he was delightful enough. 'The children came in soon after we sat down, and remained till shortly before we rose; the little girl was carried about in her nurse's arms, crowed away and seem'd delighted with the scene, the boy ran about the room, or from one to another, or talking to himself in the large pier-glasses, –

100

at one time standing by my side, playing with my sword-knot; he is a fine broad-chested child, nice-looking, though not handsome, with light hair curling stiffly all over his head; the baby is a sweet child with dark blue eyes; she was in a very full border'd cap, with plain white muslin frock, with two insertions of work; the boy also was in white with black shoes and straps and had on a broad black sash and bow,' Courthope recorded in his carefully compiled 'Journal of the Garter Mission to Berlin'.

Before dinner, Courthope relates, 'the Prince talked with me a good deal about Berlin and its early history, and the Princess ask'd me as her husband had done before, whether I was present at her marriage; I told her yes; which procession? I told her, – both, which she repeated to her husband; "ah, yes!" he said, "and I have told them I did not see them, because I saw only but you," she turned away laughing – "ah! there, she will not listen to what I say."'

Victoria, affectionately known by those close to her as Vicky, had a great and benign influence over the crown prince, an altogether more attractive personality than either his father or son. Unlike them, he was of a liberal persuasion (rejecting Bismarck's domestic policies); the course of modern German history may well have been less explosive if the cancer with which he came to the throne in 1888 had not limited his reign to only ninety-nine days, propelling his headstrong, ambitious and foolish son into power.

Lord Frederic Hamilton, a young diplomat in Berlin in the 1870s, was invited to a private farewell dinner with the crown prince and princess in Potsdam's Neues Palais before his posting to St Petersburg. They dined simply on curds and whey, veal cutlets and rice pudding. Afterwards the men drank beer and the crown prince drew on his long pipe. Hamilton noticed how 'the crown princess always laid down her needlework to refill her husband's pipe and to bring him a fresh tankard of beer'. With his luxuriant, spade-like beard the future Frederick III cut an avuncular figure, quite unlike the two Williams. His fate was to be forgotten between two so momentous reigns.

Like Vicky, Augusta, William I's queen and later empress, was a liberal opposed to Bismarck. She outlived both her husband and son, dying in 1890, the year of the Iron Chancellor's dismissal by William II after twenty-eight years at the helm of government. Lord Hamilton remembered a woman who, while beautiful in her youth, 'could not

101

resign herself to growing old gracefully'. He went on: 'She would have made a most charming old lady, but though well over seventy then, she was ill-advised enough to attempt to rejuvenate herself with a chestnut wig and an elaborate make-up, with deplorable results. The empress, in addition, was afflicted with a slight palsy of the head.'

But whatever her appearance, the highly educated former princess of Sachsen-Weimar held her English daughter-in-law in high regard. Two nights before the Garter Mission's reception and dinner with the crown prince and princess, and after the heralds had passed a very wet morning at the museums, there was a similar invitation to the palace from the king and queen. Before dinner, Courthope recalled, the queen 'conversed with me for some time about the museum and her daughter-in-law, whom she highly lauded and who was (she said) loved by all for her amicability and sweetness of temper'. As for the king, he 'was desirous to know whether he might wear the Insignia of the Bath, at his investiture, but on this point, he was told positively, not'.

'From the palace, we went to the opera, where the royal loge and a box near the stage were placed at the service of the Mission; the ballet was "Ellinor" or "See Naples and die". The scenery very beautifully executed, comprehending all the neighbourhood of Naples; the dancing most extraordinary, comprizing the national dances of most countries, – Marie Taglioni being the principal artiste, – some of the girls and children very pretty, – the dresses, rich and picturesque in the extreme: the king had desired that Lord Breadalbane should occupy his place, – the theatre crowded from top to bottom. We had returned to our hotel after dinner to doff our uniform, and don our evening costume, and the opera over, we finish'd the night at Count Redern's who open'd his picture gallery, and saloons, for a grand crush: here were congregated together our Minister Lord Augustus Loftus, to whom I had been introduced at the palace, the attachés of the embassy, and other foreign ministers, and numerous notabilities of Berlin, amongst whom was Meyerbeer the composer: – with all this work, we got home before 12 o'clock, had tea, and went to bed.'

The Palais Redern originated as a baroque palace built by Grael in 1729–36 on the prime site on the corner of the Pariser Platz and Unter den Linden. Exactly a hundred years later it was redesigned by Schinkel, raised a storey and given a distinctly Florentine appearance with pronounced rustication. Inside, Schinkel chose Pompeian motifs for the splendid decoration of its great barrel-vaulted banqueting hall. Such would have been the magnificent building known by Courthope. In 1905 it was pulled down to make way for the most celebrated of Berlin hotels, the Adlon, which backed directly on to the British embassy and was itself to be razed following war damage forty years later.

The next day saw Courthope rise early for an hour's walk and shopping before breakfast. He visited the French and German churches and Schinkel's theatre 'upon the Gens d'Armes Market', where he found 'the buildings and space on which they stand form a fine opening'. Later, after going through the programme for the investiture with the German side, Courthope set out in the company of Garter and Chester Herald for more sightseeing; this time to the Zeughaus, where he noted 'an immense quantity of flags, said to have been taken from the French on various occasions; (more perhaps than the French would acknowledge to have been fairly won in fight, and how many were picked up in the retreat, after the English had beaten the French at Waterloo, we are not told)'. Another ten years on, after France's capitulation at Sedan, there were to be a great many more.

On the Garter Mission's first full day in Berlin – 1 March 1861 – Courthope recorded his impressions of the heart of the city, a picture which is readily recognizable today except for the disappearance of the royal castle (Schloss) and the transfer of Schlüter's equestrian figure of the Great Elector to the courtyard of the Charlottenburg Palace. He will not have known another of the city's surviving central – near the Alexanderplatz – landmarks, the 'Rotes Rathaus' (red town hall), so called because of the bright-red bricks used by the architect, Hermann Friedrich Waesemann. The foundation stone for the distinctive, neo-Renaissance building with its tall clocktower (reminiscent of a north Italian Palazzo del Popolo) was laid in the presence of the king three months after the end of Courthope's mission. Clearly and not surprisingly influenced by Schinkel's Bauakademie, it was finally completed two years before Berlin assumed imperial responsibility.

'We walked out and saw all the principal exteriors of the city between the Brandenburg Gate and the Schloss: within this space are congregated together all the finest buildings and most striking monuments of the city. Of palaces, there are, besides the Schloss,

103

the modern edifices occupied by the king and by the crown prince respectively, there are the Academy of the Fine Arts, and the museum with its fine colonnade, . . . the university, the opera house, the Arsenal and the Guardhouse; (the cathedral, in the immediate vicinity of the Schloss, must be omitted from the enumeration of fine buildings, being unsightly in the extreme). Of monuments, . . . first, upon the Brandenburg Gate, stands the Car of Victory which for the space of seven or eight years sojourned at Paris, – a trophy of Gallic, not German triumph; – then comes that of Frederick the Great, the finest of the sort in Europe, or in the world, besides the equestrian portraiture of the hero himself, standing more than seventeen feet high, there are figures of thirty-one of his warrior generals, four of them on horseback and all life size; – next, between the opera house and the king's palace, are the three bronze statues of Yorck, Blucher and Gneisenau, by Rauch, and nearly opposite are statues of Scharnhorst, & Bulow, in Carrara marble, and by the same artist; the exquisite bas reliefs of all these monuments, to say nothing of the figures themselves, which are all superb, are a pleasing historical study. Beyond these again and upon the Schloss-brucke, are the eight statues in Carrara marble and on pedestals of granite, representing the idealized life of a hero . . . these are by different artists, but all are grand and effective; from the view of these figures you may turn your eyes on the one side, upon the bronze horses, standing on either side the entrance of the Schloss, and on the other, upon the gigantic basin, the amazon in front, and the horses which surmount the museum, and altho' not visible from this spot, there is another which must not be forgotten, namely the very fine one of the Great Elector on horseback, upon the other side of the Schloss.'

Courthope's verdict on Johann Boumann's weakly designed cathedral, which Schinkel had done much to improve in 1821, is uncharitably harsh: 'plain and ugly in the extreme, and more like a Methodist chapel than aught else'. Schinkel himself had a low opinion of the building, which was put up with Frederick the Great's usual involvement between 1747 and 1750. 'The cathedral church is such a thorough monument to the emptiest and worst of French show architecture that it has almost become a byword,' Schinkel wrote in 1815. Two years later he began redesigning the interior and then embellished the exterior with a main dome and two smaller ones. Not very long before it was pulled down in 1893 to make way for the pompously bombastic Berlin Cathedral that survives today, a photograph of the ill-fated building was taken; it captures a group of street urchins on its steps and the sad blotches of exposed brickwork where the plaster has fallen or flaked away. But for all its imperfections the old cathedral at least maintained the balance of architecture around the Lustgarten. All proportions were ignored by its immodest successor and abandoned completely with the later removal of the castle.

The king's investiture with the Order of the Garter followed in the Weisser Saal (White Hall) of the royal palace on 6 March 1861. 'The entire ceremony passed off without the slightest hitch and agreeable to the programme set down,' Courthope noted with satisfaction.

However, two days later – 'a deplorably rainy day again' – on the eve of the Mission's departure from Berlin, an embarrassing misunderstanding occurred. 'At 5 o'clock, there was again a dinner at the palace, but by some mistake the invitations to myself and Dendy were not delivered and I had accordingly order'd dinner for ourselves at the same time, – the royal servants insisting they were to take seven gentlemen, the mistake was discover'd; however it was too late to dress and they went without us, but just as we were sitting down to our own dinner, back comes the royal carriage, with a desire that we should come as soon as we possibly could; we therefore dressed in all imaginable haste and started, – arrived at the palace, rush'd up stairs, – found the anti-room and drawing room empty, all having sat down to dinner; before we could decide what to do, the door of the saloon was thrown open by the pages in waiting and Count Puckler (the royal chamberlain) advanced to meet us, and pointed out our seats reserved unfortunately at the further end of the table; I advanced, bowed to the king and queen in passing, who returned my salute, and then sat down by no means discomposed, altho' greatly annoyed at the occurrence.' Courthope clearly continued to fume for a while afterwards. 'We left with the crown prince and princess, the former much amused in the vestibule by my having on, what he called, a military cloak; I told him we were not quite so particular in England with regard to such matters.'

That the king should have had the Garter Mission put up in the Hôtel de Rome on Unter den Linden was not altogether surprising. Preferring to live in his modest palace facing the hotel, rather than in the cumbersome castle, he too shared the modern conveniences otherwise reserved for its guests. Up to the end of his long life – he died in 1888 having exceeded the grand age of ninety – whenever he wanted a bath he would order one from the hotel. The moment the management received the royal command a pair of muscular porters were sent bearing a bathtub across Unter den Linden to the palace opposite, where sufficient water to fill it was meanwhile being heated on the kitchen stoves. The Kaiser Wilhelm Palais (later the Altes Palais), as it came to be known, may have been without a bathroom, but it had fine reception rooms and an elegant portico of four Doric columns, with Prussian eagles, wings spread, mounted above the capitals. The royal standard signifying his presence, William had his quarters on the ground floor, looking on to the opera house. He acquired the palace in 1829 and had the interior designed by Schinkel, whose plans for the building's exterior, however, he rejected as too grandiose. The commission went instead to Karl Ferdinand Langhans, son of the architect of the Brandenburg Gate, who between 1834 and 1837 created a residence of pleasing classicism. This was the palace which in the heat of the 1848 revolution, amid the popular indignation, was so nearly burnt down, a fate it suffered on 23 November 1943 during an Allied bombing raid. The exterior was subsequently restored and the interior modernized for the use of the university.

Afflicted with bad teeth, William was a lover of simple but good food, which for a long time was provided for him by his French chef Urbain, who published several cookery books describing himself as 'Urbain, premier officier de bouche de S. M. l'Empereur d'Allemagne'. There was also a Monsieur Dubois, who was dismissed from his position during the Franco–Prussian war but allowed to return afterwards as William could not stomach the cooking of his German successor. With age the emperor's dental difficulties became grave and his speech almost unintelligible. 'The old emperor had been but indifferently handled by his dentist. It had become necessary to supplement Nature's handiwork by art, but so unskilfully had these, what are euphemistically termed, additions to the emperor's mouth been contrived, that his articulation was very defective,' Lord Hamilton remembered.

By the 1850s Berlin had already become a city of innovation, not just imitation. A well-travelled printer and publisher, Ernst Litfass,

106

came up with an original and lucrative idea that countered illegal fly-posting and quickly became one of the city's hallmarks: broad iron pillars on which advertisements could be pasted. In July 1855 he founded his Institute for Advertising Pillars. They soon came to be known as 'Litfass Säulen' (Litfass columns) or 'dicke Damen' (fat ladies). A contemporary lithograph shows the first of his brood of columns being scrutinized by top-hatted bystanders, joined by a small boy and dog whose interest in its lower level seems unlikely to have remained limited to the advertisements. Litfass himself was dubbed 'the king of advertising', and earned a fortune. He died in 1874 and, like other notables, found a place in the Dorotheenstadt cemetery, Berlin's nearest equivalent to Père Lachaise in Paris.

In 1865, four years into William I's reign, horse-drawn trams were introduced in Berlin, transforming its traffic. The following year, continuing his experiments, Werner Siemens discovered the dynamo, extending the pioneering successes of his company, which in 1879 built the first electric railway. Two years later electric trams began to operate. The first electric street lamps followed, and a telephone exchange linking initially just fifty subscribers.

Industrial and urban development was fast and furious, and like a magnet Berlin was drawing workers from far afield into its orbit. 'Anyone who saw Berlin ten years ago would not recognize it today. It has developed from a rigid parade-ground to the busy centre of Germany's machine manufacturing,' Karl Marx wrote in 1859, twenty years after studying in the city.

Growing afresh and at such a tempo, Berlin became for the first time in its history a pulsating, vibrant capital, the most modern of European cities. Its long held reputation for provincialism evaporated with the clouds of steam given off by the pistons driving its factories. As the population exploded, the city burst outwards from its late eighteenth- and early nineteenth-century core, fragmenting into the surrounding countryside. The city gates ceased to mark its limits; urban life began to overflow west of the Brandenburg Gate. In the rural suburbs the price of land rose to fifty times its previous value, allowing a good many farmers in Wilmersdorf, Schöneberg and Tempelhof to retire as millionaires.

Figures are rarely more eloquent than words, but those charting Berlin's population growth are arresting. The just 20,000 inhabitants of 1688 had risen to 145,000 by the time, almost a hundred years later, of Frederick the Great's death. After Napoleon's defeat in 1815 the figure reached 200,000, rising to 431,500 in 1849, and to 826,000 in 1871, the year Berlin became capital of more than Prussia. By 1890 the number had jumped to over 1.5 million and then up to the First World War the total continued piling up like on some inexorable meter: 2 million in 1910 and 4 million in 1914.

With its enormous expansion Berlin became a city of extremes, of wealth and poverty, of palaces and slums. While the industrialists and bankers built up great fortunes, commissioning magnificent town houses with a munificence that had rarely been displayed by the aristocracy, the workers struggled to survive, labouring up to sixteen hours a day only to spend the little time left in cramped and desolate tenement dwellings. There was a surge in crime, and prostitution flourished. In the early 1870s the police estimated there to be 25,000 prostitutes, of whom 2,223 – mostly girls aged between fourteen and twenty – were registered. A breakdown of their family background proves revealing: 1,015 were the daughters of craftsmen, 467 of factory workers, 405 of civil servants, 222 of industrialists and traders, 87 of farmers and gardeners, and 27 of soldiers.

The character of Berlin, which for centuries had been a city of independently minded and generally prosperous traders and craftsmen, had changed with its industrialization. New social tensions were introduced and a reputation for radicalism was born. The seeds of 'Red Berlin' were sown. The slums provided fertile ground for socialism. In 1863 – a year before he fell mortally wounded in a duel over an affair of the heart – the debonair Ferdinand Lassalle founded the first German workers' organization, the Allgemeiner Deutscher Arbeiterverein; twelve years later it joined forces with the Sozialdemokratische Arbeiterpartei (Social Democratic Workers' Party), which had been established in 1869 by Wilhelm Liebknecht and August Bebel in the Thuringian city of Eisenach, the birthplace of Johann Sebastian Bach in less turbulent times. But nascent socialism would have to battle with an untiring opponent: Bismarck, the *Sozialistenfresser* (guzzler of socialists) of the political cartoon.

It was to this rigidly determined and disagreeably capable man that Berlin owed its new position in the world, and Prussia the fruit of its dominance among the German principalities. Neither a Berliner himself nor a great lover of the city, as a dedicated Prussian and loyal servant of the king he yet ensured its transformation into the capital of a new formidable German empire. Count Otto von Bismarck was born in 1815, a fateful year for Europe. In 1862 King William appointed him chief minister and the rest is indeed history. Just as Frederick the Great invented the blitzkrieg, altering the map of Europe and Prussia's position on it, so Bismarck devised *Realpolitik* (practical politics) and secured a dominant role for Prussian-led Germany in the international order. In the seven years between 1864 and 1871 Bismarck engineered three successful campaigns: against Denmark in 1864; the Seven Weeks War against Austria in 1866, which saw the old imperial power spectacularly crushed at the battle of Königgrätz, emphatically asserting Hohenzollern military superiority over the Habsburgs; and the bringing of France to her knees in 1870–71. The last brought the prize of Alsace, half of Lorraine and a huge war indemnity of five billion gold francs that was to finance Berlin's *Gründerjahre* (founding years), as this period of hectic economic growth came to be called.

In October 1877, six years after becoming Reichskanzler (chancellor of the empire) and his elevation to the rank of prince, Bismarck spoke over dinner at his Pomeranian estate, Varzin, of political responsibility. 'Without me, three great wars would not have been fought, eighty thousand men would not have died, and parents, brothers, sisters, widows would not have grieved. I have meanwhile settled with God over that. But I have had absolutely no joy from everything I have done, only a great deal of trouble, worry, and toil.' It is a terrible admission from a man whose iron determination appeared unquestionable.

The young Lord Frederic Hamilton witnessed him utter 'polite platitudes' at home. 'Bismarck invited me three times to dine with him, but I never heard him say anything striking in his own house.' It was a different story elsewhere. 'With his intensely overbearing disposition, Bismarck could not brook the smallest contradiction, or any criticism whatever. I have often watched him in the Reichstag – then housed in a very modest building – while being attacked, especially by Liebknecht the Socialist. He made no effort to conceal his anger, and would stab the blotting-pad before him viciously with a metal paper-cutter, his face purple with rage.'

109

In an essay ('Goethe, das deutsche Wunder') written in 1949, Thomas Mann in weighty words described Bismarck as 'a phenomenon of a political genius of German stock who, in three bloody wars, created the Prusso–German dominion and secured its hegemony in Europe for decades; . . . a hysterical colossus with a high-pitched voice; brutal, sentimental, and prone to nervous fits of weeping, all at the same time; a giant of unfathomable cunning and of such cynical candour of speech that it was not advisable to report on it officially; a misanthrope and subduer of men through charm or force; a go-getter, realist, utter anti-ideologue; a personality of inordinate, almost superhuman dimensions who, the absolute ego, subjugated everything around him to enthusiasm and set it quaking'.

Christoph Tiedemann was, as head of the chancellor's office from 1878 to 1881, a close colleague of Bismarck, of whom he wrote: 'As with Frederick the Great and Napoleon, his ego was paired with a strong dose of cynicism, and this not infrequently led him to underestimate friends and foes. He saw in friends will-less tools of his plans, chess figures that he could arbitrarily push to and fro on the board of his politics and even sacrifice if this fit the game; in his enemies [he saw] only scoundrels and fools. Friends were of use to him only if they identified completely with him. He regarded them with mistrust as soon as they ventured to have an opinion other than his or to adopt a stance that failed to conform to his expectations.'

This giant of a man was a glutton not only for political power, possessing an appetite of gargantuan proportions and a reputation for maintaining, regardless of circumstances, a fine table. 'The prince feasts with the best of appetites and genuine Pomeranian refinement. Lobster, breast of goose and jellied goose, sprats and herring, smoked meat and turkey, one after the other makes its way into his stomach,' recorded Baroness von Spitzemberg, and Lucius von Ballhausen observed: 'After Bismarck had already consumed soup, a large, fat trout and roast veal . . . he ate three or four of those large, heavy . . . gull eggs that he had received as a present . . . And in his opinion he was still on a special diet.'

There were batteries of pipes and bundles of Havana cigars in his office in the Wilhelmstrasse, a collection of swords and daggers on the wall and an outsize sofa on which he could stretch out with the newspapers after meals. At the start of his 'rule' he was still able to survey fields of potatoes and beet from the room's two windows. By the time an ungrateful William II evicted him from the premises in 1890, 'like a thief,' he complained, and without even time to pack up all his belongings, Berlin had lost its last traces of provincialism and, thanks to Bismarck, become a most dynamic metropolis.

As a diversion from matters of state, Bismarck would ride regularly, hunt and exercise his beloved mastiffs. When one hound, Sultan, died, he could not hold back his tears, explaining he 'had nothing dearer in the world'. He was a voracious reader, but showed less interest in painting or music. 'I knew Richard Wagner, but it was impossible for me to make anything of him . . . I have given up listening to music, too; I cannot get the melody out of my mind afterwards, and then the music brings tears to my eyes and it greatly tires me when I allow myself to be moved,' he once recounted.

Bismarck's most trusted aide was his eldest son, Herbert, who entered the diplomatic service in 1874 and was state secretary at the foreign ministry from 1886 to 1890. According to Lord Hamilton, he 'inherited all his father's arrogance and intensely overweening disposition, without one spark of his father's genius'. But there was a second, less-known son, 'Bill' Bismarck, 'a genial, fair-headed giant of a man, as generally popular as his elder brother was the reverse,' Hamilton noted. 'Bili Bismarck . . . drank so much beer that his hands were always wet and clammy. He told me himself that he always had three bottles of beer placed by his bedside lest he should be thirsty in the night. He did not live to be an old man.'

For its embassy the British government had the good fortune to acquire at an absurdly low price the fine, if over-ornate residence in the Wilhelmstrasse which had just been completed for Bethel Henry Strousberg, the railway magnate who went bankrupt as the Berlin boom overreached itself in 1873 and became for a time a *Gründerkrach* (founding crash). It was strategically placed, a cricket ball's lob from Bismarck's office. The chancery was in another building on the Pariser Platz adjoining that of the Austro–Hungarian embassy. During Lord Hamilton's spell in Berlin the councillor at the Austrian embassy was known for his quarter-deck voice, the consequence of his extreme deafness. Hamilton resumes the story. 'I was at work in the chancery one day when I heard a stupendous din arising from the Austrian chancery. "The imperial chancellor told me," thundered this

111

megaphone voice in stentorian German tones, every word of which must have been distinctly heard in the street, "that under no circumstances whatever would Germany consent to this arrangement. If the proposal is pressed, Germany will resist it to the utmost, if necessary by force of arms. The chancellor, in giving me this information," went on the strident voice, "impressed upon me how absolutely secret the matter must be kept. I need hardly inform your excellency that this telegram is confidential to the highest degree."

'"What is that appalling noise in the Austrian chancery?" I asked our white-headed old chancery servant.

'"That is Count W. dictating a cipher telegram to Vienna," answered the old man with a twinkle in his shrewd eyes.'

The attention of the world turned to Berlin in June 1878 for the congress called to settle the terms of peace between Russia and Turkey. The last few weeks in the increasingly restless city had lacked neither excitement nor danger. On 11 May a journeyman plumber called Hödel fired a revolver at the Kaiser, who was passing in an open carriage. The four shots missed. Three weeks later Karl Eduard Nobiling, a farmer with a doctorate in philosophy, aimed two shots with greater accuracy at the Kaiser's cavalcade from the second floor of a house on Unter den Linden. The 81-year-old monarch was peppered with shotgun pellets and had to be treated by his doctors.

The Berlin Congress was nothing less than a grand diplomatic circus, stage-managed by the whip-cracking ringmaster Bismarck. The list of those present could have been a who's who of the leading figures in international affairs. Berlin, in its new, high profile role as a *Weltstadt* (world metropolis), was becoming familiar with such political jamborees; there had been a dress rehearsal in 1872 with the 'Meeting of the Three Emperors' when the rulers of Austria and Russia came to the newly declared capital of the German Empire for talks with their host, the king, recently elevated to Kaiser.

This time the personality who aroused the greatest interest, according to Lord Hamilton, was the now venerable Lord Beaconsfield. '"Der alte Jude", the jew who by sheer force of intellect had raised himself from nothing into his present commanding position. His peculiar, colourless, inscrutable face, with its sphinx-like impassiveness; the air of mystery which somehow clung about him; the romantic story of his career; even the remnants of dandyism which he still

112

retained in his old age – all these seemed to whet the insatiable public curiosity about him'. Wherever possible and to the delight of bystanders the top-hatted, frock-coated figure of Disraeli, leaning on his umbrella, would proceed to the congress's fixtures on foot. There was a magnificent banquet for the participants in the castle presided over in the absence of the invalid Kaiser by Crown Prince Frederick: 'immensely tall, with a full golden beard, he looked in his white Cuirassier uniform the living embodiment of a German legendary hero; a Lohengrin in real life'. The social high point turned out to be the hugely extravagant dinner given by the influential Gerson von Bleichröder, Bismarck's banker, in his palace on the Leipziger Strasse, which echoed to Wagner's music and where, to Disraeli's delight, the Château-Lafite flowed. Times in Berlin had changed since the day the British ambassador to the court of Frederick the Great had asked for another glass of wine at a royal reception and been told that no more was available, but perhaps some tea could be found.

Apart from savouring the claret, the visiting British prime minister penned a telling portrait of the congress's chief protagonist: 'Bismarck soars above all; he is six foot four I should think, proportionately stout; with a sweet and gentle voice and with a peculiarly refined enunciation which singularly and strongly contrasts with the awful things he says, appalling from their frankness and their audacity. He is a complete despot here, and from the highest to the lowest, the Prussians and all the permanent foreign diplomacy tremble at his frown and court most sedulously his smile.'

Only Britannia's redoubtable Queen Victoria seems to have been the measure of the forbidding Prussian. When she came to Berlin ten years later to visit her dear Vicky, who was then for a short while empress of Germany, and linger by the sick-bed of her dying son-in-law 'Fritz', she called on the half-crippled Dowager Empress Augusta and received the Reichskanzler. 'I had a most interesting conversation with him and was pleasantly surprised to find him so charming and gentle-natured.' These two fascinating figures, who so overwhelmed the times in which they lived, together reviewed the foreign political situation or, in diplomatic parlance, conducted a 'tour d'horizon'. Bismarck, while pointedly underlining the strength of the German army, gave the assurance that his greatest concern was the maintenance of peace. After over half an hour, the chancellor left. Smiling, he wiped the beads of sweat from his brow and declared, 'What a woman! How I could negotiate with her!'

History honoured Victoria by naming an age after her; Bismarck was recalled by memorials littering the length and breadth of Germany and by having his name bestowed on an archipelago, apples, cucumbers, sunflowers, marinated herrings, a popular schnapps and, much later, a fearfully destructive pocket battleship. In addition, an abominable monument to the first Reichskanzler, helmeted and leaning almost drunkenly on his scabbard-enclosed sword, was erected in 1901 outside the equally unendearing, neo-baroque Reichstag building of Paul Wallot, which had been completed seven years previously. The absurd sculpture by the fashionably facile Reinhold Begas – empty and theatrical by comparison with Rauch's inspired figure of Blücher – was, happily, removed after the Second World War.

Taste, that rare German commodity, was sadly eclipsed in the second half of the nineteenth century, having shone so brightly during the previous hundred years. Neo-classical elegance gave way to often ponderous flamboyance. Unlike his predecessors, the kings of Prussia, the new German Kaiser, William (Wilhelm) II, preferred his splendidly uniformed regiments and, to a sabre-rattling accompaniment, the great game of world diplomacy to tactful town planning. Down came the modestly proportioned eighteenth-century cathedral improved by Schinkel and, at the very turn of the century, up went its massive, heavy and restless neo-Renaissance successor: a hopeless but popular attempt by Julius von Raschdorff to emulate the example of St Peter's in Rome or St Paul's in London.

Berlin was never either a natural or popular capital. Other Germans were too different and had as much difficulty understanding Berliners as being understood. But military and political power was here; so were the all-important and already bureaucratic administration and, as the linchpin of its development, blossoming trade and industry with unlimited scope for expansion beyond the city's confines. In a modern free-trading society, Berlin's geographical position determined its dominance. Nowhere was better placed for dealings with Western, Central and Eastern Europe. Everywhere else was either too far west, east or south. Finer, more historic cities, such as Dresden, Munich, Frankfurt-on-Main or, notably, the older, more distinguished Austrian imperial capital, were left behind. At around this time there was a popular song in Vienna with the verse:

> *Es gibt nur eine Kaiserstadt*
> *Es gibt nur ein Wien;*
> *Es gibt nur ein Räubernest,*
> *Und das heisst Berlin.*

> There's only one imperial city
> There's only one Vienna;
> There's only one robbers' den,
> And that's called Berlin.

To very many, upstart Berlin was no more than a 'parvenupolis'.

SEVEN

WAR, CHAOS AND MORAL
LICENCE

D IPLOMATS called him 'the schoolboy' because he could not be trusted with any secret. Those that met him came away with the impression that he was a 'born actor'. He loved dressing up, strutting, posturing and parading. The celebrated Russian theatre director Konstantin Stanislavsky declared on a visit to Berlin, 'Either he was a man capable of extraordinary enthusiasm or else a brilliant actor.' His grandmother, Queen Victoria, had questioned his capability, and he hated her for reading him so many lectures. 'Her silly sermons are wasted on me, but I shall teach her a lesson she won't forget,' he is once said to have threatened in a fit of pique. 'She'll be sorry for that one day!' he blustered.

William II remained an impetuous, spoiled child till the end of his days, many years later, in a comfortable but lonely Dutch exile. To his country's misfortune, he inherited none of the good sense that both his father, Frederick, and mother, Vicky, had in generous measure. To rule was, in his eyes, all pomp and circumstance, an endless series of dress uniform changes, receptions, manoeuvres, military parades, reviews and monument unveiling ceremonies. 'He wanted every day,' it was said, 'to be his birthday.' As a youth he would sink into reverie as he looked on the toy frigate – an extremely accurate thirty-ton replica of a much larger vessel – moored on the Jungfernsee lake at Potsdam. The beautiful ship had been presented to the Prussian monarch by Britain's William IV, the 'Sailor King' – a gift from a great sea-power to one that had no navy worth the description. But the future William II's dream was to found a navy so mighty that it could challenge Britannia's yet unrivalled rule of the waves. At the same time the establishment of the Imperial Navy would

116

serve Germany's newly awakened colonial interests. In the end the Kaiser's overreaching, unreasonable ambition was to lead not just to war on an unparalleled scale, but to his own undoing and the premature demise of the German monarchy.

Queen Victoria had feared the worst even before her grandson came to the throne. At that remarkable interview with Bismarck, the queen of England asked the Iron Chancellor whether he thought William could cope with the weight of responsibility soon to be thrust upon his willing shoulders. 'I spoke also of William's lack of experience and that he had never travelled. Prince Bismarck replied that the crown prince knew absolutely nothing of government affairs but that should he be thrown into the water, he could also swim, of that he was sure,' the queen recorded.

Swimming, as it happened, was something William was quite incapable of, on account of a malformed arm, as was apparent in 1880 in an incident on the Potsdam lakes in the company of Lady Ampthill, the wife of the British ambassador. The Prussian prince had already as a nineteen-year-old pulled bow on a light Thames-built four-oar belonging to the embassy; his doctors had hoped that the exercise would strengthen his withered arm. He was keen to learn to scull and asked Lady Ampthill to coach him. The next day they met at the landing-stage where an embassy skiff was prepared. 'Lady Ampthill, with the caution of one used to light boats, got in carefully, made her way aft, and grasped the yoke-lines,' Lord Frederic Hamilton remembered. 'She then explained to Prince William that this was not a heavy boat such as he had been accustomed to, that he must exercise extreme care, and in getting in must tread exactly in the centre of the boat. William of Hohenzollern, who had never taken advice from anyone in his life, and was always convinced that he himself knew best, responded by jumping into the boat from the landing-stage, capsizing it immediately, and throwing himself and Lady Ampthill into the water.' Since he could not swim a stroke because of his disability, the life of the future Kaiser was in peril for some moments, during which the course of modern history hung in the balance. Fortunately for him, though not for the millions who were to perish in the First World War, help was at hand: a pair of secretaries from the British embassy and some German sailors from the royal yacht that was moored near by, hearing the shouting, rushed

117

to the rescue and fished an undignifiedly sodden prince from the water.

Bernhard von Bülow, one of a sequence of chancellors to serve under the impossible William after he petulantly sacked Bismarck, once remarked, 'Thank God no one outside Germany takes him seriously!'

After twenty-eight years leading Germany to greatness, Bismarck was no longer required by an emperor who, unlike his grandfather, sought to step out of the statesman's shadow. In one of the most famous of political cartoons, Tenniel in *Punch* portrayed the Kaiser watching from the deck as Bismarck, the aged pilot, leaves the great ship of state to sail on to an unknown, uncertain future. With great bitterness, Bismarck withdrew to his country estate to see out the last eight years of his long life. The year of his departure from office, 1890, was a watershed in Germany's and Berlin's history. Despite Bismarck's initial belligerence on Prussia's behalf, the world was a less stable place without his sure hand on the German tiller.

The straight and narrow conservatism that had too rigidly marked Bismarck's domestic policies retained its grip on the arts in the final years of the old century, reflecting the Kaiser's own taste. The architecture, painting and sculpture of the Wilhelmine age was, like William II, grand, pompous and empty. The new cathedral and Reichstag epitomized this overblown style, devoid of originality. The Siegesallee (Victory Avenue), leading through the Tiergarten park to the already immodest Siegessäule that had been erected in 1873, was a pet idea of William which exemplified its sculptural excess. He detailed his plan for thirty-two monuments depicting Brandenburg's rulers and their closest associates – 'thirty-two stations of national pride' – in a royal command issued on his thirty-sixth birthday. This gift from the monarch to his capital was solemnly inaugurated in 1901. The painter Max Liebermann expressed the view of a good many when he described it as 'a crime against good taste' which needed to be obscured by dark glasses. To Berliners it was the 'avenue of puppets'.

As ridiculous was the monument to his grandfather, 'William the Victorious', commissioned by the Kaiser from Begas. This appallingly elaborate work next to the castle showed the aged monarch on horseback guided by the goddess of victory, the steps leading to the statue cluttered by a collection of angels, horses and lions – 'four million

118

marks' work of bronze,' Berliners were quick to note, and they suggested a more appropriate title: 'William in the Lion's Den'.

As for painting, absurdly large-scale narrative works were in vogue.
William in his megalomania even gave directions for the castle's splendid Weisser Saal to be 'embellished' with a new frieze representing
'victorious warfare fostering art, science, trade and industry'. Art only
became exciting in Berlin with the dawn of the new century when
imperial bad taste finally came to be challenged before the Arma-
geddon of war.

Yet imperial Berlin possessed two painters of distinction: one,
Adolph Menzel, was to lose much of his early originality by becoming
too closely identified with the court and social round he depicted so
glitteringly; the other, Max Liebermann, who had studied in Paris
and fallen under the impressionist spell while retaining a love for the
Dutch school and Franz Hals in particular, was a bridge between the
salon and the daring new experiments that came with the new century.
Both men, separated by thirty-two years, lived to great ages (ninety
and eighty-eight), long enough to have embraced exceptional spans of
German history.

Like Bismarck, Menzel was born in the memorable year of 1815,
but, unlike the Iron Chancellor, he was almost a dwarf in stature and
rather repulsive in appearance. The son of a printmaker, he came to
Berlin from Breslau in 1830 and a dozen years later made his name
with the wonderfully atmospheric woodcuts he provided for Franz
Kugler's biography of Frederick the Great (*Geschichte Friedrichs des
Grossen*). The almost four hundred illustrations – suitably rococo in
mood – were brilliantly allied to the text, creating one of the finest
German books of the century. Menzel went on to produce a further
two hundred woodcuts in subsequent years to illustrate an edition of
Frederick the Great's own writings. He also painted a number of
scenes from the life of the 'Alte Fritz' that were to enjoy huge popularity and were not without merit. The best known were the *Tafelrunde* (Round Table) of 1850, which was destroyed in the Second
World War, and *The Flute Concert* of 1852.

Otherwise, he painted attractive interiors and landscapes of a fresh-
ness reminiscent of Corot, anticipating the 'plein air' approach of the
impressionists. Menzel was most strikingly modern when he turned
to the industrial revolution for subject matter and he can claim to have

119

produced the first industrial painting of importance, *Das Eisen-walzwerk* (The Iron Foundry), which the Berlin National Gallery purchased on its completion in 1875. But it was the depiction of street and court scenes that increasingly occupied his time, such as his highly regarded *Departure of William I to his Armies, 1870*, a painting full of colour and bustle which was also acquired by the National Gallery. Though somewhat repetitive, such works earned him fame, fortune and favour. In 1898 he was ennobled and allowed to precede his name with a 'von'; he became a professor, was addressed as 'Excellenz' and was invested with the Order of the Black Eagle, the highest Prussian accolade. When finally, in 1905, having outlived Bismarck by seven years, he died, the Kaiser honoured him by walking behind the funeral cortège. Considering William II's artistic taste, this was something of a mixed compliment.

Although Menzel had on occasions been a pioneer, his originality setting him apart from his Berlin contemporaries, in the end he became as conservative as those he portrayed. Max Liebermann told the story of how a Frau Bernstein proudly showed Menzel her collection of impressionist paintings, including works by Manet, Degas and Monet. Peering at them through his lorgnette, the gnome-like painter responded, 'Have you really paid money for this rubbish?'

Berlin was lagging a generation behind Paris, where by 1890 the impressionists had triumphed over their conservative critics and been succeeded by post-impressionists and symbolists. Official taste in Berlin was so stifling, with the Kaiser sneering at what he termed 'the gutter art' that deviated from his ideals, that artistic rebellion seemed to be primed with a dangerously short fuse. The explosion came on 5 November 1892, with the opening at the Association of Berlin Artists of a show of fifty-five works by the Norwegian painter Edvard Munch, who spent some time in the German capital in the 1890s. His powerful, disturbed, at times hysterical images proved too much for a public nurtured on anodyne salon art. There was an outcry, the critics roared, an emergency meeting of the Artists' Association was called and by a narrow majority members decided to call off the exhibition after only a week. The division led to the forming in 1898 of the Berlin Sezession (Secession) under the auspices of the 51-year-old Liebermann, who though no radical himself had an open-mindedness resulting from his years abroad which made him almost a father figure to younger, more daring artists. His own paintings married modern subject matter – *The Flax Spinners* or *Asylum for Old Men* – with a comfortable, dated impressionist manner that was acceptable to both the conservatives and the innovators.

Another leading member of the Sezession was Walter Leistikow, whose landscapes were particularly despised by the Kaiser, who 'as a huntsman knew more about nature than the painter'. It was the official rejection of one of Leistikow's pictures, the *Grunewaldsee* (Grunewald Lake) that had sparked the formation of the breakaway group, which also included the symbolist Ludwig von Hoffmann and, with the new century, Lovis Corinth, who came from Munich and was followed in 1901 by Max Slevogt. Then there was the formidable Käthe Kollwitz, who had been overwhelmed by Gerhart Hauptmann's 1893 play *Die Weber* (The Weavers), a work that was in disrepute at court and which she illustrated with expressive engravings. A panel headed by Menzel recommended a gold medal for her work, but this was categorically rejected by the Kaiser with the words, 'Please, gentlemen, a medal for a woman, that's really going too far. That would amount to a debasement of every high distinction. Orders and honours belong on the chests of deserving men!'

The secessionists secured premises for their exhibitions in the newly expanding area west of the centre, on the Kurfürstendamm, which until its development in the economic boom years of the *Gründerzeit* had been but a quiet country road. Apart from their own work and that of other Berlin artists – only Menzel refused to be shown in their salons – they displayed pictures by progressive foreign and, particularly, French painters. The Kaiser's disapproval was such that Prussian officers who wished to visit secession exhibitions were under strict orders to wear civilian dress, an unusual instruction in a city where military uniforms were otherwise *de rigueur*.

With this element of controversy, this tension between the blinkered Establishment and those challenging it, Berlin belatedly developed into more than Germany's political capital. With the new century it became its artistic centre, a magnet drawing talent from abroad. There were other secessions by rebel young artists – the Neue Sezession in 1910 and the Freie Sezession in 1913 – but the all-important break with official art had been made with the original Sezession, which was to survive until the beginning of the Nazi stranglehold.

In 1910 expressionism took Berlin, by now a city of two million inhabitants, by storm. The movement, which had been launched in Dresden several years earlier by a group of iconoclastic young painters, mirrored the anguished, feverish mood of the pre-war years and spread rapidly beyond the visual arts to theatre, literature and poetry. It was as thoroughly German in character as impressionism was sensual and French. It had the barbed Teutonic directness and cruelty of some of the prints of Hans Baldung or paintings of Lucas Cranach in an earlier age. If the Kaiser, now preoccupied with counting his battleships and buckling on his armour for war, had been upset by the tame imitators of impressionism, how he must have quaked over these anarchists and revolutionaries who mocked the hollow artistic values he cherished.

The expressionist group Die Brücke (The Bridge) had been formed in Dresden in 1905 and brought together Ernst Ludwig Kirchner, Karl Schmidt-Rottluff and Erich Heckel as well as Max Pechstein in 1906 and Emil Nolde afterwards. Pechstein came to Berlin from Dresden in 1908 and took over the direction of the Neue Sezession that broke away when in 1910 the Sezession rejected twenty-seven expressionist works. In March of that year Herwarth Walden became the movement's publicist, founding the expressionist magazine and publishing house *Der Sturm* (The Storm), followed two years later by a gallery of the same name which for two decades was to be a focal point for avant-garde German and European artists and writers. He brought Oskar Kokoschka to the capital. Already using his distinctive initials, O.K., Kokoschka designed a series of provocative covers for *Der Sturm* and was a leading exhibitor at the first show at the Sturm-Galerie. Meanwhile, Pechstein was joined in Berlin in 1911 by Kirchner, Schmidt-Rottluff and Heckel. Their paintings were outrageous in subject matter – hectic, loud street scenes, unidealized men and provocative women with mask-like faces and angular bodies. There was violence in their treatment and a primitive, emotional savagery in the colour.

In 1911 another group, Der Blaue Reiter (The Blue Rider), exhibited for the first time in Munich, comprising Wassily Kandinsky, Alexei von Jawlensky, Paul Klee and also August Macke and Franz Marc, both of whom were to fall in action in France only a few years later. Unlike Die Brücke, this less German circle was not drawn to Berlin and was to prove even more progressive, moving towards abstraction in 1912, the year in which figurative art was first abandoned in Paris, Munich and Moscow.

In 1913 the activities of the enigmatic Walden – whose real name was Georg Lewin and who as a Jewish communist refugee from the Nazis emigrated in 1932 to the Soviet Union, where he was arrested and disappeared in 1941 – reached a high point with his First German Autumn Salon, at which ninety artists from fifteen countries exhibited some three hundred works. It was also the year of the dissolution of Die Brücke whose artists continued on their separate ways. Some, hoping for a fundamental change in society, volunteered for the front in August 1914. And some, like Macke and Marc among the pick of the artists, never returned.

Max Slevogt, a secessionist who was eager to be dispatched to the front as a war artist, came back in a deep state of shock. War, and this war like no other, was a sobering, horrifying experience. In 1916 he produced a series of lithographs for the Berlin magazine *Bildermann* entitled *Symbole der Zeit* (Symbols of the Time). In *Wie lange noch?* (How Much Longer?) Time is portrayed as a desperate woman smearing blood-dipped fingers on a wall to inscribe the dates 1914, 1915, 1916 . . .

The Kaiser's martial taste, aspirations and ambition had earned Berlin a reputation as 'the modern Sparta' years before his troops raped little Belgium, took on the arch-enemy France again and pitted themselves against the armies of the British empire and Russia. If Prussian youth did not quite imbibe the virtues of warfare with their mother's milk, they certainly did from the nursery and schoolroom onwards. Student corporations with their elaborate drinking and duelling rituals, their cuts and scars worn with pride, completed the education and led directly into the crack regiments the Kaiser loved to review.

But alongside this Spartan image, which even survived the years of carnage and stalemate on the western front, Berlin somehow and curiously maintained a parallel reputation as 'the Athens on the Spree'. This dated from the days of Frederick the Great, when after a season of military campaigning the king would seek rest and recuperation in matters cultural and concern himself with beautifying the Prussian capital, or else his residence at Potsdam.

A German classical tradition was, additionally, born with Johann

Joachim Winckelmann's rediscovery of the glories of antiquity, and was pursued with enthusiasm in the nineteenth and twentieth centuries by a succession of distinguished academics, archaeologists and collectors. Berlin was destined to be the repository of their findings. Its famous collection of Greek vases was expanded and expounded on by the undisputed expert on early Hellenic art, Adolf Furtwängler, the father of the musician Wilhelm, who was destined to become arguably the greatest of all Berlin conductors.

Archaeology and ethnography went hand in hand with the newly acquired taste for colonialism. Imperial Germany was following the example of and now competing with the older, more extensive British empire. German archaeologists – often in the company of military missions gathering valuable intelligence – unearthed with great fervour the treasures of ancient Egypt, Babylon, Assyria, Mesopotamia and Greece, and their extraordinary finds were shipped back to the new German capital, where they filled specially built museums with exhibits that were the envy of Europe, including the celebrated Pergamon altar and the Ishtar Gate from Babylon.

In 1873 Heinrich Schliemann discovered the fabulous treasure of King Priamos in Troy in Turkey. 'Gold beakers weighing pounds, huge silver jugs, golden diadems, bracelets, necklaces, made up of thousands of small plates of gold joined together – that could only be the dazzling treasure of a powerful ruler of this land,' the archaeologist wrote excitedly of his find. He celebrated by decking out his already fetchingly attractive Greek wife, Sophie, in the extravagant jewellery from the hoard and having her photographed as a modern Trojan princess. The 3,500-year-old treasure was sent to Berlin 'to be kept safely together in perpetuity', but history was to dictate otherwise. In May 1945 Soviet troops came across it stored in packing cases in a bunker at the Zoo station and spirited it away to Russia, where it has remained ever since.

Then a few years before the storm of the First World War broke, Ludwig Borchardt discovered the painted limestone bust of queen Nofretete (Nefertiti) on a dig in the ancient Egyptian royal city of Amara. She too came to Berlin, where she has reigned unrivalled ever since as the city's *schönste Frau* (most beautiful woman).

Berlin's hectic years as an imperial capital saw a mushrooming of museums in the city as every kind of collection had to be accommodated. The area behind Schinkel's pioneering Altes Museum was soon congested with them and, being flanked by the Spree, became known as the 'Museumsinsel' (Museums Island). The development of this centrally situated wedge of marshy land, which had begun with Schinkel's masterpiece of 1830, continued with museum buildings designed by his prolific pupil Friedrich August Stüler, who had first studied theology before qualifying as a surveyor and then turning to architecture: his Neues Museum was completed in 1855 and the National Gallery, reminiscent of a raised Roman temple, was finally opened in 1876.

The Museumsinsel complex was completed in the new century by Ernst Eberhard von Ihne with his tactfully impressive neo-baroque, finely domed Kaiser-Friedrich-Museum (subsequently renamed the Bode Museum after its distinguished director) occupying the splendid corner site abutting on the Spree. Built between 1897 and 1904 in close consultation with Wilhelm von Bode, this was for its time a model museum, especially with regard to its lighting and lay-out. Among the abundance of Berlin museums which survive today, it remains exceptional.

The final gap left on the 'island' was then closed with the adjoining Pergamon Museum, which was begun in 1912 and only completed in 1930 after repeated interruptions brought by war, followed by political and economic turmoil. On account of its unique and fantastic antique riches, this soon became the most popular of Berlin's many museums.

The Kaiser's conservative and questionable views on contemporary art fortunately did not extend to the Old Masters, where he, and Berlin, benefited greatly from the appointment of outstanding director-generals of the Royal Museums. Richard Schöne held this key position from 1880 to 1906, followed by the redoubtable Wilhelm von Bode until 1920, by which time the museums were no longer 'Royal'. Collaborating with connoisseurs and experts such as Max Friedländer, they acquired a series of memorable paintings to enhance the collections, including Rembrandt's stunning *Man in a Golden Helmet*. Along with his own acquisitive skill – barring some notable misattributions – Bode was a master at persuading wealthy collectors to bequeath their prize works of art to the city. By all accounts a most agreeable scholar, Bode is portrayed as such in an oil painting by Max Liebermann: dark suited, a book in his right hand, peering through pince-nez over a nose as impressive as his great ginger moustache.

But Berlin's reputation as a 'city of the Muses' in the years leading up to the Great War, and after, was perhaps most surely based on music and theatre. While Paris and London could vie with it and often excel in artists and museums, here Berlin could outdo even that most musical of capitals, Vienna. As for the stage, with the marvellous talent of Max Reinhardt, Berlin soon achieved a modernity that was second to none.

The city which for too long had relied on musicians – generally Italian – imported for their faded fashionable flair became more discriminating, more German. Richard Wagner, who had first laid siege to Berlin in the 1840s with his *Flying Dutchman*, was lionized by the fair sex in the fashionable salons of the 1870s as Franz Liszt, by now his father-in-law and an altogether more venerable romantic, had been before.

At the charming eighteenth-century house of the Baroness von Schleinitz, Wagner went through the music of *The Ring* on two grand pianos placed side by side and was rewarded with a meal to himself. 'Then the long-wished-for moment began for his feminine adorers. The great ladies of Berlin would allow no one to wait on the Master but themselves, and the bearers of the oldest and proudest names in Prussia bustled about with prodigious fussing, carrying plates of *Sauerkraut*, liver sausage, black puddings, and herring-salad, colliding with each other, but in spite of that managing to heap the supper-table with more Teutonic delicacies than even Wagner's very ample appetite could assimilate,' related Lord Frederic Hamilton, who witnessed the bizarre spectacle. The composer's aristocratic waitresses learned that he liked strong-smelling Limburger cheese best, never touched white bread and drank only dark beer.

Finally, Wagner, the reformed revolutionary, had conquered the hard hearts of the music critics and converted a court by nature resistant to innovation, long after he had won over the Berlin public and audiences elsewhere in Germany and Europe. In May 1871 the composer, who had manned the barricades in Dresden in 1848 and, hounded by the authorities, sought refuge in Zurich, marked the new-born empire with his triumphant 'Kaisermarsch'. In March 1876, at the Kaiser's command, his seminal *Tristan und Isolde* was performed at the Royal Opera House. Five years later his *Ring* tetralogy

126

followed to great acclaim in the Viktoria Theater, in the presence of the Kaiser and 'le tout Berlin'. Angelo Neumann, the impresario who staged the colossal undertaking, described how thousands gathered in Unter den Linden to cheer the arriving carriages and especially the one bearing the composer in the company of his wife and the Baroness von Schleinitz.

It was during this Berlin stay that Wagner met Bismarck, declaring to the Reichskanzler how it was his 'eternal regret not to be able to live in the same city as Europe's greatest statesman.' To which the grand old man of German politics replied with some wit, 'Alas there is little I can do about that, for I think it hardly likely that I will be transferred to Bayreuth.'

The following year, in 1882, an especially significant musical milestone was reached with the foundation of the Berlin Philharmonic Orchestra, which, in due course, knitted into a brilliant emsemble by the meticulous Hans von Bülow and Arthur Nikisch, could claim to be without equal in the world. It stemmed from the orchestra started by Benjamin Bilse, a former military band director, that gave popular concerts of Beethoven symphonies in the hall in the Leipziger Strasse. There beer and coffee were served, men smoked cigars or brought along their pipes, and women, while watching over the children, could continue with their needlework. A rift between Bilse and some members of the orchestra led to the forming of the Philharmonic Orchestra, which Brahms and Richard Strauss were soon to conduct.

Shortly before Berlin gained imperial status an Academy of Music was founded in 1869 with the Hungarian violinist Joseph Joachim as its first director: a great bearded bear of a man, he could coax the sweetest of tones from his precious Stradivarius. Berlin had already been mesmerized by Paganini's demonic virtuosity in 1829 and by the Belgian Henri Vieuxtemps in 1837, while, among pianists, Liszt elicited hysterical adulation at his twenty-one recitals in 1842 – ten in the Singakademie, four in the opera house, three in the Hôtel de Russie, two in the Schauspielhaus Konzertsaal and two in the university lecture theatre. As a close friend of Robert and Clara Schumann, Brahms and Liszt, Joachim stood as the pivotal figure in Berlin's increasingly brilliant musical life. Brahms, whom he championed over Wagner, dedicated his Violin Concerto to him, as did Schumann,

127

Bruch and Dvořák – a rich harvest for any violinist. Joachim's performance of the Beethoven Violin Concerto was the model for a generation and the cadenza he wrote for it remains definitive today. He also instituted a distinguished tradition of chamber music in the city – carried on in the new century by the violinist Carl Flesch and the pianist Artur Schnabel – with his formation of the Joachim quartet. Its authoritative performances attracted not only musicians but leading figures in public life, such as the goblin-like Adolph von Menzel, or the daunting Field Marshal Count Helmuth von Moltke, who had directed Bismarck's wars with such success. Joachim's death in 1907 at the age of seventy-six deprived Berlin of one of its musical pillars, but by then he had schooled a new generation of considerable talent.

Joachim was one of the original conductors of the Berlin Philharmonic, which already in the year of its foundation was able to claim its own concert hall in the Bernburger Strasse – the Philharmonie – adeptly converted from a roller-skating rink. Transformed into a suitably stately home for what soon grew into a magisterial orchestra, the Philharmonie remained *in situ* until the close of the Second World War when, competing nightly with the deluge of deadly Allied bombs, Wilhelm Furtwängler was finally forced to lead his players to safer quarters. Soon afterwards the building, its galleries ringing to years of glorious music-making, was destroyed. In 1884 Brahms had come here to conduct the Berlin première of his autumnal Third Symphony. Three years later the orchestra was placed in the sure hands of Hans von Bülow, who was both an outstanding conductor and a fine pianist. He had been married to Liszt's daughter Cosima until her surrender to Wagner and their divorce in 1870, and had learned his craft conducting the court orchestras in Munich and Meiningen. Anticipating the methods of the modern maestro, he was a strict orchestral disciplinarian, insisting on adequate rehearsal time and respect for musical detail. His frantic energy on the conductor's podium was a caricaturist's delight. Bülow always conducted from memory, once telling Richard Strauss, who acknowledged a great debt to him, 'You should have the score in your head, not your head in the score.' He could surprise too, as on the memorable occasion when he unexpectedly addressed the audience after a performance of Beethoven's Third Symphony to say that the work which the composer had first dedicated to Bonaparte had been played in tribute to Bismarck – who had just been summarily sacked as chancellor. But Bülow's reign at the Philharmonie was to be cut short by illness; he resigned his position in 1892 and last played in Berlin in October 1893, on that occasion as a pianist at the opening of the Bechsteinsaal. Four months later, seeking relief from the rigours of a Berlin winter, he died in Cairo.

A series of accomplished conductors followed in his shoes at the Philharmonie, including Felix Mottl, the musical director from Karlsruhe, Ernst von Schuch, who lorded it over the magnificent Dresden orchestra, with whom he gave a whole sequence of first performances of operas by Richard Strauss, then Strauss himself and Hermann Levy from Munich. Finally, towards the end of 1895, the Berlin Philharmonic succeeded in engaging the impressive talent of Arthur Nikisch, the director of the distinguished Leipzig Gewandhaus Orchestra, on condition that he could continue to conduct in the Saxon city, with its outstanding musical tradition dating from the time of Bach and its strong association with Mendelssohn. For twenty-three years the fabulously moustached Nikisch wove his spell at the Philharmonie. 'He doesn't really conduct, he just succumbs completely to the mysterious genius he has within,' Tchaikovsky remarked. The oldest surviving recording of the Berlin Philharmonic Orchestra dates from 1913 and is of Nikisch conducting Beethoven's Fifth Symphony in a performance of spellbinding intensity.

The early blossoming of the Berlin Philharmonic forced an overdue improvement in the standards of the torpid Royal Orchestra (the opera orchestra), which in 1891 at last found a conductor of calibre with the appointment of the 27-year-old Austrian Felix von Weingartner as its musical director. Even on his début this pupil of Liszt introduced some spice to the orchestra's previously too stolid concert fare with a performance of Berlioz's Symphonie fantastique, an appropriate tribute to the French romantic composer who had himself been so enthusiastic about music in Berlin. 'Your Berlioz,' Brahms had remarked to Weingartner when the conductor called on him in Vienna before a concert in 1896.

In 1905 the Berlin correspondent of the American Musical Courier reported: 'We are constantly hearing the world's two greatest conductors, Nikisch and Weingartner. Weingartner conducts with wonderful élan, and with remarkable perfection of detail . . . he calculates his effects with unerring certainty; he is the harder worker and the great drill-master. Nikisch is more poetic, more impulsive.'

129

When Weingartner moved on from the German capital to replace Mahler as director of the Vienna Court Opera in 1908, his position was taken by the extremely versatile Richard Strauss, who remained the Royal Orchestra's chief conductor until the end of the empire. During his twenty years in Berlin he totted up the remarkable tally of 959 opera performances, ranging from Wagner to Verdi, from Bizet to Johann Strauss (in 1899 news of the death of the 'Waltz King' led him to substitute Mozart's 'Masonic Funeral Music' and *Die Fledermaus* for the intended programme), in addition to 225 concerts with the Royal Orchestra. Among his compositions, he completed his semi-autobiographical symphonic poem *Ein Heldenleben* (A Hero's Life) while living in the Knesebeckstrasse in 1898.

There was no shortage of opera in pre-Great War Berlin. Besides the Royal Opera House, the premier establishment, there were the Kroll Theatre in the Tiergarten, which since 1895 had been attached to the Royal Theatres and would accommodate visiting ensembles, and also the independent Komische Oper. It was founded by Hans Gregor in 1905 at the Weidendammer Brücke (Weidendammer Bridge) with the intention of injecting realism into productions and encouraging acting as well as singing, a goal which was only really achieved by Walter Felsenstein in the Behrenstrasse some fifty years later. The picture was completed in November 1912 with the opening of the Charlottenburg opera house, incorporating the latest in stage technology and modern facilities, which was to make its mark under Bruno Walter during the politically turbulent but artistically inspiring years of the Weimar Republic. West Berlin's flagship opera house, the Deutsche Oper, was rebuilt on the same site after the Second World War.

Between 1906 and 1913 Enrico Caruso, the king of tenors, made annual appearances at the Royal Opera, one of many illustrious names attracted to the German capital during these golden years. The lure of Berlin was such that many musicians, like the great piano pedagogue and composer Ferruccio Busoni, preferred to settle in the city.

In music, as in art, the Kaiser's taste was predictably limited. His favourite composer was the Italian master of *verismo* Ruggiero Leoncavallo, known today for his *I Pagliacci*, the constant one-act companion of Pietro Mascagni's *Cavalleria rusticana*. Leoncavallo would have been chief of military bands in Cairo had it not been for British military activities, which forced him to flee, disguised as an Arab, to Ismailia. In December 1904 much was made of the première of his opera *Der Roland von Berlin*, specially commissioned by William II and forgotten today.

Berlin's musical life was far from exclusively serious; from the 1860s the irreverent but musically brilliant *opéra bouffe* of Jacques Offenbach had a following in the city second only to Paris. In those days the Cologne-born cellist turned composer was regularly and exuberantly performed in the Kroll and in the Friedrich-Wilhelmstädtische Theater. In May 1861 Offenbach himself came to conduct the Berlin première of *Orpheus in the Underworld*, which was without doubt the event of the season. The operettas of Franz von Suppé, Johann Strauss and later Lehár were subsequently to enjoy similar success, as did Gilbert and Sullivan's *Mikado*. But Berlin had its own talent too.

Paul Lincke had the far from disagreeable experience of learning his *métier* at the Folies Bergère in Paris. He broke the Berlin ice in 1897 with *Venus auf Erden*, followed two years later by his highly popular *Frau Luna* and *Im Reiche des Indra*, lightweight but charming and colourfully exotic works which married the operetta with the musical revue, the peculiarly Berlin entertainment form that was soon to assuage the trauma of war. It was Lincke's inspired lot to compose 'Berliner Luft', the rumbustious song Berlin immediately made its own and which with blithe ease was to survive through every subsequent tribulation as the city's theme tune. Having minted a fortune from his melodies, Lincke died in 1946, aged eighty, as a no longer gay Berlin lay in ruins.

Apart from Lincke's *Schlager* (hits), the public were delighted by the shows of Walter Kollo (really Walter Kollodziejski) and Jean Gilbert (Max Winterfeld) and their catchy numbers. Perhaps none summed up the frivolous mood that gripped Berlin on the eve of war more memorably than:

> *Du bist verrückt mein Kind,*
> *Du musst nach Berlin,*
> *Wo die Verrückten sind,*
> *Da gehörst Du hin!*

131

You're crazy my child,
You must go to Berlin,
Where those that are crazy dwell,
That's where you belong!'

And as the madness mounted, the Kaiser issued an order in November 1913 forbidding officers in uniform from dancing the tango, a dance he deemed immoral.

The seeds of the 'golden twenties', when Berlin became an orgiastic modern Babylon, desperately trying to cheat memories of war with moral licence and to be distracted from the reality of spiralling economic and political chaos, were sown in these ebullient pre-war years. Cabaret, the form of entertainment that Berlin quickly adopted as its own, arrived with the new century, and the Berliner Folies Bergère followed in 1906, offering eighteen scenes with dancers alluringly bedecked in a choice of six hundred costumes.

In 1901 Max Reinhardt was behind one of the earliest cabaret theatres, Schall und Rauch (Sound and Smoke), establishing a tradition of which Berlin would never grow tired. It was the earliest in a succession of theatrical ventures which Reinhardt embarked upon with gusto after arriving in the city a few years earlier from Austria. 'Berlin is a genuinely splendid city – Vienna multiplied more than ten times,' he wrote from his address in the Friedrichstrasse. Born in Baden near Vienna in 1873, his real name was Max Goldmann. At the age of twenty-one he was taken on by Otto Brahm (Abrahamson), a champion of Ibsen and Hauptmann and leading advocate of the new theatrical 'naturalism', at the Deutsches Theater in Berlin where he was given minor roles. But if Reinhardt was only a mediocre actor, he was the greatest director and producer of his time, revolutionizing theatre first in Berlin, then in Salzburg and Vienna before, as a Jew, being driven by the Nazis to an American exile in 1938. He died in New York five years later.

Reinhardt really began his stage wizardry in earnest when he took over the Neues Theater in 1903 and, two years later, the Deutsches Theater from Brahm, who moved to the Lessing Theater and directed it in his rather puritanical style until his death in 1912. While Brahm may have carried through valuable pioneering work, it was Reinhardt who for a few brilliant years turned the Deutsches Theater into the

132

foremost stage in Germany, and Berlin into the world's theatre capital. In 1906 he had a more intimate playhouse, the Kammerspiele, built near the main theatre, for a smaller, sophisticated audience. He also dreamed of staging theatre for the masses and so, in the dying days of the German Empire, he acquired the Grosses Schauspielhaus, which, with its vast arena, the architect Hans Poelzig converted from a circus with an abundance of imagination.

Reinhardt's repertoire and taste were excitingly catholic, ranging from Sophocles to Strindberg; he had the uncommon ability to make actors give their best and he assembled a marvellous team of them. His productions were startlingly original and he was capable of producing pieces, such as Georg Büchner's *Danton's Death*, which others at the time thought unplayable. He made use of the latest theatre technology – a revolving stage, for example, in a yearningly romantic production of *A Midsummer Night's Dream* – and commissioned leading artists to produce designs: the aged Menzel for Lessing's comedy *Minna von Barnhelm*, Edvard Munch for Ibsen, and Lovis Corinth. His understanding of music led to his being summoned to Dresden to untangle the rehearsals for the first performance of Richard Strauss's *Der Rosenkavalier* in 1911. More than any other theatre director of his day, he could impart magic to the stage.

But as Reinhardt continued to fascinate Berlin audiences, upheaval was at hand. On Unter den Linden at 4 p.m. on 31 July 1914 a Guards officer, Lieutenant von Viehbahn of the Kaiser Alexander Grenadier Regiment, immaculately turned out in his uniform of Prussian blue with red and gold facings and spiked helmet, read out the public proclamation of the general mobilization order to an eagerly attentive throng of men in boaters, panamas and fedoras, women in gay summer hats and urchins with oversize caps pulled over their ears. World war was only a few days away. It had been a vintage summer with Wagner's *Parsifal* and *Ring*, as well as Richard Strauss's *Rosenkavalier*, performed at the Royal Opera House, a Shakespeare cycle directed by Reinhardt at the Deutsches Theater and, at the Kaiser's express command, a royal tournament between competing army units at the Deutsches Stadion (Stadium).

Early in August declaring hostilities became almost a daily ritual – against Russia on 1 August, against France on 3 August and then the following day, after German troops had violated Belgian neutrality

133

(raping and pillaging, according to Allied propaganda accounts), against the might of the British empire. Neither Berlin nor Europe could be the same again. The crowds that cheered the soldiers down the great lime-tree-lined avenue and through the Brandenburg Gate, showering them with roses and oak leaves, assumed that as in Bismarck's wars they would before long be welcoming them back, victorious. The Kaiser, whose sabre-rattling policies had long anticipated this moment – perhaps remembering how as a petulant boy he had riled against his Victorian grandmother – was banking on it. His generals assured him that the well-prepared military campaign could be wrapped up in six months. It was, he believed, a time for heroism of the kind Germans had previously proved themselves capable of, and he was proud at the prospect of leading the 'great Teutonic nation' to victory. And in the martial euphoria of August 1914 few would dare question the call to arms. War was initially seen even by some of the most radical opponents of the Kaiser as an opportunity for renewal. They were not entirely wrong, for war altered everything, finally bringing down the old order which had kindled it.

So Berlin, a city cracking at the seams after fifty years of phenomenal growth, its population having doubled to four million between 1910 and 1914, led Germany and Europe through the gates of hell into a conflict without parallel.

Despite the pretence of propaganda, with its compulsory scoresheet of military and naval successes, the early enthusiasm soured as the months and years passed, as the human toll mounted inexorably. Victory in six months was soon forgotten and always postponed to the following year, or 'next Christmas'. Repeated promises of an ultimate victory that never materialized cast doubt on the credibility of the whole enterprise and even the dogged Berlin pluck, which could look back on its final triumph a hundred years earlier over Napoleon's arrogance, wore thin as German manhood was unrelentingly sacrificed in the trenches of Flanders and France, or on the eastern front. Berlin's historic church bells were melted down for cannon; an elaborate fund-raising campaign for the war effort saw a grotesque giant wooden statue of Field Marshal Hindenburg, the hero of Tannenberg, erected in the shadow of the Siegessäule, but victory this time was elusive and the well-cultivated myth of German invincibility was by

1918 painfully shattered. Instead of returning with foreign trophies, a 'bread card' was introduced in February 1915, foodstuffs were either rationed or unavailable and soup kitchens became a feature of the city in 1916, feeding many of those who had waved the troops on so confidently two years earlier.

As the newspapers daily published lists of men who had met a glorious *Heldentod* (hero's death) or were posted as 'missing', and provided an interminable catalogue of casualties, the 1917–18 potato crop failed, bringing famine. As in Paris during the Prussian siege of 1870, dogs, cats and rats appeared on menus, as delicacies.

Meanwhile, Russia's 1917 October revolution was not without influence, providing inspiration to the workers' movements which were prepared to take their chance. Several hundred thousand workers staged strikes in January 1918, only to be brutally suppressed by troops. Yet by November, after the mutinies of sailors in Wilhelmshaven and Kiel and the dispatch of a three-thousand-strong Volksmarine (People's Navy) division to Berlin, members of the Kaiser Alexander Regiment (named after a Russian tsar) on garrison duty in the city fraternized openly with the workers. And the people, tired of war, marched through the streets demanding 'Peace, freedom and bread!'

Revolutionary fervour gripped Berlin even if Lenin, displaying some understanding of the German character, had predicted that there could never be a revolution in Germany because Germans would only storm a railway station after first buying platform tickets.

On Saturday 9 November, confronted by his generals and badgered by repeated telephone calls from the Reich chancellor, Prince Max of Baden, the Kaiser was forced against his will to abdicate. Changing out of one of his countless uniforms into the civilian dress in which he felt so ill at ease, William II slipped despondently away to exile in Holland, from where, three weeks later, he mailed the formal document of abdication. The Hohenzollerns, masters of Berlin for almost five hundred years, were gone, together with the monarchy and an empire that had failed to last fifty years.

On that same cold, grey, penetratingly wet Saturday in Berlin, in the midst of the fomenting, confused revolution, the hunger and bereavement, the first democratic German republic was declared. The Armistice followed two days later.

There was a legend, very much discredited, that whenever a

135

Hohenzollern was about to die, the ghost of a white lady would be seen roaming about the castle's long corridors. In the 1890s an American newspaper correspondent had even been expelled for reporting a sighting of the ominous apparition. Whether she also heralded the demise of the monarchy, or stayed on after the castle's conversion into a museum of industrial art, is not recorded.

EIGHT

THE RISE AND FALL OF
GERMANIA

D AZED, like a prisoner at the conclusion of a long sentence, Berlin staggered into the reality of a post-war, monarchy-less existence quite determined to make up for lost time and exploit its newly acquired liberty. Posters went up on the city's ubiquitous Litfass columns depicting a waltzing couple: a skeleton and a languid lady. In a warning of where licence could lead, the caption read: 'Berlin, halt! Come to your senses, your dancer is death.' The sobering message was directed principally at countering the spread of syphilis among returning soldiers and the girls and women laid off from the munitions factories. There was poverty and hunger, and prostitution seemed to many an easy alternative. After the years of deprivation, few cared for morals.

The Berlin that emerged from the huge human waste of the First World War was a revolutionary city in turmoil. Nobody was quite sure where it was going, or how it would all end. An unfamiliar air of desperation hung about the capital. Communist 'Spartacists' competed for the proletarian vote with the Social Democrats, who, surprisingly unprepared, had been entrusted with power, while the Right, licking the wounds of war, was waiting for its moment. As ordinary Berliners endeavoured to carry on their lacklustre lives, armed revolutionaries and militia groups milled around the city centre trying to exert political pressure by seizing key buildings. In the winter of 1918 Berlin's historic heart resembled a revolutionary bivouac. Sailors of the Volksmarinedivision, who had occupied the castle and the royal stables since their arrival in November, patrolled the streets along with the workers' militia. The provisional government, meanwhile, tried to restore a semblance of order by re-enlisting volunteers from among the discharged troops who had recently returned from the front, organizing them into a highly trained and well-equipped force, the Freikorps, to supplement the regular army, or Reichswehr. The mercenary corps quickly turned into a transparent instrument of the Right, and so came to be known as the 'Black Reichswehr'.

Shortly before Christmas the Social Democrat minister of defence, Gustav Noske, ordered the shelling and storming of the Volksmarine-occupied castle by regular troops, an action which left sixty-seven dead. But the authorities were not yet in control and the Spartacists had by no means given up. In Russia, they reasoned, the moderate Kerensky had been followed by the radical Lenin – a revolutionary evolution they believed could be mirrored in Berlin. By December the Spartakusbund had joined with other radical socialists to form the German Communist Party (KPD).

Early in January 1919 a second wave of revolution swept the city, provoked by the appointment of a new chief of police who was less sympathetic to the radical Left than his predecessor, Emil Eichhorn. A massive demonstration of protest on 5 January was broken up by the army. The communists, urged on by their fanatical leader Karl Liebknecht, seized the police headquarters on the Alexanderplatz, several newspaper offices and public buildings, and called a general strike. This time, however, the Volksmarinedivision and the soldiers' and workers' councils held back and, after the government sent in more than three thousand troops to flush the revolutionaries from their strongholds, the rebellion collapsed with only pockets of resistance holding out.

Leibknecht and the doughty Rosa Luxemburg, the communists' untiring theoretician, went into hiding, but were soon traced to a flat in the Wilmersdorf district of the city that was raided on 15 January. From there they were taken directly to the Hotel Eden, which was occupied by Guards Regiment officers. Following interrogation they were due to be transferred to the criminal court in Moabit, a destination they never reached. Bundled roughly into two cars, they were abused by their captors before being murdered in the Tiergarten. Rosa Luxemburg's body was thrown into the Landwehr canal, from where it was fished out weeks later. The murderers were given cynically short, derisory sentences; indeed, to the Right they were heroes. After all, only a few days before the assassins' sinister undertaking, Freikorps posters had appeared all over the city urging, 'Workers,

Citizens! The Fatherland is close to collapse. Save it! It is not threatened from outside, but from within: by the Spartakus group. Beat their leader to death! Kill Liebknecht! Then you will have peace, work and bread!'

Deprived of its leaders, the Spartacist revolution was finished and only a mopping-up operation was required to restore some order, though a brief uprising flared up again in March. Liebknecht, who might have been Germany's Lenin, together with the more endearing Rosa Luxemburg, passed instead into communist hagiography. He was remembered in a strongly expressionist, almost religious woodcut by Käthe Kollwitz, whose talent had been scorned by the Kaiser.

Four days after their cold-blooded murder, general elections were held for the National Assembly in which the Social Democrats under Friedrich Ebert consolidated their dominant position, emerging as the largest party. But the atmosphere in Berlin was considered too highly charged for the newly elected deputies to discuss the necessary drawing up of a new constitution in peace. The risk of outside pressures was too great. They adjourned instead to the genteelly late baroque, occasionally tastefully neo-classical, Thuringian city of Weimar, as Goethe, Schiller and Liszt had done before. Meeting in the National Theatre, the home of German classicism, they approved the Weimar Constitution on 11 August 1919 and the ill-fated but well-intentioned Weimar Republic was born, with Ebert as the first president of Germany and Berlin as its capital.

The experiment in democracy lasted a turbulent fourteen years before the chronic state of the economy, divisions between the parties of the Left and the rise of the Right, allowed Adolf Hitler to manipulate his way to power and assuage Germany's thirst for order and authority with the poisoned chalice of Nazism.

The fragile Weimar Republic ultimately foundered on the impossibly harsh terms exacted by the victorious powers at the peace negotiations in Versailles. Facing a dire ultimatum, the German delegation had little option but to accept the humiliating conditions. Just as Berlin's prosperity in the *Gründerzeit* had been based largely on the billions of gold francs wrung from a defeated France in 1871, so the new German republic was to be ruined by the reparations demanded, principally by the revengeful French, at Versailles. Not only did they bankrupt the economy, but, amid the legend of the *Dolchstoss* (stab

139

in the back) and the betrayal by 'unpatriotic' politicians of an army that was 'undefeated in the field', they prepared the ground for reaction by the nationalist Right.

This duly came on 13 March 1920 with the Kapp putsch. Freikorps troops carrying the old imperial black–white–red war banner and with roughly painted swastikas on their vehicles and helmets streamed into Berlin from their barracks at Döberitz and took up positions in the city centre. Some six thousand men occupied the government quarter and other strategic points. General Baron Walter von Lüttwitz, one of the instigators of the right-wing *coup d'état*, announced the overthrow of the constitutional government and the installation of Wolfgang Kapp, an arch-reactionary civil servant from East Prussia who was previously unknown in Berlin, as chancellor. However, his tenure proved short-lived. While the Reichswehr revealed its true colours by remaining conspicuously on the sidelines, waiting to see how the coup would evolve, the legitimate government and trades unions called for a general strike which left the capital without public transport, water, gas, electricity or telephones and closed banks and post offices. The coup crumbled after four days; Kapp himself bolted to Sweden, declaring 'his mission fulfilled'. The forces of right-wing reaction had failed on this occasion, but would remain dangerously active.

They engineered a series of political attacks and murders, the most spectacular of which shocked Germany and Europe on 24 June 1922. The foreign minister, Walther Rathenau, a particularly gifted industrialist turned politician, was shot in broad daylight by three former members of the imperial army while travelling in an open car from his Grunewald villa to the foreign office in the Wilhelmstrasse. One of the most brilliant and erudite figures of the Weimar Republic, Rathenau was despised by the Right for his efforts to effect a reconciliation between Germany and the Allies, and for being a Jew. Right-wing gangs had been marching through the streets of Berlin chanting:

> Shoot down the damned Jewish sow,
> Murder Walther Rathenau!

Even among those of a less extreme disposition he was not a popular figure – his all-round talent seemed to arouse jealousy – being

140

described scathingly on the Stock Exchange as 'Jesus Christ in a tail-coat'. He knew his life was in danger and when a Grunewald neighbour, the theatre critic Alfred Kerr, urged him to take protective measures, he replied that he had just sent away his three bodyguards and would trust in fate.

That year he had negotiated the Treaty of Rapallo, which established friendly relations with the Soviet Union and did much to make the Western Allies reconsider their exigent treatment of Germany. Had he not been embroiled in business – he sat on over one hundred company boards – and politics, he might have been a painter; he was also a philosopher, art collector and writer, more than matching the considerable talent of his celebrated father, Emil Rathenau, the founder of the Allgemeine Elektrizitäts-Gesellschaft (AEG), one of Berlin's industrial giants which had taken on the electrification of the German economy in the previous century.

The shooting of Walther Rathenau added another prominent name to the list of victims of the nationalist Right. The murderous tally had begun with Liebknecht and Luxemburg, and included, on the second attempt, the former finance minister Matthias Erzberger. Philipp Scheidemann, a senior Social Democrat, was lucky to survive having acid hurled at him. Finally, it led in the next decade to the notorious concentration camps at Sachsenhausen and Oranienburg, outside Berlin, where the Nazis rounded up their political opponents. Although it was politics which provoked passions, there was something of the Wild West about Berlin in the Weimar years. Amid the lawlessness that sprang from political weakness were gangs, feuds, muggings and murders; there was an abundance of saloon-bar sin and fortunes were lost as swiftly as they had been made.

More demoralizing than the upheaval of revolution and shock of assassination, or the humiliation of wartime defeat, was the misery brought by the rocketing inflation which characterized the early 1920s more than anything else. The trauma ingrained itself on the German psyche perhaps even more deeply than the years of Nazism. In 1914 one US dollar was worth 4.20 Reichsmarks. In 1922 it bought 7,500 marks and by 20 November of the following year, when the 'galloping inflation' reached its climax, an absurd 4.2 billion. A worker needed a shopping bag to carry a day's almost worthless wages to the grocer and his banknotes depreciated in value on the way. For larger purchases a wheel-

141

barrow piled with cash – the symbol of German 'hyperinflation' – became necessary. Money was carried to the bank in laundry baskets. The notes were indeed not worth the paper they were printed on. Bundles of valueless billion mark notes became playthings for children.

In economic terms the disaster was explained by the increasing outflow of foreign currency in payment of war reparations which robbed the Reichsmark of its value. The government made the classic error of printing more money in ever larger denominations, even employing newspaper presses for the purpose. The result was a vicious inflationary spiral which rendered life savings worthless and ruined all but the shrewdest speculators. Profiteers, or 'Raffkes' in Berlin parlance, who were unscrupulous enough in the desperate circumstances, could still manage to make fortunes.

For Germans it was a soul-destroying sequel to the human sacrifice of war. For foreigners with hard currency the opportunities were limitless. One evening at the Hundekeller an exuberant American ordered champagne, whisky and food for everyone. Emptying his pockets of small change, he strewed the beer cellar with cents and dimes, insisting that only naked women could retrieve the coins. A large, mature woman immediately tore off her blouse, skirt and underwear, dropped to her knees and began to crawl for the pieces. Other, more attractive girls quickly stripped bare, hurling themselves greedily into the scrum of naked flesh. 'Money doesn't stink, not dollars, anyway,' remarked the landlady.

More soberly, a Dutchman found that the neck-ties on sale in the city were extremely good value, and went home with four thousand of them.

The economic orgy was brought to a sudden, overdue halt on 23 November 1923 with the introduction of the Rentenmark, worth one trillion (1,000,000,000,000) Reichsmarks, which had been devised by Hjalmar Horace Greely Schacht, a private banker appointed commissioner for national currency following the fortuitous death of the head of the treasury. The value of money in Germany was thus re-established, but not the reputation of the new republic, nor its morals. The intoxicating inflation of permissiveness and sexual licence continued, as Berlin danced deliriously on into the decade.

'Sex was the business of the town. At the Eden Hotel, where I lived in Berlin, the café bar was lined with the higher-priced trollops. The economy girls walked the streets outside. On the corner stood the girls in boots, advertising flagellation. Actors' agents pimped for the ladies in luxury apartments . . . Collective lust roared unashamed at the theatre. When Josephine Baker appeared naked except for a girdle of bananas, it was precisely as Lulu's stage entrance was described by Wedekind: "They rage there as in a menagerie when the meat appears at the cage."'

The observations of actress Louise Brooks can hardly be questioned, for she played Lulu in Wedekind's play *Pandora's Box*, which G. W. Pabst was filming in 1928. There is added piquancy too in the knowledge that it was at the same Eden that Liebknecht and Luxemburg were interrogated by Guards officers before being taken away to their unofficial execution.

And Isherwood's Sally Bowles got her job at the Lady Windermere 'through a man I met at the Eden bar'.

As for the sensational Josephine Baker, she was as much the rage in Berlin as in Paris. 'Berlin was mad. A triumph! In the dance hall, when I made my entrance, the musicians would stop playing, and everyone rose to applaud me. In Berlin I received the greatest number of flowers and presents,' she wrote in her memoirs. She played in Berlin for only a few weeks in 1926 and 1928 – in *La Revue Nègre* at the Nelson Theatre and at the Theater des Westens, where she appeared in a new version of the famous banana costume – but is forever associated with those jazz-crazy Weimar years. Her smoky sexuality was overpowering. In the city of expressionism, she was a living expressionist.

Max Reinhardt, with his sure eye for talent, wasted little time in buttonholing Baker and offering to train her as an actress at his Deutsches Theater. 'The expressive control of the whole body, the spontaneity of motion, the rhythm, the bright emotional colour. These are your treasures . . . With such control of the body, such pantomime, I believe I could portray emotion as it has never been portrayed,' he told her.

Reinhardt introduced her to the urbane Count Harry Kessler, summoning him in the small hours to a party at the home (or 'harem', as Kessler described it) of the playwright Karl Gustav Volmoeller in the Pariser Platz. There Kessler, a diplomat, diarist, writer and art collector of distinction, saw the extraordinary Josephine for the first time

143

off-stage, naked except for a pink loincloth. Reinhardt and the other male guests were surrounded by naked women and, the count recalled, 'Miss Baker was dancing a solo with brilliant artistic mimicry and purity of style, like an ancient Egyptian or other archaic figure performing an intricate series of movements without ever losing the basic pattern . . . Apparently she does this for hours on end, without tiring, and continually inventing new figures . . . She never even gets hot, her skin remains fresh, cool, dry. A bewitching figure.'

As Baker's dance brought her into the arms of Volmoeller's dinner-jacketed mistress, Kessler fantasized about creating a ballet for her based on a story of Solomon and his Shulamite, with music 'half jazz and half oriental, to be composed perhaps by Richard Strauss'. Kessler had already collaborated with Hugo von Hofmannsthal and Strauss on the *The Legend of Joseph* ballet for Diaghilev.

With this in mind, Kessler invited Josephine to a party ten days later where the project could be pursued. She came from the evening performance of *La Revue Nègre* and the count had the library cleared after dinner, hoping that she would dance for him. But Baker was at first overawed by Kessler's elegantly dressed guests and reluctant to dance, 'embarrassed at exposing her nudity in front of "ladies"'. Kessler did not insist, but regaled her instead with his extravagant scenario for the ballet. Captivated, she undressed and started dancing next to a prize piece in Kessler's collection, Maillol's sculpture *Crouching Woman*. The count recorded: 'She began to go into some movements, vigorous and vividly grotesque in front of my Maillol figure, became preoccupied with it, stared at it, copied the pose, rested against it in bizarre postures and talked to it, clearly excited by its massive rigour and elemental force. Genius . . . was addressing genius.'

Though she loved Berlin, its outrageousness, the bright lights of the cafés which took on the appearance of ocean liners at night, and relished eating sausages pretending they were 'hot dogs', Paris beckoned and the Folies Bergère lured her back with a new show and a fabulous contract; Reinhardt's fascinating offer to turn her into a serious actress and Kessler's fantastic ballet came to nothing. Two years later Kurt Weill, whose *Threepenny Opera (Die Dreigroschenoper)* tunes were being whistled across the city, celebrated Josephine's return in his weekly column for the Berlin radio journal and offered to write songs for her. This time, though, Berlin had to make do with the banana dance.

Christopher Isherwood, whose two Berlin novels so pungently distilled the decadence of the city in those years, wrote much later: 'Wasn't Berlin's famous "decadence" largely a commercial line which the Berliners had instinctively developed in their competition with Paris? Paris had long since cornered the straight girl-market, so what was left for Berlin to offer its visitors but a masquerade of perversions?'

Stephen Spender, Isherwood's companion in the German capital – 'Christopher never wanted to pay more than a mark for a meal and was always eating *Lungensuppe* [offal soup]' – recalled: 'If you went to somewhere like Berlin you realized certain people were not leading respectable lives . . . It was a great relief to discover so little concealment about sex.

'Berlin was full of unemployed – lots of boys – they wanted a friend, prostituting themselves, but only because they needed the money. It was all rather romantic; I can't think that any of them were bad.'

The Tauentzienstrasse was a well-known stalking ground for male prostitutes and there was a profusion of homosexual bars and clubs for made-up men and monocled women. Berlin, it could be argued, was more of a latter-day Sodom than a modern Babylon. There was not a sexual appetite it could not satisfy.

Thomas Mann's son Klaus, who emigrated the moment the Nazis came to power and was to commit suicide sixteen years later in 1949, wrote: 'Berlin nightlife, my word, the world hasn't seen anything like it! We used to have a first class army; now we have first class perversions! Vice galore! A fantastic choice! Something is happening – Ladies and Gentlemen – which mustn't be missed!'

In the 1970s in London I lived next door to Charlotte Wolff, one of Berlin's leading lesbians in the 1920s and early 1930s until, pursued by the Nazis on account of her sexual preferences and for being a Jew, she wisely sought refuge in London. I used to see her – a small bird-like figure in a short beige mohair overcoat, always wearing a brown beret pulled down to her bushy dark eyebrows, a sharp nose protruding over an undisguised moustache – making her way to the bus-stop in Fulham Road, where she waited for the number 14, chattering away to her companion in heavily accented English, sporadically breaking into 'echt Berlinisch'. At about this time Dr Wolff,

145

for she was an academic of the first order and an accomplished psycho-analyst, was to her delight and excitement invited back to visit and speak in a Germany where feminism had come into vogue. She appeared on West German television recollecting and discussing those heady Berlin days before the Nazis terrorized any who deviated from their racial or moral norms. Having finally found a wider audience so late in life, she returned to London with a sense of fulfilment and died soon afterwards.

'Berlin at night, this light-filled, sparkling, champagne-bubbling, jazz-droning, noisy, too noisy, always overflowing Berlin night,' wrote Eugen Szatmari in his 1927 *Das Buch von Berlin*. He went on: 'Apart from the countless bars, dance halls, and cabarets . . . the places on the Jäger- and Behrenstrasse, where you find a night-club in every house . . . where admission is free and a thousand shapely legs are displayed . . . apart from all this, there are two kinds of places: those one talks about and those one doesn't talk about, but frequents just the same.'

Among those not talked about were the Residenzkasino near the Alexanderplatz, or 'Resi', as it was known, in which every table was equipped with a telephone allowing communication with other tables where eligible partners might have been spotted, and the Eldorado in the Motzstrasse, which 'recruits its patrons mainly from circles where the arithmetic of love is not without its mistakes' and 'men do not only dance with women but also with men, and women dance with women', each often confusingly dressed as the other.

Berlin's night-spots were notorious; by 1927 it could boast altogether 75 cabarets and night-clubs, as well as 3 large music-halls, 49 theatres and – unique for any city then – 3 opera houses. By 1929 there were also 363 cinemas and 37 film companies producing 250 full-length films a year. Aspiring actresses flocked to the city, like Sally Bowles with her friend Diana, 'to get work with the Ufa'. Some succeeded, such as the English actress Lilian Harvey, who in the 1920s became one of the most popular stars of the Universum Film AG (Ufa), Germany's largest film company.

Of Berlin's myriad cabarets, the most talked about were Schall und Rauch, which Reinhardt reopened in 1919, Grössenwahn (Megalomania), the 'Kuka', or Künstler-Café (Artists' Café), Kata Kombe and Der blaue Engel (Blue Angel). At Die weisse Maus (White

Mouse) tableaux of naked girls could be appreciated at close quarters. Or the fair sex could be viewed in greater numbers but less intimately at the extravagant revues put on at the music-halls such as the Scala or the Admiralspalast, the richly decorated theatre opposite the Friedrichstrasse station; among its shows was one depicting a model of Schadow's famous Quadriga with not just one naked Victoria but eighteen bare-breasted, long-legged maidens wearing only scant garlands of flowers around their slender waists. Such lavish variety shows, rivalling New York's Ziegfeld Follies or the Folies Bergère in Paris and featuring troupes such as the Tiller Girls, the Paris Mannequins and the Admiral Girls, were quite respectable by Berlin standards.

The most famous legs of the 1920s were first seen on the Berlin stage in a show called *Broadway*. They belonged, of course, to Marlene Dietrich, who was soon showing them off to their best advantage at a revue on the Kurfürstendamm, lying on her back and performing bicycles with her *schöne Beine*. Maria-Magdalena Dietrich had originally trained as a concert violinist, but in 1921, at the age of twenty, an injury forced her to give up the instrument. Condensing her name into the more manageable Marlene, she turned to the theatre, beginning in the chorus line. Roles in revues were followed by cinema and theatre parts, including appearances in productions by Max Reinhardt of *The Taming of the Shrew* and the musical *Zwei Krawatten* (Two Ties), where the film director Josef von Sternberg first spotted Dietrich, and her talent.

He daringly cast her as the seductress in the film which more than any other distilled the mood of the past decade, *The Blue Angel (Der blaue Engel)*, based on a novel by Heinrich Mann and with songs by the cabaret composer Friedrich Holländer, which Ufa released in 1930. Dietrich, her gorgeous, silk-stockinged legs provocatively visible up to the suspenders, top hat tilted, as the beguiling cabaret singer Lola-Lola ('Ich bin die fesche Lola' and 'Ich bin von Kopf bis Fuss auf Liebe eingestellt') summed up the Berlin experience of those heady 'golden twenties' and established her reputation as Germany's leading film actress and pin-up. The next step was Hollywood and seven films for Paramount Pictures, the most memorable of which were directed by von Sternberg.

Two years before Dietrich first captivated cinema audiences as the *fesche* (fetching) Lola, the very differently seductive, bright-voiced

147

talent of Lotte Lenya, alternating tones as acid as a sour orange with pure saccharin, thrilled theatre-goers as Jenny in *The Threepenny Opera* of Bertolt Brecht and Kurt Weill, the outstanding music-theatrical creation of the decade. Berlin succumbed to Weill's irresistible melodies as easily as it had done to those of Weber's *Freischütz* little more than a hundred years before. Everyone was either charmed or irritated by 'The Ballad of Mack the Knife' while the 'Kanonensong' echoed the ragtime rhythm that obsessed every Berlin night-club. The first performance of *The Threepenny Opera* on 31 August 1928 was an instant success, despite being damned by the critics. 'Rubbish. Junk. Irrelevant,' wrote Alfred Kerr, Berlin's leading theatre critic. But audiences did not agree and flocked to the Theater am Schiffbauerdamm to see Brecht's irreverent and provocative rendering – described by another critic as 'literary necrophilia' – of John Gay's 1728 *Beggar's Opera*. In the next five years Brecht and Weill's most notable collaboration was performed over ten thousand times in Europe, translated into eighteen languages and transferred to Broadway in 1933, the year the Nazis suppressed its performance in Berlin. With dubbing still an imperfect art, G. W. Pabst employed two casts for his 1930 film version: a German one including Rudolf Forster and Lotte Lenya, and a French one with the fine chansonnier Albert Préjean and the delectable Margo Lion, the Berlin cabaret star who had appeared side by side with Marlene Dietrich in the 1928 revue *Es liegt in der Luft* (It's in the Air).

Brecht's words married to Weill's tunes caught the mood of Berlin in the 1920s as pointedly as the savagely satirical drawings and paintings of George Grosz and Otto Dix. At the same time Berlin's post-war reputation for uninhibited modernism extended to music, with a nucleus of the Second Viennese School teaching there and the presence of an unrivalled contingent of outstanding conductors.

The most modern name in music, Arnold Schoenberg, returned to Berlin in 1925 to teach at the Prussian Academy of Fine Arts. In 1921 the Viennese-born composer, whose move to atonality and development of a twelve-note technique was to be the most decisive catalyst in twentieth-century music, declared his discovery of 'something that will assure German music pre-eminence for the next hundred years'. He had already lived in Berlin during less radical times: from 1901 to 1903, when he conducted at the Buntes Theater cabaret, and again between 1911 and 1918. When Schoenberg's 1912 song cycle *Pierrot lunaire* was first performed in the city in 1924, the uproar matched that unleashed by the Paris première in 1913 of Igor Stravinsky's *Le Sacre du printemps*. 'Cacaphonic rubbish' was the verdict of the unenlightened. Schoenberg, himself an expressionist painter of distinction, had achieved a form of abstraction in music that echoed the latest developments in the visual arts.

His close friend and pupil, Alban Berg, came to Berlin from Vienna for the rehearsals and première of his opera *Wozzeck*, based on Georg Büchner's incomplete play with its tortured tale of jealousy, murder and death. The fast-moving opera, with its short scenes of intense drama and tragic lyricism, was first performed at the State Opera on 14 December 1925 under the inspired direction of Erich Kleiber, who had gone through a remarkable tally of thirty-four orchestral rehearsals and fourteen with the whole emsemble in his attempt to prepare the performance and unravel the mysteries of the highly complex score, since recognized as Berg's masterpiece. Panos Aravantinos provided the hauntingly melancholic set designs for Ludwig Hörth's production. On 6 December the composer had written to his wife: 'How all of this – orchestra and stage – will be ready in eight days is beyond me, and I am comforted only by the conviction that Kleiber will not let anything unfinished out of his hands. He knows the success of the première depends on him.'

The most significant modern opera of the period was received tempestuously, with fervent applause and foot stamping as well as catcalls and whistles. The newspapers were full of it; the Social Democrat *Vorwärts* recognized 'an historic event . . . An audience not partial to moderns, accepted this most problematic work of new music without great resistance.' The conservative *Kreuz-Zeitung* considered 'the music not refreshing but exhausting and exciting', while the Catholic *Germania* had no doubt: 'It is a witch's brew of broken orchestral sounds, twisted throats, animalistic screeching, shouting and rattling, contradicting every concept of music.' But the revolutionary opera grew to be accepted, receiving ten performances in Berlin during its first year and altogether twenty-one up to 1932.

Another Austrian, Franz Schreker, perhaps the most widely performed modern composer of the 1920s, was put in charge of the Academy of Music which Joseph Joachim, the Hungarian violinist

149

and friend of Brahms, had founded in the previous century. Schreker's lush, chromatic compositions represented a final flowering of late romanticism and a bridge with the more daring experiments of composers such as Schoenberg.

Paul Hindemith, born in Hanau near Frankfurt-on-Main and the most notable talent among the younger German composers, arrived in 1927 at the age of thirty-two to take up a professorship at the Academy of Music, which between 1919, when it first presented Hans Pfitzner's opera *Palestrina*, and 1930, when it put on Darius Milhaud's *Christophe Colomb*, was an extraordinary forum for avant-garde music.

As for performers, that giant among pianists and supreme classical interpreter, the Austrian-born Artur Schnabel, also held a professorship at the Berlin Academy of Music. 'With Schnabel we begin at a concert and end at a communion,' Neville Cardus wrote in 1934. It was no wonder that Schnabel came to be revered by subsequent generations of pianists for his Mozart, Beethoven and Schubert.

Erich Kleiber, who was born in Vienna in 1890, came to Berlin from Mannheim in 1923 to assume the musical directorship of the State Opera on Unter den Linden, a post he held until 1935 when he joined the artistic exodus provoked by the Nazis. While championing new music, his Mozart concerts at the Linden opera house became, together with Otto Klemperer's productions at the Kroll Opera, landmarks in the history of modern Mozart interpretation.

Klemperer, known later in his long life for his measured tempi and, in the words of William Mann, his 'granite-like orchestral sonority', particularly in Beethoven, was the most daring and modern of conductors in the Berlin of the 1920s. His Mozart was greatly influenced by his mentor Gustav Mahler, sworn by all who heard him conduct to be the greatest Mozartian of them all. But at the Kroll, which he directed for four years from 1927 until it was closed down under political pressure from the Right, he was an adventurist, embracing all that was most modern in music: Stravinsky, Hindemith and Janáček. As the critics wailed at the outrageousness of *The Threepenny Opera*, Klemperer commissioned an orchestral suite of the music from Weill, the *Kleine Dreigroschenmusik*, which he performed with the Berlin State Opera orchestra at the Opera Ball in February 1929, repeating it at a subsequent symphony concert to the dismay of regular subscribers. His performance then and recording of the 'Dance of the

Seven Veils' from Richard Strauss's *Salome* had a carnal quality, an unashamed eroticism that well reflected the amorality of Isherwood's Berlin and has never really been matched in its animal lust. 'I conduct as an immoralist,' he later admitted.

Klemperer had begun his spell at the Kroll, which he considered the most important period of his career, with a provocatively modern and politically aware production of *Fidelio*; it served as a lasting prototype and a prophetic warning against the evils of totalitarianism, and the Nazi injustice that was soon to enforce its rule of terror. There were also memorable productions of Mozart's *Don Giovanni* (1927–8), *The Magic Flute* (1928–9), *The Marriage of Figaro* (1930–31) and, after the Kroll's closure, of *Così fan tutte* at the State Opera (1931–2). He did not ignore composition, though he was over-modest about his own work, taking lessons with Pfitzner in 1904 and with Schoenberg in the 1930s when he was already well established as a conductor.

Klemperer, who was born in Breslau in 1885, was not the only Mahler protégé contributing to Berlin's exuberant musical life during the 1920s. The Charlottenburg or City Opera was directed between 1925 and 1929 by one of the foremost representatives of the romantic tradition, Bruno Walter, a poet among conductors capable of infusing deep humanity and radiant warmth into his performances. Walter, whose real name was Bruno Schlesinger, began his long career as a conductor in 1894 when he was seventeen. A year later he met Mahler when the composer was chief conductor of the Hamburg Opera and Walter applied for the position of coach. Impressed by his ability, Mahler immediately engaged him as an assistant conductor and chorus master. Later under his sensitive direction, the Charlottenburg opera house flourished alongside Kleiber's State Opera and Klemperer's Kroll – a dazzling excess of operatic riches unknown in any other capital.

Berlin's musical dominance was crowned by Wilhelm Furtwängler who assumed the illustrious musical directorships of the Berlin Philharmonic Orchestra and of the Leipzig Gewandhaus in 1922, following the death of Arthur Nikisch, the two top positions in German music. 'Willi has Nikisch's place, and now he is on the very highest rung of the ladder,' Furtwängler's mother, Adelheid, noted in her diary with justifiable pride. His reign over the Philharmonic was long and glorious, marred only by his questionable decision to continue conducting under the Nazi scourge – though only out of love for music, for Berlin and his orchestra, and not for politics, in which he was perhaps too uninterested. He stayed behind while others, including Weill, Schoenberg, Hindemith, Kleiber, Klemperer and Walter, all of whom had played a role in transforming Berlin into the world's musical capital in the 'golden twenties', were forced to flee to America or Switzerland because they were Jews, or else considered by the Nazis to be musically 'degenerate'. The presence in the newly declared Third Reich of a conductor of Furtwängler's stature, as well as the greatest living German composer, Richard Strauss, who also put art above politics, provided the grateful Nazis with two of their greatest cultural assets.

After the intoxicating freedom and dangerous excitement of the post-Great War years the visual arts were equally blighted by the Nazis' intolerance and rejection of modernity for 'racially pure' but empty art that was meant to uplift by extolling perceived 'Aryan' qualities.

Hitler, himself a failed artist and minor watercolourist, shared the crassness of taste Kaiser Wilhelm II had displayed before the overthrow of the monarchy. 'Cubism, Dadaism, Futurism, Impressionism, etc., have nothing to do with the German race. For all of these concepts are neither old nor new, they are the artificial mumblings of people who have been denied the God-given attributes of the true artist and have instead a gift for deception . . . art which cannot depend on the healthy, instinctive support of popular feeling and relies on a small, interested clique cannot be tolerated. It attempts to confuse the healthy, instinctive feelings of the people instead of joyfully supporting them,' Hitler was quoted as saying in the Nazi newspaper *Völkischer Beobachter* in July 1937. Muscular, athletic men, modern warriors, were the order of the day and naked women whose cold nudity had more to do with pornography than art.

Max Liebermann, the Methuselah of German painting, looked out from one of the windows of his fine house in the Pariser Platz which he had inherited from his well-to-do father in the previous century – the Kaiser had repeatedly complained about its prominent skylight – as on the night of 30 January 1933 the Nazi take-over was marked by stormtroopers marching, torches in hand, through the Brandenburg

Gate chanting the 'Horst Wessel Song'. He turned to a guest and said in disgust, 'Pity one can't eat as much as one wants to vomit.' Shortly afterwards he admitted, 'I never look out of the window any more.' Two years later, at the age of eighty-eight, he died, having seen a good deal more than he wished, though he was spared the additional misery of another world war. But there was a tragic postscript to the life of a man who had dedicated himself to Berlin and his fellow artists – 'unser lieber Mann!' (our dear man), the popular cartoonist Heinrich Zille had punned and penned in an eightieth-birthday tribute. In 1943 his widow was roused by the long awaited knock of the Gestapo coming to take her away. Before they could force the door open, she committed suicide, aged eighty-five. The marvellously situated house next to the Brandenburg Gate – Liebermann used to explain to visitors, 'When you come to Berlin, we're immediately on the left' – was subsequently reduced to a pile of rubble by wartime bombing and bombardment.

Art in Berlin awoke with a disrespectful bang at the end of the First World War, roused by the Dada movement which had been founded in 1916 at the Cabaret Voltaire in Zurich. In April 1918 George Grosz was a co-founder of the Berlin Club Dada and, as a 'Dada-Marshal', one of the initiators of the First International Dada Fair, which was held in the city in 1920. It was an aggressive, outrageous, provocative art of happenings. Even at its most shocking, however, it was more than a fleeting statement. The collages and montages of Kurt Schwitters and Hannah Höch that employed everyday objects of deliberate banality yet had a sensitivity that pointed directly to the equally controversial work, fifty years later, of Joseph Beuys. There was no doubting the modernity of the Dadaists, any more than that of the new music of Schoenberg.

George Grosz resorted to savage satire to express his disgust with poverty, prostitution, profiteering and militarism. His strangely macabre drawings and paintings were cluttered with hideous whores, repulsively corpulent bankers and speculators, horribly maimed war cripples and decrepit but blood-lusting Prussian officers: a world of vice and violence. In 1928 he produced a notorious backdrop for Erwin Piscator's production of Brecht's *The Good Soldier Schweik*, based on Hašek's novel. It depicted a crucified Christ wearing a gas mask and army boots with the caption, 'Shut up and keep serving'.

153

He was quickly charged with public blasphemy, found guilty and fined two thousand marks in lieu of a two-month prison sentence. In his defence Grosz had pleaded: 'I have certain obligations as an artist. I belong to the entire German people and I, therefore, feel myself to have a certain mission. I have been placed on this earth as a whip, if but an artistic and thus reasonably harmless one.'

Otto Dix, peopling his paintings with characters from the same sordid world picked upon by Grosz, had been at the centre of a celebrated Berlin court case five years earlier. On that occasion his painting *Girl before a Looking-glass*, portraying a prostitute clad only in a camisole and bodice beautifying herself for business – the mirror reflecting a ghastly hag – was considered to be offensive to public morals.

'Could you not pursue the moral idea through a less crassly realistic presentation?' asked the judge.

To which the artist replied, 'I believe that I have not even been realistic enough in portraying things with their horrendous consequences.' Dix was acquitted; the offending picture was destroyed during the war.

Of all the paintings of these frenetic years, none revealed the nature of the 'golden twenties' legend more tellingly than Dix's huge triptych, *Gross-Stadt*, of 1928, with its gaudy depiction of the idle frivolity and decadence of the rich, alongside abject squalor and penury, much in the manner of a modern Lucas Cranach. If the painting came to life, which it seems on the point of doing, the jazz band of the central panel would almost certainly break into numbers from Brecht and Weill's *Threepenny Opera*, composed in the same year.

From such realism it was only a short and direct step to the *Neue Sachlichkeit* (new realism), a movement that tackled portraiture with the methods of the psychoanalyst's couch, dissecting the individual meticulously, sometimes surrealistically, in order to reveal with penetrating frankness the subject's personality, warts and all. In literature, such realism was echoed in Alfred Döblin's epic novel *Berlin Alexanderplatz*, published in 1929.

Only a year earlier, the Nazi *Völkischer Beobachter* newspaper had ominously concluded: 'This city is a melting pot of everything that is evil – prostitution, drinking houses, cinemas, Marxism, Jews, strippers, negroes dancing and all the vile offshoots of modern art.'

In architecture, Erich Mendelsohn combined the new objectivity (*Sachlichkeit*) of functional smoothness – deploying an abundance of windows and glass to provide a maximum of light – with the expressionist flamboyance of curvaceous forms to create genuinely popular New Architecture, such as his extravagantly curved Universum cinema. Many of his ideas were born in minuscule but visionary sketches drawn in the hell of the First World War trenches. They caused astonishment when they were first shown at Paul Cassirer's Berlin gallery in 1919. But his prophetic designs led to his becoming the city's busiest architect during the 1920s. In 1924 he travelled to Wisconsin to visit Frank Lloyd Wright, whose work was an inspiration to German architects well before it achieved recognition in the United States, and ten years later – an exile from the Nazis – he was commissioned to design the De La Warr Pavilion in the unlikely setting of Bexhill-on-Sea in Sussex, far away from his pioneering Berlin buildings, but a typical masterpiece none the less, with long lines, generous curves and plenty of glass looking on to the wind-stirred sea.

Back in Berlin, between 1928 and 1931 Emil Fahrencamp completed the Shell-Haus overlooking the Landwehr canal, which, having mercifully survived the rain of wartime bombs, today serves as the BEWAG (Berlin electricity company) building; a ripplingly beautiful edifice with its repeated corners, honeycombed with windows, and undulating lines, it is an exercise in architectural poetry.

For the first time since Schinkel a hundred years earlier, German architecture and design had returned to prominence with the Bauhaus and the modern movement. The pioneering school of design was founded in Weimar in 1919 by Walter Gropius, who aimed to bring 'the union of all the arts under the wings of a great architecture'. He assembled a remarkable band of modernists, including, apart from himself, the architects Mies van der Rohe and Marcel Breuer and the painters Lyonel Feininger, Paul Klee and Wassily Kandinsky. Hardly an artistic discipline or craft was neglected, whether sculpture, furniture design, typography, weaving, graphics or photography. 'Everything from the coffee-cup to city planning', in the words of Mies van der Rohe, was embraced. Advancing Schinkel's ideas into the twentieth century, the Bauhaus set out to join art with industrial production and search for new forms in architecture and industrial design. In 1926 the school transferred to Dessau into a flagship

155

ıg designed by Gropius, which helped establish the Inter-
.al Style in architecture. The Bauhaus's next move was in 1932
rlin, where Gropius had worked with Piscator on an unrealized
theatre project and designed buildings for the Siemensstadt housing
project developed for workers from the giant Berlin electrical concern,
Siemens. The lean, clean, functional efficiency of the Bauhaus was
applied not only to buildings but to ordinary household objects,
allowing Berlin's modernity to become tangible and accessible. But
the school's Berlin days were numbered; in April 1933, with
the Nazis tightening their iron grip on power, Hermann Göring, the
Prussian prime minister, closed the Bauhaus down for being a 'hotbed
of cultural Bolshevikism'. Hitler's cultural and human purge had
begun in earnest. Jews, communists, socialists, homosexuals and
Andersdenkende (those who thought differently) were driven out or
rounded up.

On 10 May 1933 a vast bonfire in the main court of Humboldt
University, facing the Opernplatz, consumed some twenty thousand
books written by authors deemed by the Nazis to be 'un-German'.
The long list included Bertolt Brecht, Kurt Tucholsky, Thomas Mann
and that most sensitive of Germans, Heinrich Heine. It was Heine,
himself no stranger to exile, who wrote: 'Where books are burnt, in
the end people will also be burnt.'

Brecht had left Berlin at the end of February, as the ashes of the
Reichstag fire still glowed. He sought refuge in Prague before travelling the world in search of a Berlin he only rediscovered in 1949.
Tucholsky committed suicide in Sweden in 1935. Thomas Mann emigrated to Switzerland, his brother Heinrich to America. The cream
of Berlin's literary, musical and artistic world was forced into exile –
so many ambassadors or beacons for a Berlin free of the Nazi yoke
scattered across the globe. Some, like Marlene Dietrich, certainly
Germany's best known actress, who were already abroad, joined the
propaganda war against Hitler, to the Nazis' acute discomfort. Soon
a cultural coalition of unusual diversity and quality was ranged against
the Nazis, but it would take time for the pen to prove itself mightier
than the sword, and only cold steel could slay the unfeeling Nazi
monster.

After proscribing authors, the Nazis next banned composers who
were either Jewish or progressive. Mahler and Mendelssohn, Schoen-

berg and, despite his defence by Furtwängler, Hindemith disappeared from concert programmes. Then painters and sculptors came under scrutiny. With the Berlin Olympics satisfactorily concluded, the modern section of the National Gallery, which had opened in 1919, was closed down by the Nazis at the end of October 1936. In the same year works by Käthe Kollwitz, Ernst Barlach and Wilhelm Lehmbruck were removed from the jubilee exhibition at the Prussian Academy of Arts. At the end of the following June Hitler ordered a nationwide programme of confiscation of 'Entartete Kunst' (degenerate art) and declared a 'remorseless war of cleaning up and destruction'. Altogether some 12,000 graphic works and more than 5,000 paintings and sculptures were removed from 101 German museums. Berlin's National Gallery alone lost 164 paintings, 326 drawings, 27 sculptures and some 600 prints. On 19 July 1937 the Nazis mounted an 'Entartete Kunst' exhibition in Munich, a propaganda show meant to deride modern, 'degenerate art', but which in fact proved a remarkable display of what German artists had achieved in the first decades of the twentieth century before their work came under the Nazi ban. In February 1938 the exhibition transferred to Berlin, where it again attracted long queues of curious visitors.

The confiscated works were subsequently sent for auction in Switzerland to raise funds for the Reich. But the 'valueless residue' which failed to sell, amounting to 1,004 paintings and sculptures, 3,825 watercolours, drawings and prints, was piled high in the courtyard of the Köpenicker Strasse fire station and set alight on 20 March 1939. Among the works lost were many by Otto Dix, George Grosz, Erich Heckel, Käthe Kollwitz, Karl Schmidt-Rottluff and Kurt Schwitters.

The Nazi witch-hunt had already begun after the stage-managed fire at the Reichstag on 27 February 1933 and continued with ever mounting fury until it reached its shattering climax on the night of 9 November 1938 amid the splintering of glass and arson of the *Kristallnacht* when synagogues and Jewish premises went up in flames. The only respite came for a few weeks in the summer of 1936 when Berlin and the Nazis, playing host to the Olympic Games, relaxed the anti-semitic, anti-socialist onslaught as long as the eyes of the world were upon them. The most slanderously anti-semitic publications were briefly withdrawn from news-stands, 'Forbidden for Jews' signs suddenly disappeared and Berlin offered once again a spirited night-life that included jazz, the 'nigger-music' suppressed by the Nazis. It was all an illusion, though much of the world came away impressed by the clean, well-run German capital and some with the naïve thought that perhaps the Nazis were not quite as bad as had been made out. It was not long, however, before it became quite clear that they were very much worse than could have been imagined.

Having conquered the hearts and susceptible souls of Germans, at once plagued by the misery of mass unemployment and economic uncertainty while yearning for the order that had been lost in the wayward Weimar years, Hitler sought revenge for Versailles and with cold calculation embarked on world war. Soon the Nazi terror was no longer confined to Germany, as Hitler's generals rolled back the map of Europe as none of their forebears had managed since Bismarck's time or the days when Frederick the Great first introduced the blitz-krieg. To many Germans, made to believe they were members of a master race, mass destruction and murder seemed almost a normal price for world domination. In January 1942 at a conference in a comfortable villa by the lakeside of Berlin's idyllic Wannsee, Hitler's closest aides decided on the chilling logistics for the 'final solution to the Jewish question', which meant nothing less than the total annihila-tion of the race long selected by the Nazis for persecution. But the tide was about to turn, even if it would take another three years and millions of lives for the Nazi spectre to be overcome. And Berlin would pay a terrible price for the role thrust upon it by the Nazis.

Already early on it was clear that Hitler would bring Berlin ill fortune – from the moment he ordered the venerable lime trees on Unter den Linden to be cut down so that they did not obscure the view of his battalions goose-stepping down Berlin's finest avenue. With his undisguised preference for Munich, he foolishly ignored the fondly held sentiment expressed in one of the most popular of contemporary songs:

> *So lang noch Unter den Linden*
> *Die alten Bäume blühn,*
> *Kann nichts uns überwinden,*
> *Berlin bleibt doch Berlin.*

As long as the old trees
Still bloom on Unter den Linden,
Nothing can conquer us,
And Berlin will remain Berlin.

The Austrian-born demagogue and dictator had, apart from dreams of world conquest, his own grand vision of transforming ill-laid out Berlin into a new, monumental capital, 'Germania', suitable for a 'thousand-year Reich'. It would excel the ancient magnificence of Luxor or Babylon. 'It will be the capital of Europe, even the world,' declared the ranting Joseph Goebbels, whom Hitler had sent to Berlin at the end of 1926 to be the Nazi Gauleiter (district leader), and who became his mouthpiece as propaganda minister. 'Germania will be a new, a bigger Berlin . . . that will give a greater Germany a new and happy future.'

In 1937 the planning of the project was entrusted to a young architect who pandered to the Führer's megalomania, the 32-year-old Albert Speer. Its centre-piece was to be the Volkshalle (People's Hall), capable of accommodating up to 180,000, which would rise to a height of some nine hundred feet and be crowned by a cupola of similar breadth – 'the Capitol in Washington would be submerged many times in this mass,' Speer noted with pride. Preparatory work began in 1938, and completion was due in 1950. The monstrous design would dwarf all Berlin's existing landmarks, causing the Brandenburg Gate to shrink to insignificance. It would be built by the Spree on the Königsplatz, renamed the Adolf-Hitler-Platz, the other sides of which would be made up by a palace for the Führer, an extension of the chancellery and by army headquarters. The nearby Reichstag, Hitler decided, should remain to provide reading rooms. To the north of the great hall there would be a huge water basin (about 1,300 yards by 440) filled with clear water – intended as an open-air pool equipped with changing rooms, sun terraces and boat houses – and surrounded by massive new buildings housing the admiralty, the town hall and police headquarters. The city's overcrowded old quarters would be torn down, with scant regard for their history or architectural merit, while Berlin's haphazard urban design – the result of its rapid growth in the nineteenth century – would be rectified by rebuilding it around two great axes, streets more than 100 yards wide and over 23 miles

159

long from north to south and 31 miles from east to west, that would cross in the Tiergarten by the Brandenburg Gate. At one point, on a level with Tempelhof airport, the street would be straddled by a great arch, 186 yards across and 128 high, designed by Speer from Hitler's own sketches. State visitors and travellers arriving at the Südbahnhof and descending its great sweep of stairs 'should be overcome, literally bowled over, by the spectacle of urban planning and so of the power of the Reich,' wrote Speer. As a whole it was, Goebbels noted admiringly in his diary, 'the most grandiose building programme of all time'.

'Look at Paris, the most beautiful city in the world! Or even Vienna! Those are cities with a bold design. But Berlin is nothing but a disorderly clutter of buildings. We must out-trump Paris and Vienna,' Hitler instructed Speer.

But the result was cold, sterile, inhuman architecture befitting a cruel, heartless regime, though not a city with Berlin's soul. How Frederick the Great, hijacked by the Nazis as one of their own heroes, and honest Schinkel would have been revolted by Hitler's lack of taste and proportion. Thanks to the distraction of war, only a few Nazi buildings of significance cast their grey shadow over the city: Werner March's forbidding Olympic Stadium built for the jamboree the Nazis made of the 1936 Summer Games, Ernst Sagebiel's Tempelhof airport and air ministry (1934–6) on the Leipziger Strasse, Heinrich Wolf's extension to the Reichsbank (ironically taken over by the Communist Party for its offices after the war) and Speer's frigid new chancellery (Reichskanzlei) building of 1938, the bomb-shattered remains of which the Russians wisely blew up when they took Berlin. From the confines of the bunker under the chancellery, laconically described by the Soviet military command as 'objective number 153', Hitler witnessed the dying days of his 'thousand-year Reich' and there committed suicide with his mistress, Eva Braun, on 30 April 1945, ten days after his fifty-sixth birthday and hours after Russian troops raised the red flag on the battered Reichstag.

Ill-fated Germania had scarcely begun to rise before she fell. Altogether the Allies dropped some forty-five thousand tons of bombs on Berlin and in the final battle for the city Russian artillery expended more than a million high explosive shells, turning the once imposing German capital, which a megalomaniac dictator and his henchmen had planned to transform into the hub of a world empire, into a brittle pile of rubble. On his way to Moscow on 25 May 1945 the American presidential adviser Harry Hopkins flew over the devastated city, scarcely believing his eyes. 'It's a second Carthage', he muttered.

NINE

DIVISION AND DISTRESS

I N THE opening sequence of Billy Wilder's 1948 film *A Foreign
Affair* members of a congressional delegation survey from the
portholes of their aircraft the scene of utter urban desolation as
they approach the shattered shell of what had for a spell been Europe's
liveliest city.

The terrible devastation inflicted on Berlin in the closing stages of
the war came almost as a cleansing after the enormities of the Nazi
years. It was the fate of a modern Gomorrah. British and American
bombers, Soviet artillery and tanks had pounded and pulverized the
former Prussian capital, purging the people of Berlin. They were left
in what a recent study calculated was 'the biggest single area of ruins
in Germany and Europe', described by Winston Churchill in 1945 as
'a reasonable amount of destruction'. Yet they managed to stagger
out of the haunted shadows and stinking rubble showing remarkable
fortitude in adversity, and somehow retaining their characteristic
sense of humour.

A Foreign Affair brought Marlene Dietrich back to Berlin, to play
a beautiful former Nazi and night-club singer, Erika von Schlütow.
Friedrich Holländer, who had written all Dietrich's most successful
songs since *The Blue Angel*, was appropriately cast as the pianist
accompanying her in 'Black Market' and 'Illusions', songs that
expressed the pathos and reality of post-war Berlin. Some eighteen
years after she had left Berlin for Hollywood, borne by the sensational
success of *The Blue Angel*, she was once again cast singing cabaret in
Berlin, to Holländer's tunes.

Her return to her native city, where, first treading the boards,
she had toiled hard enough before tasting fame, was painful. Her
wholehearted identification with the Allied cause had, in the opinion
of many Germans still confused by their own part in Nazism, gone
too far. She had spent much of the war in a sober but well-tailored

American uniform boosting the morale of troops as they battled their way across Europe, and sharing some of their discomforts. She witnessed the liberation of Rome in June 1944 before falling seriously ill in Bari when her life was saved by the timely prescription of penicillin. She was pictured in Paris looking lovely in uniform next to the formidable Patton, the cowboy general who both admired her courage and recognized her value to his troops, sending her to strategically important points. On one occasion, with her unit surrounded, she was only saved from capture by a last-minute counter-attack. During the Battle of the Bulge, fought in the Ardennes during the bitterly cold winter of 1944–5, her fingers were frostbitten. A few months later she was photographed standing by her jeep clad in an army sheepskin jacket signing autographs for battle-weary GIs in liberated Germany. It was around that time that some soldiers came up to her and asked, 'We've got a couple of Nazis over there. They're ill. Would you have anything against coming over and speaking German to them?' She found some pale-looking young Nazis who asked incredulously, 'Are you the real Marlene Dietrich?' On her saying, 'Yes', everything was forgiven and she sang 'Lili Marlene', her wartime signature song, to the whole field hospital.

Many were the occasions when, despite sensible walking shoes and a regulation below knee-length military skirt, grateful GIs hoisted her high above their shoulders like some football hero, to reveal those legendary legs. French troops treated their Josephine Baker, also elegant in uniform, more gingerly. Dietrich and Baker were sex symbols of a very different order, but each had dazzled pre-Nazi Berlin, and both were made members of France's Legion of Honour for their valuable roles in the war effort.

Dietrich had already braved the difficult return to Berlin in September 1945 – her first visit for thirteen years – for an emotional reunion with her mother and those friends she could trace amidst the dusty ruins. She went on to Biarritz and there learned of the death of the mother she had only just rediscovered.

Bertolt Brecht came back to Berlin and described it still in 1948 as 'a pile of rubble near Potsdam'. He settled in the Russian-administered eastern half of the city, eventually being offered agreeable accommodation in the Chausseestrasse, which today houses the Brecht archives, overlooking the French and Dorotheenstädt cemeteries and the

163

tranquil spot where he and his wife, Helene Weigel, were later to be buried. *The Threepenny Opera*, which the Nazis had delighted in banning, was performed as soon as some sort of a cast could be mustered and a stage found. After a while Brecht was able to take over one of the few Berlin theatres that had escaped relatively unscathed, the charming Theater am Schiffbauerdamm, having founded his Berliner Ensemble on the very day in 1949 that the communist East German state was established.

In its misery Berlin was desperate for distraction and soon theatre and concerts were often easier to come by than food and other basic necessities. In the early days of occupation there was calculated encouragement from highly educated Russian 'cultural officers', who for their own political motives endeavoured, now that Nazism was crushed, 'to make Germans again out of Germans'. The Russians also had a high regard for and knowledge of Goethe and Schiller, and love of Beethoven. Moreover, they could offer in return, among others, Pushkin, Gorki and Tchaikovsky. There were more than enough talented singers and instrumentalists in the Red Army to help make up orchestras and ensembles, or provide soloists. On 15 June 1945, scarcely six weeks after the cessation of hostilities, the City Opera gave its first post-war evening of ballet. Meanwhile, opposite Knobelsdorff's noble but bomb-battered Royal (or State, as it was known after the end of the monarchy) Opera House, cows were still grazing in the court of Humboldt University and where the grass pushed through on Unter den Linden. The Tiergarten, Berlin's Hyde Park, was divided into allotments growing badly needed vegetables. Ten days later the Deutsches Theater in the Schumannstrasse, where Reinhardt had presided over the golden age of German theatre, reopened with Schiller. The audience was packed with senior Soviet officers, and the ancient Arthur Werner, who had recently been installed as mayor, was conspicuous in one of the theatre boxes wearing his outdated wing collar.

This policy of returning to the vanquished their cultural dignity was developed with vigour by the Americans and British when in July 1945, under terms confirmed in February at the Yalta Conference, they moved into the sectors of Berlin set aside for their administration. The Americans saw it as part of their concept for the 're-education of the German people'. Just as the Russians brought back and delegated responsibility to Germans who had chosen exile in Moscow, among those now in American uniform were a good few who had emigrated from Hitler's Berlin as he unleashed his racial and cultural purges.

By the end of 1945 Berlin theatres had incredibly managed 120 new productions; the following year the total rose to 196.

Music played a major role in bringing the city back to life. In a generous gesture of reconciliation Yehudi Menuhin, the New York-born violinist of Russian–Jewish extraction who as a child prodigy in pre-Nazi days had delighted concert audiences on either side of the Atlantic and in Berlin, returned to demonstrate forgiveness and solidarity. When, forty-four years later, the Berlin Wall came down and the city's people were again brought together, he made a point of playing for them once more.

Famous conductors followed his example and returned from exile as others who had stayed, such as Wilhelm Furtwängler and Herbert von Karajan, who was to succeed him at the Berlin Philharmonic, resumed their work after clearing initial Allied hurdles. But there was a host of complications; while those who conducted under the swastika waited to be rehabilitated, conductors who had been forced from their posts by the Nazis were not automatically reinstated. It was perhaps an irony that the ones who had continued to perform for the Nazis enjoyed a degree of acceptability in German and Berlin's post-war musical life not accorded to those who to their credit had either left in protest or been impelled to flee. So Bruno Walter remained more appreciated in New York, and Otto Klemperer, after wartime exile in the United States, in London. Erich Kleiber died in Switzerland in 1956 after years in America. Fritz Busch, whom the Nazis hounded from the Dresden Opera in 1933, died in London in 1951 after helping establish opera at Glyndebourne as its first musical director. A year later his younger brother, the violinist Adolf, who had taught in Berlin before the Nazi takeover, died in America. The German musical tradition in Germany had fallen to the conductors who had continued performing in Hitler's Germany: Furtwängler, Karajan, Knapperts-busch, Böhm and Jochum.

Seemingly unfairly, controversy still surrounds Furtwängler's decision, as Germany's senior conductor, to remain in Berlin and not to relinquish conducting during the Nazi years. He was often enough at loggerheads with the Nazis, for whom he had no sympathy. In the

165

wake of the so-called 'Hindemith affair' when he defended the composer against Nazi accusations – 'no one from the younger generation has done more for the reputation of German music in the world than Hindemith' – over all three columns of the front page of the *Deutsche Allgemeine Zeitung* of 25 November 1934, and the newspaper had to respond by printing Goebbels's counter-blast, Furtwängler felt compelled to stand down from his musical posts and withdraw to the solitude of his holiday house in St Moritz. However, the musical director of the Berlin Philharmonic stood as the most important representative of the city's cultural life and was too valuable to the Nazis; he was stopped at the border and barred from leaving. By April 1935 he was conducting at the Philharmonie again. He did what he could to protect Jewish members of his orchestra – at first he had managed to retain the Philharmonic's leader Simon Goldberg, a Jew, and Bertha Geissmar, his Jewish secretary – while in February 1934 he even celebrated the 125th anniversary of the birth of Felix Mendelssohn as if the Jewish composer had not been banned by the Nazis. Despite this and the fact that Furtwängler stood for a better Germany, he was to be forever associated, particularly in America, with those Philharmonic concerts that were conducted under the swastika.

More charitably and accurately, Menuhin wrote much later: 'Shortly after the Second World War, I had the good fortune to meet in Furtwängler a human being who seemed to embody all that is great and noble in the German tradition. It was a privilege to be able to discover with him, amidst the ruins of Berlin, the beginnings of a new Germany.' In due course Furtwängler completed the cumbersome denazification process and was given permission to resume conducting; his deeply felt concerts in the Titania-Palast, used as a provisional concert hall following the old Philharmonie's destruction in the bombing, became symbolic of Berlin's cultural rebirth.

The Austrian-born Herbert von Karajan, whom the Berlin Philharmonic unanimously chose as its 'Chief Conductor for Life' following the death of the legendary Furtwängler in 1954 at the age of sixty-eight, is less easy to defend, except as a masterful musician. He was an intensely ambitious opportunist of immense talent, who quickly realized that a great many doors could be opened with the help of the Nazis. He consequently became a paid-up member of the Nazi Party at the earliest opportunity (in April or May 1933, according to records),

166

preceded concerts by playing the 'Horst Wessel Song' – hardly justifiable on musical grounds – and watched his career take off. He moved from the post of Kapellmeister at the Ulm opera house, which he had gained in 1929, aged only twenty-one, to Aachen in 1934, becoming Germany's youngest Generalmusikdirektor. In April 1938 he conducted the Berlin Philharmonic Orchestra for the first time, and, following performances of *Fidelio* and *Tristan und Isolde* at the Staatsoper that year, a Berlin critic wrote of 'Das Wunder Karajan' (the Karajan miracle). His meteoric rise under the Nazis may have been boosted by his value to an anti-Furtwängler faction led by Goebbels, which sought to undermine the position of the 'politically obstinate' senior conductor. Furtwängler himself was deeply suspicious of his young rival and did what he could to block Karajan's performances with what he considered, not unreasonably, to be 'his' orchestra. But by 1942 Karajan's star with the Nazis was on the wane, possibly because his second wife, Anita Gütermann, was found to be part Jewish, and he left Berlin to Furtwängler, turning to conducting in Italy with the encouragement of the Italian maestro Victor de Sabata.

Karajan himself defended his Nazi membership as merely a means of securing the Aachen directorship. 'Before me was this paper, which stood between me and almost limitless power and a budget to provide for an orchestra with which I could do however many concerts I liked. And they were saying that I must be a member, that maybe I would do a concert for them once in a while, that's all. So I said what the hell and signed. But afterwards people said, "Of course you are a Nazi."'

In fact his denazification was to prove less painful than Furtwängler's; it was neither to last quite as long, nor was it later to be so haunting. He had the good fortune of striking a close bond with Walter Legge, whom he met in Vienna soon after the war when the Russians were barring him from conducting. In 1946 Legge signed Karajan up for a series of recordings for EMI Records which enabled him to conduct the Vienna Philharmonic while still subject to a public performance ban. It was to prove a very solid foundation to a formidable and prolific recording career that by the 1960s was to give Karajan an international standing never previously attained by a conductor. By October 1947 Karajan could celebrate his denazification with a

167

performance of Bruckner's Eighth Symphony in the Vienna Musik-verein; he inscribed a pocket score of the work which belonged to Legge with a dedication to the man who had helped him survive the exigencies of the past eighteen months: 'To my second musical self and dear friend in memory of a long awaited day.' Soon Legge had engaged Karajan as the unofficial principal conductor of the new orchestra he set up in London, the Philharmonia.

Although initially in the shadow of Furtwängler, no musician was to become more closely identified with post-war Berlin's musical life than Karajan after his return to the city. During a reign, some would say a dictatorship, of over thirty years he moulded the Berlin Philhar-monic into his own brilliant, superbly accomplished musical instru-ment, transforming a traditionally magnificent band into perhaps the top – and certainly the best paid and equipped – orchestra in the world. During the years of division that followed those of distress, Karajan and the Berlin Philharmonic, travelling the world, came to relish their role as West Berlin's cultural ambassadors *par excellence*. His death at the age of eighty-one, only four months before the breach-ing of the Berlin Wall in November 1989, anticipated the dramatic ending of an era.

While for many years the generously subsidized, Karajan-led Berlin Philharmonic was recognized as king in the realm of musical culture, the eastern half of Berlin, encompassing the old heart of the city bounded by the Brandenburg Gate, also had its cultural strengths, succoured in the immediate post-war period by the Soviet authorities. The exquisite Schinkel-inspired Singakademie behind the Neue Wache was quickly repaired and reopened as the Maxim-Gorki-Theater; after a time the rebuilding of the gutted shell of the once proud State Opera was begun and satisfactorily completed by 1955. Brecht was able to move his Berliner Ensemble into the Theater am Schiffbauerdamm in 1954. Most significantly, as it turned out, the old Metropol theatre in the Behrenstrasse, running parallel to Unter den Linden into the Friedrichstrasse, was restored with Russian help to reopen as the Komische Oper on 23 December 1947 with a vintage production of Johann Strauss's *Die Fledermaus*, brimming over with intoxicating effervescence to delight and distract Berliners during times that remained all too bleak. It was the first of many memorable productions for the Komische Oper by its extraordinarily talented

168

founding director, Walter Felsenstein, a name worthy of mention in the same breath as that earlier god of Berlin theatre, Max Reinhardt.

The Vienna-born Felsenstein's great gift was the ability to bring an opera production to life – 'the humanization of opera', he called it – through brilliant stagecraft and impeccable ensemble. The Komische Oper's success under Felsenstein was the sum of its parts; singers were coached to act credibly as well as sing, and they were unlikely to be let down by either the production or the orchestra. The aim was to create complete 'music theatre' accessible to the people. As a repertory company of the very highest order, the Komische Oper had no need to import outside talent and could rely on coordinated and commited teamwork to succeed. If Felsenstein had learned from Klemperer's pioneering productions at the Kroll during the late 1920s, he took their immediacy even further, whether in that first *Fledermaus*, in a famous *Carmen*, Janáček's *Cunning Little Vixen* or a legendary version of Offenbach's *Bluebeard*, which for more than 350 performances and over 25 years mesmerized audiences with its original cast, its seemingly tireless durability threatened only by the repercussions and rationalization of German reunification.

During the long, grey years of communist rule, the East Berlin skyline was at least pleasingly decorated by the distinctive calligraphy of the Komische Oper's blue neon logogram, and the street by the simple orange and green display board on the Friedrichstrasse where the evening's performance was daily proclaimed. Felsenstein's inspiring rule came to an end with his death in 1975, but his spirit lived on, first with Joachim Herz and then most markedly with Harry Kupfer's revelatory productions. The Komische Oper, in its warmly cosy, red plush and gilded stucco, *fin de siècle* theatre concealed behind an uncompromising façade dating from its 1966 renovation, maintained a reputation as not just East Germany's premier opera house but one of the most consistently original in Europe.

As shortly before Christmas 1947 the champagne corks popped on-stage and the fittingly Russian Prince Orlofsky of Johann Strauss's operetta invited his guests to raise their glasses in a toast as the Komische Oper opened with Felsenstein's exuberant *Fledermaus*, Berlin was only a few months away from becoming the scene of a new international crisis.

The city was still in ruins – not surprisingly, since a fifth of all its

169

buildings had been demolished and half of them damaged. Out of 1.5 million homes only a quarter had come through the war unscathed, while two fifths were completely destroyed. Of the seventy-five houses on the Leipziger Strasse, seventy-two were devastated. The scale of destruction made clearing up painfully slow and it often fell to women – 'Trümmerfrauen' (ruin women) in headscarves and aprons, armed with buckets and shovels – as their menfolk were dead, missing or still held as prisoners of war. Berlin's familiar landscape took on a new appearance as several artificial hills, among them the *Teufelsberg* (Devil's Mountain), were raised out of the thousands of tons of rubble which could not be recycled for rebuilding work.

Despite regular raids by the police, a black market thrived. Cigarettes became 'harder' than any currency: just four were worth forty marks, or the equivalent of a Trümmerfrau's weekly wages. The black market was inevitably fuelled by Allied soldiers rich in rations and cigarettes, leaving them able to buy almost anything that could be offered for sale: bric-à-brac rescued from the rubble or feminine company. And then more precious even than cigarettes were the nylon stockings that street-wise GIs secreted from home – the key to any girl's heart in those austere years. Following the lifting of an early fraternization ban, the lot of the Allied soldier who had fought his way across Europe was not altogether disagreeable in a city where women outnumbered men by two to one. Girls were no longer compelled to dance with each other and there were more than enough to go round at such perennial night-spots as the Femina, which, unlike its surroundings, had somehow survived the bombing.

By the end of 1947 the post-war honeymoon was wearing thin and the simmering tensions between the Soviet-run eastern zone, where communism was being applied, and the western sectors finally boiled over in the summer of 1948. In an attempt to squeeze the Western Allies out of Berlin, the Russians enforced a blockade of their enclave, isolated 110 miles inside communist-occupied territory. The Cold War had begun in earnest.

The countdown to crisis began in June 1948 when the Soviet attempt to extend its currency reform to West Berlin was vetoed by the Western Allies, who responded by introducing the Deutsche Mark into their sectors. On 16 June the Russians withdrew from the Allied Kommandatura and three days later they tightened checks on all

170

routes into the city. On 24 June the Soviets went further and imposed a total blockade on passenger and goods traffic into the western half of Berlin in an attempt to starve it into submission.

But they underestimated the resolve of West Berliners to defend their newly gained democracy, and, even more decisively, the determination of the Western Allies, who retaliated by organizing an airlift such as had never been seen before. By 25 June the first flights were dispatched to beleaguered Berlin, launching the swiftly improvised operation.

For over ten months it kept two million West Berliners supplied with their most urgent requirements. By the time Stalin finally abandoned the blockade on 12 May 1949, a total of 277,264 flights had brought in 1.83 million tons of supplies, including 944,000 tons of coal vital for industry and for morale during a bitterly cold winter. The incredible operation, which not only the Russians had thought impossible, reached its perfectly synchronized logistical climax on 16 April 1949 when 1,344 aircraft landed in West Berlin at meticulously orchestrated intervals of 62 seconds bearing almost 13,000 tons of supplies. The American Air Force and Britain's Royal Air Force, which only a few years before had bombed Berlin to pieces, killing an estimated fifty thousand, had won the respect and affection of West Berliners for saving them from threatened Soviet take-over and the loss of their liberty. After successfully sustaining the airlift, the Western Allies were no longer considered the 'occupying' but instead the 'protecting' powers. However, the hazardous operation to keep the city supplied had a price: thirty-nine Britons, thirty-one Americans and eight Germans were killed in airlift accidents.

One of the most remarkable episodes in Berlin's chequered history had come to an end, to be best remembered by the richly symbolic photographs of scrawny Berlin schoolboys in short trousers and pig-tailed girls waving from the Teufelsberg and other mountains of war rubble at the 'Rosinenbomber' (raisin bombers) as they came into land laden with life-saving supplies, including chocolate for the children.

During those tense months of East–West confrontation the world was not far from war, and not for the last time Berlin had proved to be the flashpoint.

At the height of the crisis Ernst Reuter, the Social Democrat mayor of West Berlin, called on the 'people of the world to look on this city'

171

in a long remembered address to a vast array of Berliners outside the ruined Reichstag building on 9 September 1948. His message was heard in the free world and in a gesture of solidarity seventeen million Americans subscribed to the casting of a 'Liberty Bell' that was presented to West Berlin in October 1950. Exactly forty years later as Germany and Berlin were formally unified, its peal rang across a no longer divided city.

As a precaution against subsequent siege, the Allies and West Berlin authorities organized a huge emergency stockpile of fuel and foodstuffs, which was cellared in the bowels of the city for forty years until, in a sequel of some irony, with Berlin and Germany once again safely reunited, the supplies were released for distribution to help hard-pressed Russians, their economy on the brink of total collapse, see through the winter of 1990.

Following the creation of the Federal Republic (West Germany) during the summer of 1949, the communist German Democratic Republic was founded in the Soviet-supervised eastern half on 7 October with East Berlin as its 'capital'. The borders between the ideologically divided German states remained open until 1952 when the communists began sealing off what came to be known as the 'inner-German' frontier with extensive obstacles, barbed-wire fences and minefields to prevent 'flight from the Republic', which had become an offence under East German law. But Berlin still remained open and for another nine years East and West Berliners could cross freely between their sectors, or East Germans could make their way to the West via Berlin. The theatre – Brecht's Berliner Ensemble, Felsenstein's Komische Oper or the Staatsoper, which reopened in 1955 – would lure West Berliners to the eastern half of the city for entertainment, while work and a good wage would draw East Berliners to the West. It was an unnatural, uneasy state of affairs which could not persist indefinitely.

Soon Berlin was to lurch into its next and bloodiest crisis. On 17 June 1953, shortly after the death of Stalin, the communist stranglehold on Eastern Europe first came to be tested. Building workers employed on the construction of housing for Communist Party functionaries in the Stalinallee (subsequently Karl-Marx-Allee) were called on to accept a ten per cent rise in their work norms that was tantamount to a salary cut. Infuriated, they sent a workers' delegation to

172

Otto Grotewohl, the communist premier, who had no time for them. Almost instantly, like a match to powder, the spark of discontent ignited an explosion of popular protest and strikes across East Berlin. Thousands marched, demanding, 'We want free elections!', 'Down with the government!' and 'Grotewohl and Ulbricht out!' As word of the demonstrations spread, the streets filled and when the despised Volkspolizei intervened, they were pelted with paving-stones; in a memorable moment a young man ripped down the red flag from the top of the Brandenburg Gate, earning wild cheers from the assembled crowd.

By midday the protest had turned into an uprising. At one o'clock, with the communist authorities fearful of losing control, the Soviet city commandant ordered an immediate state of emergency and in rolled the tanks. For the second time in less than a decade the battered streets of Berlin shook to Soviet armour, the ominous whining of diesel engines and death rattle of the steel tracks awakening painful memories. Resistance was futile, but in their anger some workers and students hopelessly defied the military force, only to pay with their lives. It was a dress rehearsal for Moscow's ruthless crushing of dissent by armoured intervention in Budapest three years later, and in Prague in August 1968.

Of the 17 June uprising Brecht, whose endorsement was sought by the communists, wrote questioningly: 'Would it not be simpler for the government to dismiss the people and elect another?'

Yet without meaning to, the communist East German regime was indeed dismissing its people. In ever increasing numbers they preferred to abandon their regimented lives in the East for the opportunities offered by the West. Berlin became a staging post for emigration westwards. In 1950 some 50,000 eastern refugees arrived in West Berlin; by 1952 the figure had doubled, reaching a peak of 300,000 in 1953, the year of the short-lived uprising. Of these more than 257,000 travelled on to West Germany. During the decade as a whole, close on one million East German refugees chose this route to the West.

Faced with such numbers, the West Berlin authorities were compelled to develop the reception of refugees into a well-orchestrated procedure, setting up a permanent camp at Marienfelde, which in later years would welcome those fleeing from other oppressive regimes, whether in the Middle East or Third World. West Berlin

173

was maintaining a liberal tradition dating from the late seventeenth century when the Great Elector opened his arms and capital city to the Huguenot refugees from France.

The steady flow westwards of East Germans was crippling the communist German state's economy. The majority of those turning their back on the East were young, well-trained, skilled workers who the communists could ill afford to lose. By the summer of 1961 some 1,500 East German refugees were arriving daily in West Berlin. An additional 56,000 Berliners, while still living in the East, had their jobs in the West. From the inception of the German Democratic Republic in 1949 to 1961 a total of about 2.7 million East Germans left for the West. The communist authorities could hardly allow such a ruinous loss to persist; drastic steps were needed to staunch the haemorrhaging.

But the infamous response was more radical than expected. Suddenly on 13 August 1961 the border between the eastern and western sectors of Berlin was sealed by Volkspolizei, border troops and workers' militia, and a menacing wall of barbed wire, then of bricks and concrete, went up, cleaving the city completely in two. The Berlin Wall had come into being, rigidly cutting off streets and inhumanly dividing houses and families. Passage between East and West was no longer possible; those who tried to escape were shot at and, if caught, punished with long prison sentences. The isolation of East Germany and East Berlin from the West was complete.

The mastermind behind the Berlin Wall was the future East German leader Erich Honecker, at the time the Politburo member responsible for security in the government headed by the sinister, goatee-bearded Walter Ulbricht. In a fine example of sophistry, the ultimate obstacle to prevent citizens from voting with their feet and leaving the communist state was described as an 'anti-fascist protection barrier', necessary to keep out pernicious western influences. It was Honecker who, a few months before he was ousted in October 1989 as East Germany's peaceful revolution gained momentum, foolishly predicted that the Wall would still be there 'in another hundred years', as idle a boast as Hitler's promise of a 'thousand-year Reich'. Honecker himself, an active communist since his youth, had languished for ten years in Nazi gaols.

Prompted by the mass exodus of East Germans to the West via a

174

more liberal Hungary, Czechoslovakia and Poland, Honecker's eventual fall was itself perhaps proof that the Wall had prolonged communist East Germany's survival by almost a generation. In 1989, as in 1961, East German industry came close to paralysis because of the loss of skilled labour to the West.

The Wall, snaking relentlessly for a length of altogether 103 miles around and through the city, segregating West Berlin from East Berlin and East Germany, was the most lasting trial Berliners were ever called on to endure. They had to learn to live with the absurd reality of not just political but physical division. For the first time since it was built in 1791 Berliners were barred from passing through the city's very symbol, the Brandenburg Gate, blocked by the Wall a hundred yards beyond its western side, and fenced off a similar distance to the east, leaving it solitary and forlorn in a no man's land. No longer was the Brandenburg Gate Berlin's pulsating aorta.

In the Bernauerstrasse the back of the terraced houses was in the East, the front in the West, leading to unforgettable scenes of families jumping out of windows into the outstretched arms of waiting West Berliners, or being forcibly dragged back by the communists. Some fell to their deaths.

In 1962 a class of eleven- to thirteen-year-olds in the northern West German town of Flensburg were asked to portray Berlin's division. They painted a picture with the caption, 'The worst thing – that people could learn to live with the Wall. Moss and spiders thrive on it.' The schoolchildren were right, but Berliners still had to find a *modus vivendi* with the monstrous concrete creation that divided their city and separated them from friends and relatives. And so, during its unwelcome life of 28¼ years, the Wall gained an acceptability it did not deserve.

In June 1963 in a powerful demonstration of solidarity with the beleaguered people of West Berlin, at a time when the Cold War was at its frostiest, President Kennedy arrived. The communists draped sheets of red cloth between the columns of the Brandenburg Gate to obscure his view of the East. Half a million Berliners streamed to come and listen to him outside the Schöneberg Rathaus, which had become the seat of West Berlin's government. He closed his speech with words which immediately became etched in his audience's memory: 'All free men, wherever they may live, are citizens of Berlin,

175

and therefore, as a free man, I am proud to be able to say, "Ich bin ein Berliner!" [I am a Berliner!]'

Subsequent American presidents, as well as British prime ministers and French leaders, would come to West Berlin in later years and renew their countries' pledge and commitment to defend the isolated city, which the composer György Ligeti described as 'a surrealist cage in which those inside are free'.

Meanwhile, the Wall remained, only to be reinforced and made even more escape proof. Nevertheless, to some courageous East Berliners, impatient at being cooped up in the communist bloc, it was an obstacle to be surmounted by whatever means ingenuity and opportunity would suggest.

The crew of an East German passenger vessel on the Spree plied their captain with enough drink to ensure he was inebriated, locked him in his cabin and took the boat and their families across the water frontier under gunfire from communist border guards.

In September 1963 an East Berlin post office worker and two friends crashed a post van through the Wall and ended up on the front door-step of a house in West Berlin.

Seven years later an enterprising Frenchman squeezed his East German fiancée into two suitcases which had their side panels cut out and left her on the luggage rack of an interzonal train.

There were other instances of girlfriends or children crammed into car boots, of successful escapes through tunnels, using fake Russian and American uniforms, with cables and pulleys, an empty radiogram and even a hollow plastic cow destined for an agricultural exhibition.

But there was tragedy too as almost eighty East Germans lost their lives trying to overcome the barrier. Among their number, two are remembered in particular for the callousness of their deaths. Peter Fechter, aged eighteen, who a year after the Wall went up was shot by border guards and, despite his anguished cries for help, left alone for fifty minutes to bleed to death in its shadow. Shocked bystanders on the western side of the Wall were powerless to help. Then in 1980 Marietta Jirkowski, eighteen years old and three months pregnant, was shot eight times in the stomach.

About 120 East Germans are known to have been wounded trying to escape and over 3,000 attempts ended in failure and trials in East Berlin courts. Yet during the twenty-eight long years of the Wall's

37. (*Above*) The Bode Museum in 1991. Originally the Kaiser Friedrich Museum built between 1897 and 1904 on the tip of the 'Museumsinsel' by E. von Ihne in a pleasing neo-baroque style, it was later renamed after Wilhelm von Bode, its distinguished director from 1906 to 1920. Making maximum use of its retricted triangular site, it was a model museum for its time both in lay-out and use of lighting. Beyond lies the Pergamon Museum, housing the extraordinarily rich collection of antiquities and built between 1909 and 1930 by Ludwig Hoffmann to a plan by Alfred Messel.

38. The house built for Johann Gottfried Schadow in the Kleine Wallstrasse (today the Schadowstrasse) at royal expense in 1805. The decorative medallions and reliefs were a tribute from his pupils. From his studio on the first floor – another storey was added to the building later in the nineteenth century – Schadow could look back on to the Brandenburg Gate and his most famous work, the Quadriga, surmounting it.

39. The house on the corner of the Friedrichstrasse and Clara Zetkin Strasse where Karl Marx once lived and where, until shortly before East Germany's peaceful revolution, a fine old barber's shop survived on the ground floor. A plaque recording Marx's presence was rudely ripped off in the wake of the revolution, leaving only the relief medallion portraying his head.

. (*Right*) Schlüter's masterly
uestrian portrayal of Frederick
illiam, the Great Elector, cast in
'00, which today dominates the
urtyard of the Charlottenburg
lace. A late nineteenth-century
py of the imposing statue now con-
nts visitors in the entrance hall of
e Bode Museum.

. (*Below*) The hectic political
mosphere of the Weimar Republic:
ocial Democrat campaigning for the
'20 Reichstag elections in the Pots-
mer Platz. On the Litfass column
e diversity of Berlin's night-life is
ident, including, among much else,
advertisement for a revue of scant-
y clad chorus girls at the Apollo
heatre. Entertainment of a pugilistic
nd is promised by a sticker on the
mp-post.

42. (*Above*) The vast stalactite-like interior of the Grosses Schauspielhaus, built on the site of the old circus by Hans Poelzig for theatre director Max Reinhardt in 1919, pictured here in 1925.

43. (*Below left*) The sensational Josephine Baker in 1925, shortly before her first Berlin visit.

44. (*Below right*) Jazz, which had swe Berlin off its feet in the 1920's, was co demned by the Nazis as corrupting 'nigg music'. This catalogue cover for the Dü seldorf 'Degenerate Music' exhibition 1938 caricatures the hero of Ernst Krenek jazz opera *Jonny spielt auf* (Johnny Strik Up). His lapel is adorned with a star of Dav instead of a carnation.

5. (*Above left*) The popular jazz band the Weintraub's Syncopators rehearsing in Berlin in 1931. Two years later, following the Nazi seizure of power, members of the band, along with many gifted musicians and artists, were forced into exile.

46. (*Above right*) The Potsdamer Platz, Berlin's Piccadilly Circus, by night in 1930, as Isherwood would have known it.

47 (*Below*) Marlene Dietrich as the irresistible Lola Lola in Josef von Sternberg's *The Blue Angel* of 1930, the film – based on Heinrich Mann's novel – which made her a star and led to Hollywood. In this celebrated pose she sings 'Ich bin von Kopf bis Fuss auf Liebe eingestellt', known in English as 'Falling in Love Again' and, more than any other, her signature song.

48. (*Above*) The Kurfürstendamm in 193
showing the fashionable Café Kranzler an
a black-uniformed Nazi sitting at one of i
tables.

49. (*Left*) The corner of Unter den Linde
and Friedrichstrasse bustling with activit
in 1935.

50. (*Below*) The same corner in July 194€
with horses providing reliable, petrol-fre
transport. The pre-war café has bee
reduced to a heap of rubble, but on th
left the Schweizer Haus and the statue o
William Tell on its corner have survived.

51. Knobelsdorff's noble opera house in 1945, severely scarred by shrapnel and wrecked by bombing. Outside a Russian officer crosses Unter den Linden. The opera house first suffered serious bomb damage as early as April 1941, but was repaired and kept open for propaganda reasons until it was gutted by fire in the furious air raids of February 1945. Restoration began in 1952 and Berlin's premier opera house was reopened in 1955.

52. The battered Neue Wache in 1945 with a sign in Russian pointing the way to Potsdam.

53. and 54. Changing the guard at the Neue Wache in 1936 and 1979, the balletic goose-stepping ritual remaining the same whether under Nazism or communism. During the Nazi years the former guardhouse served as a war memorial; the communists converted it into a shrine to the victims of fascism and militarism. On the right of the later photograph may be seen the abominable foreign ministry building for which the communists sacrificed Schinkel's Bauakademie.

55. Unter den Linden decorated for the state visit of Benito Mussolini in 1936, showing the equestrian statue of Frederick the Great, whose martial virtues and invention of the blitzkrieg were revered by the Nazis. Propaganda placed Frederick alongside Bismarck as one of Hitler's great forbears. In 1942 the film *Der grosse König* went as far as putting into Frederick's mouth quotations from Hitler's speeches. Yet, as Thomas Mann noted, had Prussia's most memorable monarch lived in Nazi times, 'Frederick would have been arrested by the SS for being a Freemason,' quite apart from his homosexuality.

56. Rauch's statue of Frederick the Great in front of the Altes Palais (formerly the Kaiser Wilhelm Palais) in 1991.

57. (*Top left*) Wilhelm I's palace in 1870. Alongside on the left is the royal library commissioned by Frederick the Great and disrespectfully known to Berliners as the 'Kommode', or chest of drawers, on account of its form. On becoming king and later Kaiser, Wilhelm preferred to remain in the palace he had occupied as crown prince rather than move to the more pompous and pretentious castle. He used to look out from a corner window, and be seen surveying Unter den Linden, his people and the soldiers marching past.

58. (*Bottom left*) Unter den Linden in the rain: changing of the guard in 1900. On the right is the Prince Heinrich Palace, originally built for a brother of Frederick the Great and later occupied by the university.

59. (*Above*) March past in the same year and viewed from an almost identical position on the Opernplatz. On the left is the former Kaiser Wilhelm Palais.

60. Wilhelm II, German Kaiser and king of Prussia (1888–1918), photographed in 1896. As in all official portraits his withered left arm is deliberately obscured. At other times, invariably in one of his countless uniforms, he would conveniently rest his crippled hand on his sword hilt, worn on the left.

61. New Year's parade at the start of the momentous year of 1914. The Kaiser is shown on the Schlossbrücke, with the castle on the left, accompanied by his six sons, the crown prince Wilhelm, Eitel Friedrich, Adalbert, August Wilhelm, Oskar and Joachim.

Der Kaiser mit seinen 6 Söhnen
der Kaiser, Kronprinz, Eitel Friedrich, Adalbert, August Wilhelm,
Oskar, Joachim.

2. Unter den Linden in 1901: the statue of Frederick the Great, the Opera house, the Crown Prince's Palace and, in the background, the Castle. Curiously, some of the traffic is moving on the left-hand side of the road.

3. Unter den Linden in 1914, showing the royal banner flying above the Zeughaus, the Cathedral dome in the background and the Crown Prince's Palace on the right.

4. The bottom end of Unter den Linden: the Brandenburg Gate and Pariser Platz in 1911.

65. The Brandenburg Gate in 1901, scene of an early motor rally. During the monarchy the central passage of the Gate was reserved for the Hohenzollerns. The house immediately to the right of it belonged to the painter Max Liebermann; its studio skylight offended the Kaiser, who saw it daily as he set out for the Tiergarten on his morning ride.

66. Barely recognizable, the shattered Brandenburg Gate, Pariser Platz and Reichstag amid the debris of war, 1945.

67. The Brandenburg Gate in 1962, a year after it was sealed off from the West by the Berlin Wall. The Quadriga is back in place, but the communists have stripped the eagle and Iron Cross designed by Schinkel from Victoria's staff. The Pariser Platz has become a no man's land patrolled by armed border guards and populated only by rabbits. Beyond the Gate the grey concrete Wall runs forbiddingly.

68. The Brandenburg Gate in 1991, over a year on from German reunification and exactly two hundred years after it was completed. Coinciding with the anniversary, the Quadriga was returned restored and with Victoria's insignia reinstated. Meanwhile, the Reichstag on the right prepares to resume its role as Germany's parliament in time for the new century.

69. Unter den Linden and the Brandenburg Gate in an aerial photograph of 1915: the boundary of old Berlin.

existence more than 4,900 East Germans succeeded in beating it.

After the initial shock of the Wall had subsided and when, with its growing impermeability, the number of escapes dwindled to only a tiny trickle, the eleven-foot-high concrete barrier was given an additional use, at least on its western side. It became a vast canvas or bleached blackboard on which artists, poets, vandals and lovers would express their sentiments, sometimes savagely, often wittily. During the last decade of its existence it became a gaudily painted and sprayed, graffiti-covered stage curtain to the increasingly unreal communist world that lay behind. On the eastern side it was regularly given a new coat of white paint – notably before state anniversaries – providing a sharper background for border guards to shoot at would-be escapers.

Culturally, the severance of Berlin by an intractable wall was like cutting a worm in two: both halves went on wriggling. Far from stifling Berlin's intense cultural life, the Wall, or the will to overcome it, served as a strange stimulus.

As the self-declared 'Haupstadt der DDR' (capital of the GDR), independent and sealed off from the West, East Berlin made itself a very visible shop window for communism. Among the wares it took pride in displaying were the arts, particularly music, in which, through calculated encouragement, education and subsidy, it soon excelled. The support and promotion of artists and athletes became a recognized means of flying the socialist flag abroad and winning international recognition for the communist German State. And in return for performing this valuable role, artists and athletes were well rewarded, becoming privileged members of socialist society who were offered superior housing, salaries and, the greatest prize, access to travel and foreign currency denied to ordinary East Germans.

So conductors like Kurt Sanderling and Kurt Masur, singers such as Theo Adam, Peter Schreier, Reiner Goldberg and Jochen Kowalski, the horn-player Hermann Baumann or trumpeter Ludwig Güttler became shining stars in the East German musical firmament. When in the autumn of 1989 it came to revolution, Kurt Masur stood out, using all the influence of his position as chief conductor of the distinguished Leipzig Gewandhaus Orchestra, to side with the people; Ludwig Güttler quickly identified with Chancellor Kohl's Christian Democrats and lobbied for the reconstruction of Dresden's

177

Frauenkirche, reduced to rubble by the Royal Air Force in February 1945 during the tragic destruction of the erstwhile 'Florence of the Elbe'.

In the visual arts, the communists' dictated preference for 'socialist realism' left artists in a backwater compared with the radical-experimental, often American-influenced paths being struck in West Berlin. The communist arbiters of taste would hardly have sanctioned *Die Neuen Wilden* (The New Savages) or the *Heftige Malerei* (Angry Painting) exhibited in West Berlin in 1980.

As for architecture, they could never make up for their earlier wanton destruction of the eminently restorable royal castle – where bomb damage did not prevent an exhibition of French impressionists from being mounted in 1946 – and Bauakademie of Schinkel, though during the 1980s the benefits of conservation and careful restoration belatedly dawned upon the old men of the Politburo, in time for Berlin's 750th anniversary, celebrated separately but comprehensively by East and West in 1987.

The castle, a rich chronicle of Berlin's history, was replaced by the Palace of the Republic, which like a huge, dull cake box encased a vast auditorium capable of seating five thousand, quite apart from the sizeable chamber of the Volkskammer, the communists' rubber-stamp parliament. There was also a theatre, numerous restaurants and a night-club. Built by an architectural collective between 1973 and 1976, it was a building with everything except inspiration. The only concession to being raised on the finest site in Berlin, the former preserve of the electors of Brandenburg, kings of Prussia and finally emperors of Germany, was provided by its glistening sides of brown glass reflecting the restless image of the bombastic Berlin Cathedral opposite.

The sacrifice of the Bauakademie, which so expertly embodied in brick Schinkel's encyclopedic architectural knowledge and understanding, for the vapid Ministry for Foreign Affairs was even more incomprehensible. Unlike the royal castle, ideology did not enter the argument. Resembling a long polystyrene packing case, the ministry, which was built by another collective from 1965 to 1967, upset the harmony which Berlin's architects were so careful to maintain around the city's noble core in the eighteenth and nineteenth centuries, and which even wartime bombs did not quite obliterate.

178

The Leipziger Strasse, one of Berlin's life-giving arteries and the principal commercial street before its wholesale destruction in the war, was transformed into a succession of massive housing blocks – relieved only and inadequately by the coloured Meissen tiles specially commissioned to decorate their exterior – offering tantalizing views across the Wall of the not so distant West.

Meanwhile, grandiose but grim Stalinist-style housing following the Moscow pattern had been raised with the utmost conformity all along the Karl-Marx-Allee to the Strausberger Platz and beyond to the Frankfurter Tor (Frankfurt Gate).

Named in honour of the visiting Tsar Alexander I in 1805, the Alexanderplatz, 'the quivering heart of a cosmopolitan city' described in Alfred Döblin's 1929 novel, was completely redesigned in the 1960s when the war-damaged remains were pulled down and a Lego-land of building blocks substituted, creating a cold concrete jungle overseen from a dizzy height (365 metres – one for every day of the year) by the bulbous eye of the television tower, East Berlin's most inescapable landmark. Among the crushing horizontals, abrupt verticals and endless repetitive lines of windows, the hallmarks of modernism, stands architecture with a more acceptable pedigree, but which set a misguided example for less original architects: the Berolinahaus and old Centrum department store, built in 1928–31 to designs by Peter Behrens, best known for his outstanding industrial building, the much acclaimed turbine hall built in 1909 for AEG in Wedding in the west of the city.

In the early 1980s the East Berlin authorities adopted a more responsible attitude to architecture and embarked on a tactful reconstruction of the Gendarmenmarkt, renamed the Platz der Akademie, and an inspired restoration of Schinkel's once majestic Schauspielhaus, which, together with the French and German cathedrals on either side, still lay in the ruins left by a long finished war.

At the same time the oldest quarter of Berlin, the Nikolaiviertel, surrounding its most ancient church, the Nikolaikirche, was mercifully spared the fate of the nearby Alexanderplatz and allowed to retain some individuality in a carefully planned reconstruction completed in time for the city's 750th anniversary in 1987. Here Günter Stahn and his team of architects aimed to re-create in modern terms the medieval character of the cramped quarter with its narrow, cobbled streets and

179

alleyways, houses squashed into one another and quaint shop fronts. In an antidote to the grey concrete unanimity of the Alexanderplatz, colour was used, with houses picked out in a variety of pastel shades. It was as if a piece of music by Heinrich Schütz had been re-orchestrated by Hans Werner Henze. But though it is easy to question the aesthetics of the redevelopment, or even whether it succeeds, it did prove popular with East Berliners, particularly the fifteen hundred fortunate enough to be allocated accommodation there, mostly Communist Party functionaries, including the notorious East German spymaster Markus Wolf.

When it came to rebuilding the war-devastated city, the East Germans were not alone in transgressing in taste or judgement. In the West, the Hansaviertel developed for the 1957 International Building Exhibition was not altogether convincing, while the reconstruction of the Kurfürstendamm was often brash and vulgar, though suitable for its role as West Berlin's most glittering boulevard, its commercial magnet. Where it meets the Tauentzienstrasse, the broken tooth of the spire of the ruined Kaiser-Wilhelm-Gedächtniskirche (Kaiser Wilhelm Memorial Church) – echoed by a hexagonal modern tower honeycombed with dark coloured glass, itself matched by a great bee-hive-like cube for the main body of the church – is strangely disturbing, sandwiched between West Berlin's relentless traffic lanes. To Berliners the new additions have become the 'Lippenstift' (lipstick) and 'Puderdose' (powder compact). A hundred yards along the gold crucifix of the church is dwarfed by the huge star of Mercedes-Benz gyrating confidently above the Europa-Centre tower block, West Berlin's principal temple of Mammon, riddled with numerous boutiques, cinemas showing sex films, bars, restaurants and discothèques. Put together in the 1960s, this was the neon-lit face of Berlin that winked and smiled at the eventual triumph of capitalism over communism late in 1989.

On the Bismarckstrasse another modernist box, as dismal as any on the Alexanderplatz, was devised for the Deutsche Oper, West Berlin's flagship opera house, which opened in 1961 with Mozart's *Don Giovanni* on the site of the old Charlottenburg or City Opera that Bruno Walter had directed with such distinction during the 1920s.

The Berlin Philharmonic, by now West Berlin's best known cultural asset under its jet-set maestro Herbert von Karajan, was more fortunate in its breathtaking Neue Philharmonie, the work of veteran architect Hans Scharoun, who already long before the war had earned plaudits for his housing designs for the Siemensstadt suburb. The 1957 Philharmonie design, completed in 1963, combined scintillating asymmetrical curved lines with strong horizonals in an intensely original design. Inside the concert hall the stepped, jagged terraces of seats succeeded in exciting the eye while the almost perfect acoustics delighted the ear. It was a building tailor-made for Berlin's celebrated orchestra.

Mies van der Rohe, the last director of the Bauhaus, followed with his New National Gallery building, which opened its doors five years later, in 1968, in the shadow of Stüler's pleasingly harmonious red brick Matthäuskirche of 1844–6. With space around to breathe, it was a building well suited for a modern gallery.

If van der Rohe's building was short of charm, there was an abundance in Hugh Stubbins's exuberant Congress Hall design, completed in 1957, which Berliners immediately saw as 'die schwangere Auster' (the pregnant oyster), a fitting description of a building which later, proving to be structurally unsound, collapsed.

As the giant cranes shifted around the Berlin skyline, in search, it seemed, of new feeding grounds for themselves and their ancillary herd of pile-drivers and cement-mixers, the division and distress which marked Berlin's long-running postscript to war was coming to an overdue end.

In the West there was an exciting measure of the madness, a dash of daring, the raciness that had made the city so notorious in the 'roaring twenties', a whiff of the famous decadence. There were the revues, bars, cabarets and night-clubs. But there were new influences too, especially from across the Atlantic. Some of New York had rubbed off. Though only half a city, West Berlin could rightly claim to be more cosmopolitan than any other in Germany.

Meanwhile, in the culturally accomplished but less dynamic, in many respects backward East, there was a new questioning, stirred by change in Moscow, which the blinkered, arteriosclerotic German communist leadership completely misjudged. This time, unlike in June 1953, the Russians would remain discreetly in the background. The Soviet Union was turning to its own problems and willingly surrendering an empire.

Berlin had staggered through its near obliteration in 1945, survived the blockade of 1948–9, witnessed the 17 June 1953 uprising and borne with fortitude the building of the Wall in August 1961. Now, exactly forty years after the foundation of East Germany, communist rule there was about to collapse, exhausted.

TEN

UNIFICATION, A NEW START FOR THE TWENTY-FIRST CENTURY

O N THE eventful night of 7 October 1989 East Germany's leading singers and instrumentalists were called on to perform at a gala performance for the fortieth anniversary of the foundation of the communist German state. In the absurdly capacious auditorium of the Palace of the Republic, more like a modern circus manège than any theatre, the party loyalists were stacked high in the ever ascending rows of seats to pay homage to the motley array of Warsaw Pact leaders assembled below. All would be regaled by communist Germany's rich vein of musical talent. The occasion was meant to be the cultural highlight of the 'birthday' celebrations in which Erich Honecker and his cronies took particular pride.

Outside, braving the autumn chill, stood a crowd that was prepared to be critical, to cheer Gorbachev the reformer and jeer the unbending Honecker and vainglorious Ceauşescu. The people's enthusiasm was reserved for the reforming Russian and not his host.

East Germany's leading counter-tenor, the Komische Oper star Jochen Kowalski, was among those expected to perform. 'We saw the demonstrators outside as we arrived. It made us feel profoundly uncomfortable and unhappy, for we shared their feelings. To justify things to ourselves we said to one another that we were singing for Gorbachev. But he went early, leaving us performing for Ceauşescu and the other fogies sitting there. It was catastrophic. I forgot the words; they stuck in my throat.

'Then on 19 October we had a chance to stage our own demonstration in the Church of the Redeemer, one of the Berlin churches in the forefront of the popular revolt. It made us feel much better for we were also part of the revolution.'

Just two months earlier, during a rare visit by the Komische Oper

183

to London, Kowalski had thrilled Covent Garden audiences with his Orfeo in Harry Kupfer's daring modern staging of Gluck's masterpiece, which deservedly won East Germany's leading opera company an Olivier award.

Once the gala was under way in the Palace of the Republic, and the Warsaw Pact leaders were safely cocooned within its confines listening to Mozart and Mendelssohn, the truncheon-wielding Volkspolizei moved in roughly on the demonstrators, herding them into vans to be taken away for detention. But, as the rapidly snowballing weekly Monday demonstrations in Leipzig showed, the people were no longer so timid. On that momentous 7 October the revolution first embraced East Berlin and turned communist Germany's milestone anniversary into its last; the GDR's fortieth birthday was to prove its death day.

Just eleven days later, on 18 October, Erich Honecker was toppled, making way for his former 'crown prince', grinning Egon Krenz, whose half-hearted attempts at 'reform communism' and utter lack of credibility gave him no more than six weeks in office. As the boiling cauldron of dissent spilled over deeper into Eastern Europe, other communist leaders were thrown out ignominiously, none more so than Romania's Nicolae Ceauşescu, made to face a Christmas firing squad.

East Germany's extraordinary revolution was remarkable in many respects. It was the first in Germany's long and often cruel history to be bloodless. It was a quite unplanned, naturally spontaneous expression of frustration and anger at the years of grey tyranny the communist regime had forced upon its citizens. Its timing, moreover, caught the West as completely off guard as the ageing communist hierarchy, who, in between sipping the finest French cognac and first-growth claret, watched the revolution unfold with disbelief from the comfort of their well-supplied luxury dachas and hunting lodges outside Berlin. In the end nothing fuelled popular fury more than the exposure of the continuous litany of their corruption. The leaders who, under the mask of communism, had made such demands of the people, had merely profited at their expense, outraging the residual sense of Prussian honesty, decency and duty that remained imprinted on the East German character.

Prompted by the example of Russian glasnost, the people dared to express long harboured but suppressed resentment. Communist authority was openly questioned. It was more even than the

184

all-pervasive Stasi (Staatssicherheitsdienst, or State Security Service) secret police could begin to contain or cope with.

On their summer visit to Covent Garden the Komische Oper had included Felsenstein's 26-year-old but evergreen production of Offenbach's *Bluebeard*, the most durable and best known of all his stagings. And it was Offenbach's intended satire of France's Second Empire, turned by Felsenstein into a general parody of the corruption of the ruling classes, which strangely mirrored the revolution being enacted that autumn on East German streets. As the Komische Oper's *Bluebeard* packed the theatre for the 350th time, a few streets away an angry crowd was heckling Egon Krenz out of office. 'The people rule,' sang the opera chorus, calling their corrupt rulers to account, 'the people march, according to old tradition', and so they did in their hundreds of thousands on the streets of Leipzig, East Berlin and the length and breadth of East Germany, kicking out the corrupt communist leadership and demanding democracy.

In Berlin's twentieth-century calendar there is one date which stands out like no other: 9 November. Three times during the traumatic century it wrote itself unforgettably into history: on 9 November 1918 the beleaguered Kaiser abdicated, marking the end of Hohenzollern rule and the abolition of the monarchy in Germany; 9 November 1938 witnessed the infamous *Kristallnacht* when the Nazis went on the rampage burning down synagogues, beating up Jews and smashing their premises; finally and joyously, on the night of 9 November 1989 the Berlin Wall was suddenly opened, signalling the end of Germany's harsh division.

After their years of isolation in the communist bloc, East Germans did not hesitate before venturing to 'Test the West', as an ubiquitous cigarette advertisement advised. Endless lines of spluttering Trabant and Wartburg cars – modest in every respect except their foul exhausts – queued to drive through the Wall on maiden trips west. For days the western half of Berlin was invaded by visitors from the East, its glittering avenues – and none more than the Kurfürstendamm – paralysed by curious easterners transfixed by the abundant display of consumer luxuries they could ill afford. Returning with his parents from a first foray into the West, a ten-year-old East Berlin boy was asked for his impression. After a moment's thought he replied with reason, 'It's rather crowded there.'

Army engineers and border guards equipped with pneumatic drills, sledgehammers and bulldozers worked through the night, and early on Sunday, 12 November, a stretch of Wall was cleared at the Potsdamer Platz, the Piccadilly Circus of old Berlin, allowing, in the presence of the mayors of East and West Berlin and briefly the West German president, a fresh wave of East Germans to surge westwards in exploration of unfamiliar territory. The doors of the nearby Philharmonie were opened to them for a hastily arranged morning concert of music by Beethoven directed by the Argentinian-born Israeli conductor and pianist Daniel Barenboim. The Berlin Philharmonic can never have played to a more deeply grateful audience.

Barenboim himself, who only shortly before had been passed over for the vacant position of chief conductor in succession to Herbert von Karajan – the players decided in favour of the Italian Claudio Abbado – later landed the position of artistic director of the Staatsoper. The size of his annual salary shocked poorly paid East Germans (though he argued he could earn as much in a month of piano recitals and concerts) and particularly those members of the opera company who were made redundant as western rationalization was applied.

With three opera houses, reunited Berlin had to juggle with its resources and prevent duplication or toe-treading. The Deutsche Oper delayed a planned new production of Wagner's *Parsifal* to avoid clashing with Barenboim's Staatsoper début with the opera in October 1992. He in turn put off plans for *Die Meistersinger* so as not to compete with a new staging of the work at the Deutsche Oper. Harry Kupfer remained at the Komische Oper, but was also engaged to work at the Staatsoper with Barenboim, whose declared aim was to give Berlin's oldest theatre the same standing in the world of opera as the Berlin Philharmonic had among orchestras.

Not only singers and musicians who had been well established in East Berlin before the demise of the Wall were vulnerable. Even Felsenstein's much loved Komische Oper production of *Bluebeard* incredibly seemed doomed and destined to be discontinued with the new broom of reunification, becoming but a musical relic after an amazing tally of 363 performances. Happily it was saved by its resounding success during a tour of Japan in June 1991. 'The company love the piece and defended it here by every possible means,' reported

186

the Komische Oper's chief dramatist, Hans-Jochen Ganzel, following the decision to keep it in the repertoire.

United Berlin also had four major orchestras to accommodate and with which it could aspire to reclaim its pre-war position as Europe's musical capital. There were the Berlin Philharmonic and the Berlin Radio Symphony Orchestra in the West, the Staatskapelle and Berlin Symphony Orchestra in the East, quite apart from the not to be underestimated orchestras of the Deutsche Oper and Komische Oper. The Radio Symphony Orchestra had Vladimir Ashkenazy, another distinguished pianist turned conductor, as its musical director, while the Berlin Symphony Orchestra came under Claus Peter Flor, a gifted young East German conductor. With Abbado, the Berlin Philharmonic adjusted to the post-Karajan era in good time for the twenty-first century. The players became more than orchestral perfectionists, developing their own distinctive character under a chief conductor who was markedly more democratic and less overbearingly egocentric than Karajan. With the Neue Philharmonie undergoing an overhaul, Abbado provisionally took them into the more dignified and elegant, if less acoustically sophisticated, surroundings of the Schauspielhaus concert hall. There on the last day of 1991, exactly two years after Berliners had prepared to fête their first New Year without the Wall for over twenty-eight years, Abbado directed a stirring performance of Beethoven's incidental music to Goethe's play *Egmont*, including, most appropriately, the spoken passage beginning, 'The wall opens . . .'

The removal of the Wall inevitably brought a transformation of the city's cultural character, long split by politics. In the East under communism the arts were made highly accessible. This started with education, where noticeably more attention was given to music or art history than in the West. Moreover, there were fewer distractions, with less television, and videos the exceptional preserve of the privileged. As a result there was more time and a better grounding for old-fashioned entertainment such as concerts, opera, ballet, theatre, books and museums. For not much more than a few marks it used to be possible to have the finest seats – stalls or dress circle – in any of East Berlin's theatres or concert halls. Culture was easily affordable.

But with unification many of the state subsidies were stripped away and art in the East was expected to become viable overnight. Suddenly

187

much higher West Berlin prices became applicable throughout the city and nights at the opera had to be rationed. Concert halls and theatres, which had played to packed audiences during the bleak years of communism, emptied as East Germans preferred to be otherwise distracted or found it hard to afford seat prices which had often tripled.

'People are demonstrating their new-found liberty by saving up for video recorders and watching pornographic films at home,' said a young actress at East Berlin's Das Ei (The Egg) cabaret, whose own job was under threat. 'It is sad but understandable.

'Faced with wholesale unemployment and worried about rent and other price increases, theatre and concert-going has become a luxury it never was under communism.'

For one freshly redundant engineer I met at the Staatsoper box office who had come up with his family from Frankfurt-on-the-Oder for a Saturday night performance of *Fidelio*, inability to find a buyer for the spare ticket of a sick relative was a blow indeed at the new prices. He would not be returning for some time. Previously he had brought his family to Berlin twice a month for a combined expedition of shopping and the opera.

Then there was the pensioner in the gods of Knobelsdorff's fine theatre who had not missed a performance there since it reopened in 1955. 'Sadly I'm going to have to give this up,' he said during an interval of Offenbach's *Tales of Hoffmann*. 'The seat prices have become as steep as the stairs!

'I witnessed some great music here and, you know, I used to come until your British bombers finally stopped the opera in February 1945 – they had already nearly succeeded in 1941. I remember Furtwängler conducting here and of course in the old Philharmonie – those were days for music lovers! I have not heard the Berlin Philharmonic play for over thirty years. Perhaps I will again now. That at least would be a consolation!'

The end to Berlin's division resulted in more than a multiplication of opera houses and orchestras. It left a prolific array of altogether more than 150 chamber music ensembles, over 1,000 rock groups, 27 theatres, and 29 state-run museums – 15 situated in the eastern half of the city and 14 in the West.

Berlin had never lost its taste for cabaret, even if it could no longer bask in the notoriety of the 'golden twenties'. Like a cactus, political cabaret thrived in the arid, repressive atmosphere of the communist East, where at the Distel (Thistle) or Das Ei every possible innuendo and allusion was eagerly seized on by over-aware audiences. So finely tuned was the satire, and so daringly close to the borders of acceptability, that Politburo members seeking to test the popular pulse were known to make an appearance in Distel's cramped auditorium. It assumed the role of jester at the court of communism.

Freedom of speech on the western side of the Wall made the political skit less compelling, the allusion tamer, but none the less the Stachelschweine (Porcupines) and Wühlmäuse (Voles) prickled, maintaining an old Berlin tradition of irreverence. Otherwise, cabaret in the West was all too often reduced to banal sex shows, such as at the establishment in the Neue Kantstrasse where the focal point was a transparent, bubble-filled bath on stage in which the club's hostesses would frolic, singling out members of the audience to join them. No artistic talent was required.

In the East the nearest equivalent was old-fashioned striptease, strongly balletic or acrobatic in character, played out to middle-aged mixed audiences in the basement of the same Palace of the Republic where the Volkskammer (parliament) used to meet, or in an opulent setting at the top of the Grand Hotel, communist East Berlin's answer to the old Adlon. Such entertainment was a direct, if small-scale spin-off from the colourful and popular revues staged at the Friedrichstadt-Palast, the theatre completed in the mid-1980s on the site of the Grosses Theater (remembered for its distinctive forest of simulated stalactites dripping from the vast expanse of roof), which Hans Poelzig adventurously built for Max Reinhardt in 1919 in place of the old market hall of 1869 that had become a circus. Battered in the war, what remained of Poelzig's exciting work was eventually pulled down to make way for the new Friedrichstadt-Palast, a cardboard-like creation which represented the communist planners' best attempt to create popular architecture. If the result was facile, it nevertheless provided a flashy modern setting for East Berlin's most successful variety show and proved that all that glittered was not necessarily western. The long-legged chorus girls in star-spangled sugar-fairy costumes, with shimmering sequins or extravagant ostrich feathers circumscribing or highlighting their bare breasts, were the true

189

successors to the troupes that tapped and did splits on the stage of the pre-war Scala theatre. Berlin still had its answer to the Folies Bergère, at least in the East.

In the more rarefied world of museums, the dismantling of the Wall allowed the ending of the often absurd anomaly of collections split between the two halves of the city: a legacy of war and the ideological differences that followed. As the Allied wartime bombing of Berlin intensified, its splendid museum collections were spread all over the country for safekeeping. But with defeat and the subsequent division of Germany many works of art ended up either lost or stranded in the wrong sector. The bulk of Berlin's Rembrandts surfaced in the West, the Poussins in the East. A third of Botticelli's illustrations for Dante's *Divine Comedy* emerged in the East, two thirds in the West. During the years of communist rule in East Germany missing items were often listed in its museum catalogues as 'illegally held in West Berlin'.

Politics and art became inseparable, and the same lawyers and politicians who negotiated tense Cold War spy exchanges became involved in complicated art swaps. The neo-classical statuary that once again adorns the Schinkel-designed Schlossbrücke (incongruously called the Marx-Engels-Brücke in communist days) straddling the Spree was, for instance, exchanged for the pattern books of the Königliche Porzellan Manufaktur.

Reinhold Begas's untypically fine Carrara marble statue of Schiller reappeared in 1986 on the commanding spot outside the Schauspielhaus it had first occupied in 1871, after more than forty years in the western half of the city. In return East Berlin released twenty-nine late eighteenth-century relief portraits by the sculptor Johann Peter Echtler, which he had executed for the tea salon of the Pfaueninsel Castle on the Wannsee. Among them were depictions of Moderation, Innocence, Peace, Abundance, Virtue and Gratitude. West Berlin also regained the Calandrelli Nymph, which used to grace a fountain by the Villa von der Heydt on the Landwehr canal.

Reunification ended the need for such complicated barter arrangements and allowed at least some restitution of pieces missing or misplaced from Berlin's complex jigsaw of museum collections. Other works of art remained untraceable, their fate unknown: destroyed or long spirited away by the victorious wartime powers to Russia or across the Atlantic.

Some fragments of the famous Pergamon altar – considered one of the seven wonders of the antique world – which German archaeologists began to excavate in Asia Minor (Turkey) in 1878 and proudly sent back to the capital of the Reich, were stored in the western half of the city during the war. Now they could be added to the altar's stunning relief frieze, depicting the gods battling the giants, that forms the dominating centre-piece of the museum of antiquities in the East, to which it has given its name.

A ring from the priceless Ottonian 'Gisela jewellery', which found its way to the West, could be reunited with other parts of the treasure at Schloss Köpenick on the outskirts of East Berlin.

The 3,350-year-old bust of the Egyptian queen Nefertiti, long held to be Berlin's most beautiful woman, separated since the war from her husband, King Akhnaton, was destined to re-join him in East Berlin's dignified Bode Museum.

There were unexpected discoveries too. The veil of secrecy was lifted over a mysterious but choice collection of twenty-eight mostly small-scale works by French masters, among them Delacroix, Corot, Courbet, Monet, Renoir, Seurat and Gauguin, which had been put away in a cupboard in the East Berlin National Gallery for twenty years. The provenance of the pictures, some of which were last seen at Paris auctions in 1941–2 before going on show at the National Gallery in 1991, remained an intriguing riddle.

Packed into a battered suitcase and a cardboard box, the paintings, pastels and drawings were deposited at the end of the war with a Magdeburg clergyman, Heinrich Solbach, by a former soldier, who instructed him to look after them until their owner from Paris came to collect them. By 1971 nobody had appeared to claim the hoard, and Solbach, who has since died, went to the Institute for the Conservation of Historic Monuments in Halle with his tale, but without revealing the name of the man who had entrusted him with the pictures. The former East German culture ministry ordered the 'strictest secrecy' and discreetly passed the collection on to the 'provisional safekeeping of the Berlin State Museums', where they remained until their rediscovery after unification. With no such pictures missing from any public French museum or gallery, they were assumed to have come from an unknown private collection.

Post-unification, the cluster of East Berlin museums congregated on

191

the Museumsinsel, among them the Bode and Pergamon, the National Gallery and Schinkel's magnificent Altes Museum, came under the sway of the richly funded Stiftung Preussischer Kulturbesitz (Prussian Cultural Heritage Foundation), set up in 1957 to run the museums in the western half of the city, and were quickly earmarked for a grant worth 660 million pounds for refurbishment and repairs, some of which had become pressing. Due to the lack of adequate exhibition and storage space, valuable furniture and works of art were piled high in unheated attics and cellars, constantly at risk from leaking roofs and pipes. Sophisticated but costly temperature control and security systems were the exception, not the rule, in the East.

The duplication induced by division resulted in two National Libraries: one on Unter den Linden in the East – a muscular edifice completed in 1914 with a reposeful inner courtyard invigorated by the spurting jet of a fountain before a portico of four mighty Ionic columns refreshingly wrapped in a luxuriant abundance of cascading creeper – and the altogether more modern, functional affair designed by Hans Scharoun which opened in 1978 on the Potsdamer Strasse, just across the Wall in West Berlin.

On 15 February 1944 a sizeable British bomb scored a direct hit on the domed reading room of the Unter den Linden library, blasting it apart and leaving the hands of its clock stopped at half past six, where they have stood ever since. By the following May all its windows had been blown out and forty per cent of the building destroyed. But in a programme undertaken between 1942 and 1944, its three million printed texts, seventy thousand written and half a million autograph manuscripts were evacuated to twenty-nine safe places scattered across the Reich. Some 1.8 million volumes remained in the West at the end of the war, forming the basis of the Staatsbibliothek Preussischer Kulturbesitz (Prussian Cultural Heritage National Library).

The autograph score of Beethoven's Eighth Symphony, for example, which before the war was to be found in its entirety in the Unter den Linden archives, was afterwards spread more widely. The first two movements (including the Allegretto scherzando of soufflé lightness, inspired by the steady beat of the metronome's prototype) remained in the Deutsche (formerly Preussische) Staatsbibliothek (German Library) in East Berlin, the third movement was held by its western counterpart (the 'West-Stabi') in the Potsdamer Strasse, while the finale ended up in Poland.

The two Berlin libraries, which under the terms of German reunification were themselves formally united from 1 January 1992, possessed between them the world's richest collection of Mozart autograph manuscripts. In a dress rehearsal for their imminent merger, the libraries suitably celebrated the bicentenary of the composer's death in December 1991 with a joint exhibition of his original scores in the Potsdamer Strasse premises. Never before had so much material in Mozart's own hand been shown publicly.

Berlin's rich Mozart inheritance, notable not just for quantity but for its outstanding quality, dates back to 1841 when the Prussian capital gained part of the Georg Poelchaus collection and was subsequently added to item by item until in 1873, in a major coup, the Johann Anton André collection of 135 Mozart manuscripts was secured for twelve thousand Reichsthalers. André himself had managed to acquire a good share of the legacy left by Mozart's widow, Constanze. It comprised manuscripts relating to all his major operas, with the exception of *Don Giovanni*, numerous symphonies, masses, piano concertos, serenades and the Clarinet Quintet.

With the libraries' merger it was agreed that all pre-1956 publications as well as music, maps, *incunabula* and works for children should be stored in the Unter den Linden building, while all other books and those for lending would be housed in the Potsdamer Strasse. But initially much valuable material would have to be transferred from East to West as the Unter den Linden library underwent a thorough restoration, and temperature control was introduced into storerooms where damp-infested plaster was flaking off. The first two autograph movements of Beethoven's Eighth Symphony were reunited with the third, Tempo di Menuetto, in the security of the Potsdamer Strasse's atomic bomb proof, climatically controlled steel safe.

Among the museums the change wrought by the collapse of communism and German reunification was most drastic at what had been the bastion of Marxist historical theory, the Museum for German History, generously housed in the Zeughaus, Berlin's finest baroque building. It responded swiftly to the political upheaval – as early as November 1989, well before the revolution had run its course – by shutting off

193

the recently expanded section entitled 'Socialist Fatherland GDR' that included a carefully argued and illustrated defence of the 'anti-fascist barrier', or Wall. It also successfully resisted early suggestions that it should revert to being a military museum, displaying weapons and uniforms, as in pre-war days, and defended its role as a history museum, underpinned by its vast and diverse collection.

Its storerooms were packed with some 450,000 items ranging from prehistoric times to the present and including weapons, costumes (among which was Frederick the Great's favourite frock-coat), every-day utensils from the seventeenth to the twentieth centuries, 60,000 drawings and posters, as well as a library of 180,000 volumes. The museum had the original document of the constitution set out in 1848–9 by the Frankfurt National Assembly, Germany's first parliament, with the signatures of all the deputies, as well as the ninth-century *Heliand* manuscript, the oldest written document that exists in German. The Old Saxon poem, dating from 830, tells of Christ appearing as a popular German king.

Finally, the Zeughaus was closed for much of 1991 as surviving displays were dismantled and the last remaining cobwebs of the Marxist interpretation of history were brushed away. It reopened that autumn as the Deutsches Historisches Museum (German Historical Museum), having with some irony been swallowed up by the very museum that Christoph Stölzl was charged with forming in West Berlin as an ideological counterbalance to the communists' now defunct Museum for German History.

The face of Berlin's eastern half was changing, if at first only superficially. On the corner of the Friedrichstrasse opposite the concrete and glass pile comprising the Metropol Hotel there used to be a vintage barber's shop which, had it been in London's Curzon Street, would have been considered terribly smart and been graced with a royal warrant. Deep, mechanically complex swivel chairs dating from the 1920s, long mirrors, their edges foxed with age, shiny steel lockers resembling safe deposit boxes in which towels were steamed for an immaculate shave, chrome hand-held hair-driers, looking monstrously like some secret weapon from the Great War, and an arsenal of scissors were all variously and skilfully employed by the two unusually taci-turn, white-coated barbers, shuffling in a well-practised manner around their clients in the chocolate-brown painted premises. Each as

194

old, it seemed, as Erich Honecker, who preferred to have his sparse white hair trimmed in the greater comfort of the well-appointed VIP complex at Wandlitz, outside Berlin, they charged only a mark or two for their services, prices fixed since pre-war, Prussian times. Sadly, even with the protective economic cushion of communism, the days of such an establishment were numbered and a few months before the revolution its metal shutters were rolled down for the last time.

On the building's otherwise blank, windowless wall on the side facing the Friedrichstrasse was a tablet and relief medallion recording that Karl Marx had lived here during his time in Berlin. One night soon after the final collapse of communism the memorial was ripped away and the word 'Hurra!' chalked triumphantly in its place.

Communist-imposed names began to be removed from streets, squares, places and underground stations. A list of 190 was considered for change, and in most cases it was decided they should revert to their pre-war nomenclature.

In November 1991, two years on from East Germany's autumn revolution, the towering statue of Lenin which had become so familiar to those living amid the modern blocks of the suburb of Friedrichshain began to be pulled down on the instructions of the city government and removed at an absurd cost of 500,000 Deutsche Marks, five times more than had been estimated. The austere 63-foot-high statue, fashioned out of blocks of red Ukrainian granite by the Russian sculptor Nikolai Tomski and unveiled in April 1970 before a crowd of 200,000 by the then East German communist leader Walter Ulbricht, proved harder to remove than expected. The sure construction of the 400-ton communist colossus made the dismantling of the altogether 125 granite blocks unusually difficult. Having removed the head, the original firm charged with the operation gave up, making way for another. There were also some Berliners who objected to the 'ideologically motivated' decision to get rid of Lenin who, they argued, formed part of eastern Germany's heritage and warranted recognition as an historic monument. But in the end their protests only delayed his downfall by a few days; the statue's own resilience proved a greater obstacle. It had been easier to give the Lenin Platz, in which the granite image of the communist revolutionary had stood glowering for more than twenty-one years, a new name: United Nations Square.

195

There was no place any more for either Marx or Lenin in the new Berlin, and gradually their last memorials vanished.

Opposite the Pergamon Museum another curious piece of Berlin history was overturned during these post-revolutionary days. Facing the great Doric-columned portico of the museum is a series of unassuming, inconspicuous bungalow-like buildings which served as police barracks. On the narrow strip of grass in front was a stone with an inscription whose tale conjured up the germ of a Cold War thriller:

In these barracks served our comrades,
murdered by West Berlin agents.
People's Police Sergeant Helmut Just, 2.7.1933 murdered 30.12.52.
Sergeant Peter Göring, 28.12.40 murdered 23.5.62.
Sergeant Egon Schultz, 4.1.43 murdered 5.10.64.

For a few months after the overthrow of communism the memorial survived unnoticed, bypassed by otherwise preoccupied museum visitors strolling down the quiet Kupfergraben. Yet after a while it too was toppled, like the system which had put it up.

Vandalism was a bad habit which came with the collapse of communist authority and the feeling of impunity it brought, particularly among the growing number of young unemployed. It began inauspiciously on the first New Year's Eve after the opening of the Wall. As the fireworks ripped joyously into the night sky and the bottles of Sekt (German champagne) popped, dozens of young people climbed scaffolding to surmount the Brandenburg Gate and gouge their names or initials into Schadow's copper Quadriga, or, worse, tear off the horses' reins and rob Victoria of her crown of laurels.

Soon the white marble pedestals bearing the neo-classical statues that again adorned Schinkel's Schlossbrücke were scrawled with coarse graffiti or defaced by gaudy stickers promoting discothèques. As the months ticked by and world politics took complicated new turns, the palace in which William I, the first German Kaiser, preferred to reside and where once the revolutionary mob of 1848 had inscribed their angry slogans, had smeared on its Unter den Linden side the words, 'Freedom for the Balts!'

Then, as the Gulf War approached its climax, even the stately equestrian statue of Frederick the Great opposite was not spared.

196

'Fight the war – Desert!' was crudely painted by some objector across the bottom of the base supporting Prussia's greatest warrior.

A few yards down Unter den Linden past the opera house was the surest evidence of the change from communism to capitalism. The dingy, cramped kiosk which for years had stood outside the Operncafé, much more elegantly accommodated in the former Princesses' Palace, was replaced by a long, glass-sided cabin offering cakes, rolls filled with smoked salmon and West German bottled beer at inflated prices. The tables and seats under the parasols remained unoccupied, not even watched over by Rauch's pensive marble portrayal of Scharnhorst which had been removed for restoration, leaving only the pedestal forlornly behind. Before the introduction of the market economy, it had been different. The tiny kiosk was besieged by a well-disciplined queue waiting for the limited fare it had on offer at minimal prices: fat, thick-skinned sausages, half-litre glasses of thirst-quenching East German beer, outrageously coloured cakes, inferior, thin coffee and, in winter, watery grogs laced with Nicaraguan rum. The tables were always occupied and Scharnhorst still surveyed the scene.

For those living around the Gendarmenmarkt, as the Platz der Akademie came to be called again, on the Friedrichstrasse and Leipziger Strasse, a decade of sleeplessness as pile-drivers and pneumatic drills opened their daily barrage – Sundays excepted – on the dot at 6 a.m. was to continue into the twenty-first century. No sooner was the project drawn up by the former communist authorities for the reconstruction of the surrounding area nearing completion than their capitalist successors ruled that it should come down – even if the new buildings were, in the manner of the Nikolaiviertel, not inappropriate to the finely restored architecture they framed, and were certainly a great improvement on previous efforts by communist architects. Their façades were elaborately decorative, mixing oriental with *Jugendstil* elements and liberally incorporating coloured building materials, a continuation of the popular but insubstantial style developed with the construction of the Friedrichstadt-Palast theatre. But their use of the prestigious site was deemed commercially inadequate; they did not include the modern prerequisite of underground garage space and, anyway, funds dried up in the wake of the revolution and building work had to be suspended.

Instead, international architectural practices were invited to tender their designs for the Friedrichstadt-Arcade complex that would occupy the prime area between the Friedrichstrasse and Schinkel's Schauspielhaus, flanked by the matching German and French cathedrals, whose height was not to be exceeded. The ideas submitted were practical, self-confident and occasionally breathtaking, displaying the latest in architectural virtuosity. Different architects were chosen to raise three interrelated blocks: for the corner of the Französische Strasse, Paris-based Jean Nouvel designed a glass block that would house a completely transparent Galeries Lafayette department store, making much play of mirrors, light and news screens; for the shops and office building in the centre, the Chinese-American Ieoh Ming Pei, best known for his sensational glass pyramid above the Louvre's Cour Napoleon, produced a plan for the French construction company Boygues that experimented daringly with glass vaults; and for the American property concern Tishman Speyer, the Cologne architect O. M. Ungers planned to complete the complex with an equally adventurous office block and a fanciful interpretation of a gallery. It was extravagant architecture for a new century.

Meanwhile, at the end of the square facing the German cathedral, the luxury Dom Hotel, begun under the communist regime but only completed after reunification, its foyer a cooling arrangement in glistening marble, glass and palms, more suited to a warmer climate, was taken over by the Hilton group.

The overall aim was to create an ensemble around the Gendarmenmarkt, conceived by Frederick the Great as one of Europe's loveliest squares, that was at least as fashionably smart as the bustling Kurfürstendamm in the west and to bring life back to Berlin's desolate eastern half. Unter den Linden, still waiting to regain its former glamour, required similar treatment but, already thoroughly built up, did not offer the same architectural scope.

The Potsdamer Platz, the star-shaped hub of pre-war Berlin through which an incessant flow of traffic used to pass day and night, had been reduced to a barren no man's land by the Berlin Wall, becoming part of the notorious 'death strip' that snaked alongside. Only the scars of the redundant tramlines survived and, at the further end, a grass mound, the remains of Hitler's chancellery bunker dynamited by the Russians, where rabbits had made a cosy warren. Now, without the Wall, the Potsdamer Platz was a focus of feverish attention and speculation, the subject of keenly fought architectural competitions. The result was to be lorded over by Berlin headquarters for Daimler-Benz – not merely the maker of luxury limousines but Germany's giant aerospace and armaments manufacturer – and for the huge Japanese multinational Sony Corporation.

Next to the Zoo station in the western half of the city the British architect Richard Rogers was scheduled to build for brewers Schultheiss and Dortmunder Union a twenty-storeyed 'Zoo-window' that would include twin towers with glazed lifts running on the front of the building and a vast glass-covered atrium. Facing the so-called Kranzler-Eck (corner), the Chicago-based German architect Helmut Jahn planned a towering complex for the Victoria Insurance company.

'The real heart of Berlin is a small damp black wood – the Tiergarten,' wrote Christopher Isherwood. There the city's transformation for the twenty-first century required a network of tunnels to be excavated to accommodate a new generation of rail links.

Elsewhere, Berlin would become a city of skyscrapers in a turn of the twentieth century bid to redress the transatlantic urban imbalance. In 1891 Mark Twain described Berlin as the most modern city he knew, one which 'made Chicago seem old'. Now a Berlin which had slipped behind would strive to catch up with cities like Chicago and regain its reputation for modernity. Already in the 1870s the French journalist Victor Tissot had noted that 'everything Berlin has to show is modern and brand-new'.

In Erich Kästner's delightful detective story for children of 1930, *Emil and the Detectives*, there is a marvellously exaggerated picture of the ultra-modern German metropolis. 'You'll be staggered! They now have houses in Berlin that are a hundred storeys high, and they have to make fast the roofs in the sky so they don't blow away!'

As the newly re-established German capital, to be the seat of government of the most economically powerful country in Europe from the mid-1990s, and as a leading contender to host the Olympic Games in the year 2000 (for which a determined 'Berlin 2000' campaign was launched), Berlin attracted an avalanche of investment and the latest, most daring architectural ideas.

But amidst all this modernity there were also some politicians,

199

planners and historians who were not shy of displaying a reactionary streak. Perhaps as the most visible evidence of the ideological victory over communism, they suggested that the Palace of the Republic (or 'Ballast of the Republic', as some wits called it), which closed in 1990 following the discovery that it was dangerously infected with injected asbestos imported from Britain, should be pulled down and replaced stone by stone by a replica of the royal palace, the Berlin castle, whose site it occupied and which the communists, using thirteen tons of dynamite to eradicate five hundred years of history, had themselves razed out of political spite. Such a costly (estimated at up to four billion Deutsche Marks) and impractical proposition failed to take into account that the castle was not an especially attractive building and that its sole merit, lost once and for all with its destruction, lay in its visible agglomeration of history, its catholic mixture of styles.

Then there were those, mostly art and architectural historians, including the director of the German Historical Museum, Christoph Stölzl, who formed an association to rid Berlin of the ghastly Ministry for Foreign Affairs building and restore in its place Schinkel's weighty Bauakademie. 'It pointed the way for modern architecture,' argued Uwe Lehmann-Brauns, a Christian Democrat cultural expert. 'Its restoration does not revolve around a solitary reconstruction but the completion of the city's historic centre.' Detailed plans of Schinkel's late masterpiece (1831–6) existed, as did a number of original parts, rescued and deposited in East Berlin museums when it was demolished by communist planners in 1962. A reconstructed Bauakademie could, like the original, have shops occupying its ground floor and once again house the museum dedicated to Berlin's greatest architect.

And yet Schinkel, anything but a reactionary himself, would almost certainly have advocated a more progressive response. He had, after all, stated his view clearly: 'Being historical does not mean clinging solely to what is old or repeating it, for that would be the death of history; to act in the spirit of history one must continue with the past in giving rise to something new.'

As in its nineteenth- and early twentieth-century heyday, Berlin's future would lie rather in its modernity, not in harking back to an often problematic past. It was never a beautiful city and, despite Schinkel's inspired efforts, rarely elegant. But it had a character and energy which made it unique in Germany and Europe. There was an historical inevitability about its progress towards becoming capital of a newly proclaimed German empire in 1871, and then of a reunited Germany in 1990.

Although modest Bonn, the birthplace of Beethoven, with a history dating back more than two thousand years and the early civilizing influence of the Romans behind it, argued that its western situation, together with over forty years of problem-free rule as the provisional federal capital, was a sound reason for its continuing as the seat of government, members of parliament decided otherwise, voting to move to Berlin in time for the new century. For them to have done differently would have been perverse. In spite of its undoubted good service, Bonn remained but 'a small town in Germany' while Berlin was the Gross-Stadt (big city).

For all its pleasant green spaces, woods, lakes and great suburban tracts, encompassed in a Gross (Greater) Berlin from 1920, now that the deadening effect of East–West division has been lifted, Berlin is once again 'the' German metropolis, pulsating with new life, a city of five million and the most noteworthy urban concentration between Paris and Moscow. Isolated no more by ideology, it remains a window to the East and a door to the West. And as with the turn of the twentieth century the European sphere or influence extends eastwards, Berlin, primed with investment, opportunity and enthusiasm, is well poised to dominate the twenty-first century like no other European capital. London, Paris and New York have to acknowledge the reappearance of a real cultural rival, commandingly placed in Central Europe.

'The United States of America may perhaps have a Berlin. Berlin, however, lacks the United States of Europe. One should establish them as quickly as possible. Not only on account of Berlin, but for Europe's sake,' Herwarth Walden, the indefatigable champion of expressionism and founder of the gallery and magazine *Der Sturm*, advocated with astonishing foresight as early as 1923.

And more than a hudred years after they were written, Theodor Fontane's words took on a new significance: 'The fact cannot in the end be denied that whatever happens here or not affects directly the world at large.'

No longer divided, Berlin was able to resume its interrupted, almost

201

forgotten role as a vital European city and cultural dynamo. It was rewarded by becoming the capital in more than name of a new, increasingly self-confident Germany. Once again the continent would ring to the cry of 'Berlin! Berlin!'

SELECT BIBLIOGRAPHY

Baedeker's Berlin u. Potsdam, Leipzig, 1878.

Baedeker's Nordost-Deutschland, Leipzig, 1902.

Blauert, Elke, *Nicht mehr vorhandene Bauten Karl Friedrich Schinkels in Berlin und Potsdam*, Berlin, 1991.

Brayley Hodgetts, E.A., *Berlin: Germany's Clean and Spacious Capital*, London, 1922.

Dudman, John, *The Division of Berlin*, Hove, Sussex, 1987.

Eckardt, Wolf von, and Gilman, Sander L., *Bertolt Brecht's Berlin: A Scrapbook of the Twenties*, London, 1976.

Eckhardt, Ulrich (ed.), *750 Jahre Berlin: Stadt der Gegenwart*, Berlin, 1987.

German Historical Museum, *Bismarck: Prussia, Germany and Europe* (essays), Berlin, 1990.

Goethe, Johann Wolfgang von, and Zelter, Karl Friedrich, *Briefwechsel* (selected by Werner Pfister), Zurich and Munich, 1987.

Gottschalk, Wolfgang, *Altberliner Kirchen*, Würzburg, 1985.

Hamilton, Lord Frederic, *The Vanished Pomps of Yesterday*, London, n.d. (1920s).

Hammond, Bryan, and O'Connor, Patrick, *Josephine Baker*, London, 1988.

Hessel, Franz, *Spazieren in Berlin*, Munich, 1968.

Hürlimann, Martin, *Berlin*, Zurich, 1981.

Isherwood, Christopher, *Mr Norris Changes Trains*, London, 1935.

Goodbye to Berlin, London, 1939.

Kieling, Uwe, *Berlin: Baumeister und Bauten. Von der Gotik bis zum Historismus*, Berlin, 1987.

Krammer, Mario, *Berlin im Wandel der Jahrhunderte*, Berlin, 1956.

Kugler, Franz, *Geschichte Friedrichs des Grossen*, illustrated by Adolph Menzel, Berlin, 1842.

Lammel, Gisold, *Daniel Chodowiecki*, Berlin, 1987.

Johann Gottfried Schadow, Berlin, 1989.

Lemmer, Klaus J. (ed.), *Karl Friedrich Schinkel. Berlin und Potsdam: Bauten und Entwürfe*, Berlin, 1980.

Macaulay, Lord, *Frederic the Great*, Edinburgh, 1842.

Masur, Gerhard, *Imperial Berlin*, London, 1971.

Mittenzwei, Ingrid, *Friedrich II von Preussen*, Berlin, 1979.

Navacelle, Thierry de, *Sublime Marlene*, Paris, 1982.

Ploetz Verlag, *Preussens Grosser König* (essays), Freiburg, 1986.

Rose, Phyllis, *Jazz Cleopatra: Josephine Baker in Her Time*, London, 1990.

Rothfels, Hans (ed.), *Berlin in Vergangenheit und Gegenwart*, Tübingen, 1961.

Schäche, Wolfgang, *Architektur und Städtebau in Berlin zwischen 1933 und 1945*, Berlin, 1991.

Schebera, Jürgen, *Damals in Romanischen Café. Künstler und ihre Lokale im Berlin der zwanziger Jahre*, Leipzig, 1988.

Snodin, Michael (ed.), *Karl Friedrich Schinkel: A Universal Man*, New Haven and London, 1991.

Tissot, Victor, *Reportagen aus Bismarcks Reich* (trans. Erich Pohl), Stuttgart and Vienna, 1989.

INDEX

205

215